From one student of Oklahoma's
wild, wayward politricks to
another,

☒ How To Win Elections Without Hardly Cheatin' At All

ACKNOWLEDGMENTS

Sincere thanks and a deep bow to Helen Hauan, my true love, conscience and editor; Marie Dooley, dear friend, secretary and researcher; sweet Margaret Buckley, grammarian, typesetter and spelling champ; Harry Culver, generous friend, without whose loan of materials the Hall-Rogers chapters materials the Hall-Rogers chapter would not have been would not have been authentic; Dayton Blair and Ted Coombes for helpful insights; and special thanks to the wonderfully helpful people at the Oklahoma City and Oklahoma State Libraries who permitted me to impose upon them shamelessly.

MIDWEST POLITICAL PUBLICATIONS
P. O. Box 780080, Oklahoma City, Oklahoma 73178
Phone 405/843-7351

CONTENTS

1

THINGS I COULD GO TO HELL FOR

All the ways of a man are clean in his own eyes.
Proverbs 16:2

Life's not fair, there's no free lunch and you just think you're sexy. If you don't believe me, run for public office and find out for yourself.

I can tell you how to win a major or minor election without hardly cheating at all. Save you a lot of money to boot. But you won't listen. Not if you're new to politics.

First thing every big-shot in his first political race does is surround himself with a bunch of for-hire yes men. They tell him he's smart. Naturally the fool believes 'em.

So he spends a million bucks of his and his friends' money with all the wrong people. Later, licking his loser wounds, he realizes politics, like old age, ain't for sissies.

You can't win an election without plenty money. Neither can you buy an election, except once in awhile.

All those sneaky tricks you learned in business won't work in politics. And the more money you have, the less chance you'll get honest advice from "media experts" you hire to run your campaign.

Advertising agencies make the big money from their 15 per cent commission for placing your advertising. So most, if you let 'em, will start spending your money way too early. They'll burn you out as a candidate before the real campaign begins.

I've been deeply involved in 25 or more statewide and national campaigns, plus a bundle of lesser races that cause more pain than the big ones. Most campaigns where I handled media were successful.

So why isn't everyone in politics eating cheese from my mousetrap?

For starters, I don't take on just anyone who comes along. Nor do I bill myself as an all-wise media expert. There ain't no such animal.

I also turn down politically ambitious people I don't know. When I didn't and they got elected, I was sorry.

I'm a Democrat who doesn't handle Republican campaigns. I'll vote Republican if the Democrat is known to me as a highbinder. Happens often enough to make me uncomfortable about being basically a one-party man.

"Why the hell don't you work for Republicans same as Democrats?" I'm asked. "What's the difference?"

Not much, I admit, but you gotta draw lines somewhere. It's hard enough to convince people my work isn't a branch of the world's oldest profession. So I refuse to keep a red light in my window blinking WELCOME, STRANGER to everyone passing by with political lust in his heart.

Political publicity-advertising is different from selling peanuts, popcorn, silk underwear and magic face creams. Not *much* different but what difference there is *makes all the difference* between winning and losing.

You gotta believe in a candidate's integrity to do him a good job. You'll also not hate yourself the morning after election if you only sleep with politicians in whom you have some trust.

Public Relations probably got started when the first pimp met the first prostitute. But I'm trying to upgrade the profession a little and can't think of a better place to start than politics, where sainthood is also rare.

It may sound corny but there's we, the people, to consider. I've never aided a candidate I *knew* intended screwing the public but admit guessing wrong on occasion. Makes you feel like a spreader of V.D.

So I don't take a candidate's business unless I figure he's about as honest and sincere as I am. Which leaves plenty room for human frailties.

Sound pious? Maybe so but it's hard enough to pick decent candidates when you're right up close, look 'em in the eye, and know their voting records if they've held office. If it's that tough for me, who mingles with 'em intimately, how can the poor voting public, at the mercy of our sex and sensation-seeking media, get solid information about prospective public servants?

Sad to say, you can't. Not unless you learn to read between the lines of certain publishers' front page editorials, slanted news stories and the ratings hype on TV. Only a teeny part of the public escapes the daily drudgery enough to keep up with what's really going on politically.

Fewer and fewer people vote, especially the young and minorities. This is lamented by professors of something called Political Science and members of other strange cults.

Personally, I don't worry about damage to the republic by those who don't vote. What scares me is those voting for a handsome face, slick spiel, some personal selfish reason or, worst or all, for no reason whatever.

We'd get better public officials if only those with a reason for voting did so. We'd also get better public officials if candidates ran their own campaigns and didn't believe so strongly in polls and other "media-expert" hocus pocus.

Classic example: In 1964 I handled labor's side of the bitterest campaign ever foisted upon Oklahomans. I was labor's spokesman in the battle to decide whether Oklahoma got a so-called "right-to-work" law.

The opposition, Oklahoma's millionaire crowd that usually loses elections, even easy ones, would have won that one had they been smart enough to go fishing.

Right-to-workers had us beat hands down. But they couldn't resist doing what big shots with dollar signs for eyes always do in politics — surround themselves with high-price "media experts" and imported radio-TV announcers and actors to explain to we Okie boobs why low wages and "more freedom" beats high wages and putting up with an often knuckle-headed bureaucratic union.

We dumb Okies fooled 'em. Outlawing the union shop was rejected May 5, 1964 by a vote of 376,555 to 352,267. Right-to-workers depended on their hired hands. We didn't.

We got 25,000 low income people, many pool hall dead-beats, registered to vote for the first time. I guarantee no high tone "media expert" is going to do this kind of tough job for you. It's too much work and there's no big commission money in it.

We followed up election day, dragging those people out of honky-tonks to strike their first blow for liberty.

Some folks tell me this was a disservice to Oklahoma. I say the Big Cigars of Oklahoma's Chivas Regal crowd should have followed our example.

They could have gotten their labor-hating supporters out in greater numbers. Instead they gloated in the press, which favored them 99 to 1, over the many favorable polls provided by their "media experts." They spent tons of money with all media, which were supporting them wholeheartedly editorially and every other way.

When they got beat they cried like babies, claimed we cheated. They cheated themselves.

Turn over all your strategy and organizing to overrated "experts" like they did and you'll always get beat. Magicians and those claiming to be are at heart all fakers, including most "media experts."

I'm not known for bragging on Republicans, except maybe Abraham Lincoln. But a fine Oklahoma Republican who would have gone to the U.S. Senate, and who might be president by now, went down to defeat because we got our vote out of the pool halls that May day long ago.

I regret that.

I'm talking about Bud Wilkinson. Bud is maybe the greatest football coach ever and a man with ideals and courage. He lost his Senate race to Democrat Fred Harris by a scant 21,390 votes, about the same margin by which we defeated "right-to-work."

Wilkinson would have buried Harris under normal conditions. But Lyndon Johnson was swamping Goldwater at the top of the ticket and our crowd of newly registered pool hall voters was stamping that ol' rooster, making him crow his head off for Fred Harris.

I suppose I could go to hell for that.

Bud Wilkinson, smiling and virile athlete-coach-candidate, was new to politics. Had he run a second time he would have won. Instead he chose to join Richard Nixon's team. Sometimes even the greatest coach hits a losing streak, especially when he enters a new sport.

After that Bud decided football is more predictable than politics, which it usually is. Except Bud wound up in St. Louis, where it ain't.

Things I Could Go To Hell For   5

Bud's a great coach. He could have become a greater political figure if he hadn't picked up loaded dice.

Politics and football are both games of inches and good and bad bounces. Bud got a lifetime of political bad bounces his first two times out.

My friend Ed Edmondson's timing was also way off when he tried for the U.S. Senate. After 25 years in Congress during New and Fair Deal days, Edmondson was branded part of the problem. Voters wouldn't listen to his new solutions.

LIBERAL SPENDER was branded right between his eyes, even though his views on saving the world had changed dramatically, even as yours and mine. Ed's opponents never let voters forget what Ed *used to believe*. It was exactly what most people voting against Edmondson *themselves believed at the time*.

People don't vote according to the way things are. They vote according to what things *seem to be* after watching the 6:00 o'clock news.

My sins are many. I've covered the waterfront of political strife and turmoil — newspaper reporter, editor and smalltime publisher, radio-TV newscaster, press secretary for two Oklahoma governors, involved in three presidential and a carload of state political races.

I recite these misdeeds so you'll know I'm at least smart enough *not* to file claim as a media or political expert. Media experts are mostly wide-eyed younger people who, after a couple campaigns, decide they know the magic formula for winning elections.

Like born again Christians or new converts to Catholicism, Judaism, Islam or the Moonies, one victory makes them zealous "experts." They're eager to convert you to their new salvation, particularly since they, as media experts, are going to relieve you of sizeable wads of greenbacks in return for redemption.

These true believers carry classy raised-type business cards reading: MEDIA DEMOGRAPHICS CONSULTANT. If you're running for high public office, my advice if you read such a card: Run for your life while clutching your pocketbook.

All people working in every medium are different individuals. You may be an expert on Mike Wallace if you're his wife or best friend. But that won't make you an expert on Sam Donaldson. They're two different breeds of cat, or rat, depending on your viewpoint.

Political "experts" who claim they can sell you to all media as a prize package are selling you at least nine parts bullshit to one part steer. Any salesman will tell you you gotta know the territory. Nowhere is this truer than in politics. Most candidates start out totally ignorant and many remain that way.

Dumbest thing of all, which rich candidates regularly do, is rush off to Washington, New York or Los Angeles seeking "media experts" to run a campaign in Oklahoma, Idaho or Ohio. Why? Because they don't know their asses from third base about politics, the media or voters.

"What's the most important thing you've learned from all your years in politics?" is a question I get from college students.

"What I've learned," I tell 'em, "is that nothing is what it seems to be and the best answer to most political questions is 'Maybe.' " Every campaign is vastly different from all other campaigns. There are no magic formulas.

I've been immersed in but one political blood bath worse than the '64 "right-to-work" campaign in Oklahoma. It was four years later in Dick Daley's Chicago, handling media for the Democratic Party during the wild '68 Democratic Party Convention which finally nominated Hubert Humphrey after LBJ bowed out.

That's when Mr. Jane Fonda (Tom Hayden), Rennie Davis, Abbie Hoffman and other assorted kooks claimed to be fighting against the war in Vietnam by starting their own war in the streets of Chicago.

After that bloody Democratic convention, I knew for sure you can manipulate the media. The media *begs* to be manipulated. On a dull day, they're all streetwalking, looking for just anyone and anything to pick up and take home to the 6:00 o'clock news.

Saturdays and Sundays the media, TV in particular, are starving for just about anything to present as news. That's when politicians can best sell their staged media events.

Hokey things like standing with a dead fish in hand beside an allegedly polluted stream. Or featuring political athletes with protruding bellies walking through the county "to get closer to people and learn their problems first hand."

Ratings decide what goes on TV. Big ratings bring big bucks advertising. Viewers dig sex, gore and gossip. So that's what we get. The media can be manipulated any day of the week if you're willing to put blood on the floor, overturn police cars, take off your clothes in public, curse our highest elected officials or incite to riot. These are basic "hard news" stories of today's journalism.

So it's hard for politicians with a shred of modesty to gain attention. Most smile and fawn on bended knee, lips prettily puckered, behind any news type in the area. This rarely does much good. News people mainly like strong, forthright opinions, preferably like their own.

I've found leveling with the media is the best way to get

Things I Could Go To Hell For

their help. I don't mean playing George Washington, telling the whole truth and nothing but. Instead, lay it on the line hard and honestly on one or two important controversial issues. Keep the rest to yourself until after the election. Then you can afford to be honest some more. But too much honesty on every big and little campaign issue that comes along will kill you faster than dishonesty.

Voters know what they like and it's not always the hard, unvarnished truth.

For answers on how to win elections without hardly cheating at all, I go again to that '64 Oklahoma "right-to-work" election. The AFL-CIO was putting up big bucks for the NO side, me running the campaign. Early polls showed we didn't have a prayer. Down 2 to 1 with the state's union-hating voters.

After these disheartening polls, taken by Lou Harris and other costly national pollsters, I began getting regular visits from "media experts" hired by George Meany. They all came to tell me why we couldn't win.

"Look at the poll results," they said. "Why, look here, one-third of our own union members think right-to-work is OK. All our demographics show you're dead."

"Then why don't we hold a funeral, sing some hymns and forget it?" I asked.

"Because Meany wants to make as good a showing as possible in this Bible Belt State," sniffed one genius. "We'll do all we can for you, but face it, this Oklahoma thing's hopeless."

What each of these wise birds did was spend about two hours telling me how smart they were, then 15 minutes giving me ridiculous campaign ideas that wouldn't work in New York, much less Oklahoma.

"A bar in this hotel?" was the next order of business. There was. My office was then in Oklahoma City's old Biltmore Hotel. So we repaired to the bar for further consultation.

"Any girls around?" was the next important thing to come up.

I don't introduce girls I know and like to hot-shot Washington and New York hustlers. So our conference soon broke up. These marvels would party a night or two, then go back and submit their bills to George Meany's office for advice to the ignorant, me. I had a half dozen visits from such "experts" during the year this campaign was in progress. The advice they gave, had I taken it, would have sunk us.

Some of my union clients were our biggest obstacle to victory in that campaign. I fought them as much as the opposition. Which is not to say I'm smarter than the law allows. Like you, I know about half what I think I do. But when it comes to politics, the half I know is tatooed deep in my hide.

One thing I've learned is they lied to me about the world's oldest profession. It's politics, not prostitution. My proof is Chapter 1 of the Holy Bible itself, where the serpent talks Eve into eating fruit off the forbidden tree.

"God doth know," tempted the wiley serpent, "that in the day ye eat thereof, then your eyes shall be opened, and ye shall be as gods, knowing good and evil."

Eve bought this politician's pitch promising something for nothing. Ever since, we children of God and the devil have been holding elections and deceiving each other.

Small wonder Eve got in so much trouble with her Equal Rights Amendment. Say what you will of Eve, however, Mr. Serpent was earth's first creature to recognize his true talents, working at the job ideally suiting his nature. He was our first

Things I Could Go To Hell For

phony politician, offering up false promises with softly hissing forked tongue.

Mr. Serpent did his part to populate our world. And does he have pull! His relatives are in high places around the world.

I see a few slithering around congress and state legislatures, sliding woolybooger amendments into bills, then coiling up innocently in the sun. Nobody wiser until disaster strikes months, or even years, later.

Wise fellow legislators quickly learn to shun this breed. Those who don't wind up themselves without a political pit to hiss in.

POLITICAL FAMILIES UNITE . . .

Oklahoma's two most prominent political families joined when this photo was taken at the wedding of Mara Kerr, daughter of Mr. and Mrs. Bill Kerr, to Mike Mashburn, son of Gov. and Mrs. George Nigh. Since then the family has grown by addition of daughter Ayla to the Mashburns. Pictured (l. to r.) are Georgeann Nigh, Mara, Mike, Donna Nigh and Gov. George Nigh.

2

HOW TO WIN ELECTIONS
WITHOUT HARDLY CHEATING AT ALL

Politics is perhaps the only profession for which no preparation is thought necessary.

Robert Louis Stevenson

Beguilging campaign talk has fooled most of us following in Eve's and Adam's faltering footsteps. Guile is the heart and soul of politics, especially since TV.

I've learned some tricks of the political trade myself after more than 30 years deep inside its machinations. The basics:

    1) The name of the game is 51 per cent.

    2) No money for second place.

    3) Honesty is the best policy, most times.

Keep these three precepts in mind and you really *can* win most elections without hardly cheating at all.

Being honorable and truthful *is* the best way to go. The most honest campaign *usually does win.* Thank God, because there is plenty sidestepping in the most sincere campaign you'll ever see.

The reason honesty isn't always the best policy is because we voters aren't honest either. We lie to ourselves, mistaking selfish interest for the state and nation's welfare. Too many politicians think they must learn how and why we lie to ourselves so they can recite our lies back to us. That, they believe, is how to get those extra votes that make the difference.

Political polls were born from this desire of politicians to learn voters' every bias. First sad rule of modern politics: Never take a position without first taking a poll. Nearly every important politician follows this rule.

Why else do you suppose our Congressmen and U. S. Senators consistently send you those costly questionnaires, asking your opinion on everything under the sun? At taxpayer expense, naturally.

Personally, I'd like to know *their* opinions before revealing mine.

The great ambition of too many politicians today is to become perfect echoes. Becoming a perfect echo of majority opinion, the theory goes, will get you elected forever.

Don't believe it.

Many officeholders openly boast their one duty is to vote wishes of their constituents. Since most constituents are profoundly ignorant on both major and minor issues, we'd be smart to vote such copycats into another line of work.

I'm happy to report it's beginning to happen. Partly because polls are too often saying one thing, voters thinking the opposite. Which is losing elections for those betting their all on the latest poll.

President Reagan won in '80 because he took strong positions on just about everything. I doubt if any voter agreed with him entirely. Don Nickles let it all hang out in Oklahoma and got elected U. S. Senator on bullheaded sincerity alone.

Like good whiskey, polls are healthful up to a point. Lavish use will deceive and destroy. I recommend two jiggers of polling during a campaign, not the whole fifth professional pollsters try to pour down your throat if your bankroll can stand it.

I predict a lot of candidates placing their main faith in polls are gonna get dumped the next few years. Voters have caught onto the system of always holding a wet finger in the wind. We saw the first big bunch of weathervane candidates go down in 1980.

Polls were off 30 per cent and more during the '80 presidential primaries. Most candidates taking strong positions and explaining what they believe got elected in '80.

I hope this trend continues. We've had all the leadership by public opinion polls this nation can stand.

Such leadership has made us a nation of greedy grabbers, all hands outstretched, palms up, toward City Hall, County Courthouse, State Capitol and U. S. Congress. We've become a nation of 230-million squeaky wheels screeching for grease.

We learned this from our politicians, told by their polls it is more blessed to give if you want to receive votes. That's the give-to-get theory most politicians still swear by. But it isn't holding up anymore.

Some cases in point:

The lady mayor of Chicago, Jane Byrne, got burned by too much faith in polls.

First she pledged undying support to President Carter in October of '79. A couple weeks later Byrne confessed she suddenly had the hots for Teddy Kennedy.

The wind had changed, latest poll showing Kennedy leading Carter. So what could a poor girl do who wanted to get ahead but change candidates?

"I'll whip his ass!" said Carter of Kennedy when queried about polls favoring the Massachusetts senator. Then he proceeded to do so.

Mayor Byrne, Kennedy and the media all got fooled on that one. Wonderful! There is still hope for the Republic.

In New Hampshire that year, pollsters and the media agreed Reagan and Bush were in a tossup race. Election day

Reagan clobbered Bush, 2 to 1.

Polls said Reagan would get 42 per cent of the vote in Florida. He got 57 per cent.

The wise guys said Reagan would be lucky to come up with 43 per cent in Georgia. Written in the Georgia dust when it settled election night were the words: REAGAN, 73 PER CENT.

Still worse in Alabama. Pollsters predicted Reagan 39 per cent; voters gave him 70 per cent.

So it went week after week in '80. Pollsters and media proudly predicted and predicted, later explaining and explaining why they were wrong.

But how do you explain Kennedy leading Carter 60 to 30, then a few months later Carter leads Kennedy 2 to 1? Better to use a Ouija board.

Same thing in Oklahoma. ZINK LEADS IN POLLS screamed the headlines. But Don Nickles came in on a wing and Moral Majority prayer. Then Nickles took the pants off Coats, the Democrat, although early polls said Andy Coats had it in a walk.

All the many candidates I've helped were firm believers in polls showing them ahead. Polls showing them trailing were, of course, unscientific.

The truth is polling is only slightly more scientific than crapshooting or flipping coins. If you have money to burn, a poll or two can be useful. But don't bet the ranch on any of 'em.

Too much polling actually gets a candidate confused, uptight and worrying about ghostly subconscious minds working in the night and waking up changed next morning. Which is exactly what happens to voters during election campaigns.

There's a better way to win elections than standing firmly behind whatever the latest poll says is popular. Coming up

How To Win Elections

with something honest, from your guts, works better.

Some honesty is what intelligent voters are looking for today and they influence more votes than their own. When your stand on every issue is always on the 51 per cent side of the latest poll, smart voters smell you coming. And they don't like the odor.

I'm not against polls. I just believe it's ignorant to base your whole campaign strategy on polls. You'll get beat every time. Better to project yourself as a leader, taking a firm, intelligent stand on one or two important issues.

Voters will buy logic. That's why they change their minds so much from week to week.

There are so many polling pitfalls. Who's preparing the questions? How are they worded? Will they elicit true answers?

Today's poll is not tomorrow's vote. Think back on how many front-runners didn't make it. Where are the George Romneys and Ed Muskies now? Tiny footnotes in history.

President Carter's pollster, Pat Caddell, blessed with perfect hindsight, claims his poll showed Carter lost 10 points the last 48 hours. When that can happen, and it does, why take polls as your Bible on either issues or voting trends?

Polls are false prophets often as not.

The Washington Post's final poll a couple days before the '80 election showed six big states too close to call — Florida, Illinois, New Jersey, Pennsylvania, Ohio and Texas. The *Post's* same poll said Carter would carry New York over Reagan by 16 points.

Yet Reagan carried New York and all the other six "too close to call" states, with margins as high as 16 points in Florida, 15 in Texas.

Polls are great hype for newspapers and the 6:00 o'clock news but they won't elect you to high office.

I like to do a poll not earlier than 60 to 90 days before an election, getting a feel of voter sentiment on issues my candidate plans to feature. If it's your first time out, no need buying a poll to learn nobody knows you. A serious candidate should be able to figure that out himself.

Not being known can be your greatest asset. Nobody's yet sore at you. So you have a shot at every vote out there.

That's why underdogs win so often. Especially in races without an incumbent.

Incumbent Senators and Congressmen are a whole different ballgame, having to do with their franking privilege and bundles of taxpayer money only they get to use in big doses for campaigning.

Walter Lippmann, wise political analyst, gave the bottom line on polls.

"Effective government," he declared, "cannot be conducted by legislators and officials who, when a question is presented, ask themselves first and last not what is truth and which is the right and necessary course but 'What does the Gallup poll say?' "

Amen. Everything wrong in America today would be helped a little if we had fewer polls by officeholders and political candidates.

Issues are more important. Should you take a firm stand on each and every one? Not if you expect to get elected.

What you need is one or two issues of your own, setting you apart from the crowd. I'm not talking about opposing sin and sloth. Leave that to preachers and other candidates.

Get yourself known as the candidate who's for or against something generating heat. Be for or against unions for state employees, for or against legalized betting on the ponies or liquor-by-the-drink, for or against trusts that let some industries escape taxes others pay, for or against limitation on state or local taxes. Taking a firm stand on one or two tough issues will put you in the ballgame.

You will be demonstrating leadership, in gravely short supply these days. A leader is what we voters are looking for, not another fence-straddler.

A modern Chinese proverb fits here: He who stands in middle of road gets hit by trucks going both ways.

I repeat, the name of the game is 51 per cent. You need friends *and enemies* within the electorate to get 51 per cent or a tad more.

The candidate most likely to win a major race is willing to *speak forthrightly on one or two highly controversial issues on the side where his strong belief is.* If you don't have any strong beliefs, play some other sport.

We, the people, are getting smarter. More of us are learning to read between the lines of newspapers and see behind the boob tube pictures.

No longer do we expect agreement from a candidate with our every personal prejudice. We're looking for leaders who are for and against things and know the reasons why.

About time. Too long our leaders have been followers. Instead of them leading us, we've been leading them through our replies to pollsters. The sad payoff is so much spending for every greedy, grabbing human desire that our nation's close to bankruptcy.

I think voters today understand our problems better than politicians.

So get yourself a good love-hate issue if ambitious to be governor or U. S. Senator. Just be sure more than half the logic on your big issue lies with your arguments. A noble stand for causes which can no way attract 51 per cent of voters is for martyrs.

Vigorously attack the snarling wolves who disagree with you. These scoundrels are out to destroy our state and nation. Only your courage and forthright brilliant conclusions can, in the nick of time, save us.

Cowchip politics doesn't work like it used to. You gotta believe in what you're pitchin', so bring more than your pitchfork to the campaign.

I'm convinced a majority of winners in big races for awhile now will be true believers, speaking from the heart and soul. What you need to go with that, in smaller states like Oklahoma, is a minimum $600,000 at today's prices for a governor or U. S. Senate race.

Otherwise forget it. Running for office without the minimum amount of money is like baking bread without yeast. The bread will never rise and neither will you.

There are no cinches in politics, no matter what some media marvel tells you. Running for office is riskier than wildcatting or tomcatting. It can lead to bankruptcy and divorce.

I'm talking about big races, Congress on up. Lesser statewide races, like Corporation Commissioner, are a cup of tea. If you can rustle up $75,000 to $100,000 and spend it wisely and at the right time, you should win.

I'll go double or nothing with you on my fee in such a race. Providing, of course, you have an honest American name like Jones, Smith or Jackson. Wojelowski won't get it in these races, no matter how much you love your mama or how smart you are. We voters don't trust furriners.

Candidates in secondary races aren't people. They're only names.

Among Oklahoma names I've touted in Corporation Commission races alone are Rex Privett (Remember that croaking frog?), Norma Eagleton (Keep an eagle eye on your utility rates.), Harold Freeman (A free man), and Wilburn Cartwright (Hitch up your cart right.).

Blame me for your high utility rates. Except every last one of my candidates swore, "Marty, I'm gonna stick up for the ratepayer."

I believed 'em, just like you. Trouble is, few utility regulators are any match for the utilities' lawyers and lobbyists. Those sly ones can explain putting into their rate base a new jet airplane, used mainly for bigshotting by utility executives at football games and other special events, and make it sound like they're carrying chicken soup to the sick.

So I just bought 1100 shares of utility stock to comfort me in my old age. If you can't lick 'em, join 'em. Now I'm in better shape to tolerate utilities' indecent requests for 17.5 per cent rates of return.

Nine out of ten voters are flying blind after they get past Governor on the state ballot. Strictly looking for a trustworthy name and slogan. So if you have 100-grand to drill your name into one of the vacant spots in voters' heads, you're in like Flynn.

Here's my guaranteed formula on a race for secondary state office:

Rule 1:   Husband your campaign chest carefully and keep charge of it yourself.

Rule 2:   Don't believe too much of what your advertising agency or media experts tell you.

Rule 3:   Forget about issues.

Rule 4:   In radio-TV spots, talk in high-sounding generalities, inserting your name three times in the opening, three times at the close and at least once in every sentence in between.

Timing is everything. On this point, the candidate will be in direct conflict with his advertising agent. The ad man doesn't make money for himself until he starts spending yours. So he says, "Get your name out early."

Don't believe it. Dumbest thing you can do. In a secondary race, the last ten days is almost the whole campaign. That's when 80 per cent of your money should be spent.

What to buy? Small newspaper ads, short TV spots and at least one good 60-second radio spot featuring a play on your name every other breath. I omit billboards because they're too expensive and will all be bought up anyway by candidates for governor or U. S. Senator.

When Rex Privett's frog spots started running back in '72, I caught hell from a lot of people who claimed we were frivilous. Rex's sharp wife, Pat, stuck with me, though, and I think those spots made the difference. Here's what one of our radio frog spots said:

FROG:	Ribbett, ribbett, ribbett
PRINCE:	Dumb frog! Not ribbett, ribbett, ribbett. It's Privett, Privett, Privett.
FROG:	(Doing better): Brrivett, Brrivett.
PRINCE:	Still not it. Privett, Privett, Privett. With a "P", Privett. *I* was a frog once, before I became a prince ... and learned to *talk* right ... and *vote* right.
FROG:	(Excitedly): Brivett...Brivett...Brivett.

PRINCE:	You think that beautiful princess woulda kissed me and changed me to a prince from a frog if I couldn't even say Privett? I said the *whole* name—Rex Privett. Rex Privett for Corporation Commissioner. *That* impressed her. (Again, proudly) Rex Privett for Corporation Commissioner.
FROG:	(Trying hard) Pp...rivett. Pprivett, Pr-rivett, Privett!
PRINCE:	By George, you've got it! Hey, frog, look. That doll of a princess, comin' right this way. Hi, princess...
FROG:	Beat it dummy. Give *me* a chance. (Hastily) Privett, Privett, Privett.
PRINCESS:	(Mae West style): Hi, frog. How 'bout me makin' you a prince?
FROG:	Vote Privett! Vote Privett! Vote Privett!
PRINCESS:	My favorite candidate. You're a real prince. There. (kissing sound)
FROG:	(On slow fade) Purrivet ... Purrivett ... Purrivett ... ahh ... Prrrivet.

How's that for facing the issues? Besides Pat Privett, a lot of kids liked our frog spots and were imitating frogs all over the Oklahoma landscape that summer. Many in Rex's campaign headquarters, however, insisted to the end we should be slaying dragons instead of making princes from frogs.

All I can say is, if we'd used our 60-seconds to tell folks the most important thing about utility rates — which is that utilities scheme to throw everything including the kitchen sink into the rate base—Rex Privett would never have served on the Corporation Commission.

Thus doth our democracy work its wondrous way.

If you're shooting for the big time, governor or U. S. Senator, it's more complicated. You've got planning, praying and preaching to do. First get acquainted with media people who'll be writing and talking about you.

The State Capitol press room is the biggest hurdle. Those reporters, more than anyone, decide who becomes governor or Senator. You can't win without most of them on your side or at least neutral.

Thinking about cosying up to Eddie Gaylord of the *Oklahoman?* Forget it. You take the political reporters' bosses and give me the capitol press room. I'll beat you to death.

Those reporters have their ways, more subtle and effective than the blunt axes and sledgehammers wielded by an Eddie Gaylord. Get to know them. Each has a different fingerprint, just like you and me. They'll be dealing with your prejudices, so you better know how to deal with theirs.

Harry Culver has covered the capitol for UPI at least 25 years and Jerry Scarbrough did a long haul for AP, succeeded now by Ron Jenkins. Each is a different personality. Harry worries about the underdog, Scarbrough about the Texas football team. Both would always give you a fair shake if you spoke your mind. So will Ron Jenkins.

Jim Young of the *Times* and Mike Hammer and John Greiner of the *Oklahoman* have Eddie Gaylord for a boss. It's not how they planned the world but they bear their cross stoically. Ed Montgomery did a lot of fine political writing for the *Oklahoman* before becoming an OU journalism professor. I guess I dare call him a liberal now that his job's not at stake.

You need to read the *Oklahoman's* editorial page each day before taking press statements to *Oklahoman* writers. They won't do you in without cause but they're writers, not editors. *Oklahoman* political writers speak only to managing editor Jim Standard. Standard speaks only to the lord, Gaylord.

After conversations with the lord, strange things can happen to a political writer's story. Don't forget political writers also read the editorial page and know the publishers' sacred cows. Be smart enough to do the same, and interpret properly, if you expect to win an important Oklahoma election. Otherwise you'll be pissing into the wind a lot.

Chuck Irvin, the realist, and Warren Veath are on guard for the *Tulsa World*. My old buddy *Phil Dessauer* was the *World's* managing editor until 1981, when he got run over by one of management's sacred cows. Alex Adwan runs that paper's editorial page and is Oklahoma's class editorial writer.

My friend Jim Young handles it all for the *Oklahoma City Times*. Jim learned the ropes from Otis Sullivant and Ray Parr, two of the best ever at lassoing politicians.

After a brief flirtation with politics, Paul English is back in the UPI fold at the capitol. It's where I think he now realizes he wants to be.

John Greiner and Mike Hammer do their homework. A bow for their news coverage of Gov. Nigh in '82, when their boss was bombing George, as usual, in front page editorials.

Mike Carrier and Marilyn Duck of the *Tulsa Tribune,* who succeeded Will Sentell, are bright newcomers to the capitol. The *Tribune* doesn't hire dummies for those jobs.

Young of the *Times* and Carrier and Duck of the *Tribune* have early deadlines. You give 'em a good story at 8:00 a.m., maybe you'll wind up on page one. An hour later you might not make the paper.

Don't forget there are more afternoon than morning

papers in Oklahoma. So alternate your political propaganda handouts equally between morning and p.m. papers. You get to favoring one group too much and the other will soon find things wrong with you. They have their turf to protect.

A tip of the hat to fellow members of the Over the Hill Gang, Ralph Sewell and Howard Wilson. Sewell is retired Assistant Managing Editor of the *Oklahoman* and Wilson, who covered the capitol for UPI in the '50's, is now home from California. They were recently joined by Ed Montgomery.

Sewell, Wilson and Montgomery are syndicating capitol political stories to the smarter Oklahoma Press Association publishers. Philosophers at this stage, you can trust them to be kind and gentle but not patsies.

I'll say it one more time, this bunch is the creme de la creme of Oklahoma journalism. They're a little cynical from buffeting hot crosswinds blowing daily through capitol corridors. But they're pretty trustworthy.

Don't get me wrong. You can trust most political writers if you know the rules by which they play. But don't let anyone con you into talking "off the record." There ain't no such animal. Reporters say privately, "A phonograph needle is the only thing you can keep off the record." Believe them.

The reporter you talk to off the record may not print your story first. But he's not violating your confidence when he tips off a buddy. The buddy, in turn, will do the same favor for him when he learns something "off the record." They'll always wind up with an off-the-record story in type.

Investigative reporters also get into politics a lot. They're after truth, honor, justice and whatever dirt they can dig up on someone the publisher wants gigged. So when anyone like Jack Taylor, formerly of the *Daily Oklahoman,* calls, best thing to tell him is good-bye. Taylor's job was previously held by present *Oklahoman* managing editor Jim Standard.

There's a rich, bright fellow at Shawnee, Gene Rainbolt, who owns more banks than I have shoes and socks. Rainbolt can tell you about "off the record" and investigative reporters. He had already been burned a time or two when Jim Standard of the *Oklahoman* called him one day for a friendly chat, so Standard's press room buddies tell me.

"Got nothing to say," declared Rainbolt firmly.

"It's off the record," promised Standard. "Just a friendly visit. I won't print a word."

"Trouble is," responded Rainbolt, "I keep remembering about the snake and frog."

"I promise, not one word in the paper," Standard kept on.

"Let me tell you about this snake that got run over by a truck," interjected Rainbolt. "Poor snake got smashed flat by an 18-wheeler and, though barely alive, did manage to weakly call for help."

Standard tried to interrupt but Rainbolt plowed ahead with his sad tale.

"Mr. Frog was hopping alongside the highway and heard the snake's distress call," Rainbolt said. "He was leery but his tender frog heart couldn't resist a dying fellow creature's plea.

" 'Please help me, friend,' cried the snake, sighting Froggie out of the corner of his one good eye. 'Pull me off this road before another truck finishes me off.'

"Froggie was fearful but saw the snake's terrible condition and took a chance. Timidly grabbing the snake's tail, he dragged him to the highway's shoulder.

" 'Oh, thank you, dear friend. You'll never regret it,' promised the snake. 'But look above. Buzzards. Please find me cover or they'll be eating me.'

"Tender-hearted Mr. Frog carefully pulled his new friend's torn body down the embankment to a safe shady spot under a huge rock.

" 'There you are, friend!' said Froggie proudly, 'No buzzard can get you now.'

" 'Wait, pal,' Mr. Snake cried pitifully. 'Surely you aren't leaving me here to starve. I haven't eaten since yesterday.'

"So generous Froggie hops to a nearby pond and is soon back with plenty food for the snake, although flies and mosquitoes aren't his preferred diet.

" 'I'll love you forever for this,' swears Mr. Snake. 'Promise you'll return tomorrow and nurse me in my terrible ordeal.'

" 'Don't worry,' replied Froggie. 'I won't desert you.'

"For ten days Froggie brings flies and mosquitoes to Mr. Snake, who slowly mends. On the 11th day, Froggie is happy to find his friend nearly recovered, a bright new sparkle in his eye.

" 'Got your breakfast,' says Froggie brightly. 'My, you do look fine today.'

" 'Feeling great,' Mr. Snake replied, 'but I'm so tired of this food.'

" 'Like something different? I'll get it for you," said Froggie, happily noting Mr. Snake coiling and raising his head, sure sign of recovery.

" 'What I'm dying for,' hissed Mr. Snake as he struck, 'is some tender, tasty frog legs.'

" 'No, not me!' screamed Froggie, frantically struggling to get free. 'I pulled you off the road, saved you from the buzzards, fed you, nursed you back to health. You said you loved me, that we'd be friends forever.'

" 'I know and I'm sorry but it's your own fault,' Mr. Snake replied, smacking his lips. 'You knew all along I was a snake.' "

A long pause when Rainbolt finished his sad tale of Froggie and Mr. Snake.

"I know you have good intentions," Rainbolt broke the silence, "but whenever I'm tempted to talk to an investigative reporter, the sight of that terror-stricken frog in the snake's mouth, eyes bulging, comes before me. Snakes change their skins but not their nature. Just like investigative reporters."

No interview. Very wise on Rainbolt's part. Specialty of investigative reporters is making white into tattletale gray.

When a political candidate gets a call from a metropolitan paper's ace investigative reporter, mark this down: That paper plans to swallow Mr. Candidate whole.

When that happens, you have but one choice. Take the paper on head first. Scream foul and bloody murder at the top of your lungs. Make the newspaper your campaign issue.

Every large paper has plenty unforgiven sins. Dig up ghosts of past candidates unfairly killed. Remind voters how the legislature was browbeaten into exempting all media from sales taxes the rest of us pay.

Should the paper be the *Daily Oklahoman,* mention their real estate interests, enhanced in value by fine taxpayer roads and highways nearby, and certain public trusts that can't be trusted which they help sponsor. To say nothing of news they cover up and news they fail to cover at publisher Eddie Gaylord's direction.

Any campaign taking the pants off a mighty press lord has a good chance of winning, especially now that TV is so important. I've been deeply involved in a couple such campaigns that succeeded.

Pride is the first of the seven deadly sins, followed by "a lying tongue and hands that shed innocent blood." They still aren't convinced in the *Oklahoman's* ivory tower that their tactics can backfire. So when they take after an innocent victim, like they did George Nigh in the '78 and '82 governor's races, they use a dull meat ax instead of a stiletto.

Their ax draws blood but needn't be fatal. Not if you aren't afraid to fight back and start fighting them early in your campaign.

Hesitate until two weeks before the election and you're too late. They'll bury you with last-minute claims of high crimes you allegedly committed or are getting ready to commit. And the yokels will buy it.

Timing is everything in campaigning. I've never been in one where all the candidate's main advisers, meaning those donating the money, didn't clamor to devise high strategy. They think campaigning consists of equal parts show biz and magic. What it mainly consists of is deadly drudgery.

Get past timing and there's not much strategy left.

When running for governor or U. S. Senator, spend at least a year beforehand speaking to any and every group that will listen. But only as a private citizen with words of wisdom, not as a candidate.

Before each speech, send a photo and press release to the town's newspaper and radio station. The day of your speech, take a statement of your pertinent remarks to the paper and radio station. This is the drip, drip, drip of building a groundswell.

For crying out loud don't announce for office until it's

nearly filing time. Keep 'em guessing while you're out in the hustings stirring up a draft for yourself. If you announce early, publicity you get will be mostly bad.

Once you announce, you're a candidate. *Candidates* are expected to answer specific questions about every issue. Each time you answer for the record, somebody gets sore. And you'll be answering too many questions if you're out there as an early-bird candidate.

Start answering media questions on controversial issues six months before a campaign starts and I'll order flowers for your political funeral. The first announced candidates are the only game in town, so they get played to death. Worse still, voters tire of them before the campaign ends.

You might want to follow George Nigh's smart example when he was elected governor of Oklahoma in '78. He got voters to sign a petition *asking* him to run. Many advantages to this. People who sign your petition are pledging their support. Few will break the pledge, once made.

Petition signers were a prime source of Nigh campaign workers and contributors. They also provided membership for the various Nigh campaign committees formed in every village and hamlet. Such committees are worth stories in the local paper. They show growing strength and bring doubters, looking for a winner, down off the fence.

The wise candidate reluctantly admits, many months before filing, "Yes, I'm considering the race. Many fine people are urging me to run."

A couple months later, "Yes, I'm greatly encouraged and closer to a decision. But I want to be sure about everything, especially financing."

A few weeks before filing, when everyone's asking, "Will

he or won't he?"—put one toe in the water.

"Support is building fast everywhere and that includes finances, which is vital," you announce. "I'm holding a series of meetings with supporters over the state the next couple weeks, after which I'll announce my decision."

While holding these final meetings in the larger cities, you can get a ton of helpful publicity.

"If the rest of the state is half as enthusiastic as here in Lawton," you tell the Lawton media, "I'll be running faster than a roadrunner."

Use variations of this pitch everywhere. Milk it, because the free publicity mainly ends when you become a candidate. So does the free ride on evading issues you want to duck, and ducking controversy early is vital. Voters don't zero in on candidates and issues until the last few weeks. Keep your powder dry until then or you'll end up a TV rerun.

Voters will know more about you than they care to if you start campaigning too early. The fresh new candidate who hasn't yet spoken his piece captures voters' attention at the end. He's apt to get the most votes because his political song just started playing. You don't remain No. 1 long in politics or on the music charts.

There is a time for a candidate to be born, which is not the day after you conceive. Nine months between conception and birth is about right for politics, too. Don't admit pregnancy until you're showing pretty good, about five or six months along.

The first six months you campaign for speaking experience, free publicity and to impress the pros, media and potential financial angels. Eight weeks campaigning is plenty for Aunt Minnie and Uncle John before they go vote. The public can stand no more. Campaign longer and you'll wear out both your workers and the voters.

When you can delay no longer and finally make your announcement, do it with a 21 gun salute. Let the world know you're in the race with money, marbles and chalk. Bounce your candidacy announcement off the media in every major city in one day.

In Oklahoma that means an 8:30 a.m. press conference in Oklahoma City, then by plane to Ada, Lawton and Ardmore, winding up in Tulsa at 2:30 p.m. for your final press conference. You'll thus make everyone's 6:00 o'clock news and both afternoon and morning papers. Everyone's happy and you get maximum coverage.

Warning. Don't sell your soul to TV. The pencil press, until recently King of the Hill in political journalism, is extremely jealous of that new kid on the block with his minicams, helicopters and other fancy toys. Don't stir this jealousy. Newspaper writers, who do politics in depth, still determine which candidates get considered seriously.

Timing is critical in the final eight weeks of hardest campaigning. Do a slow buildup to the last ten days, when all weapons should be firing at machinegun pace. Don't let some ad agency spend big money eight weeks out. Most of the paid media ads need to be concentrated the last three weeks. This keeps you fresh and gaining, looking like a comer and likely winner election day.

A word about campaign workers. Search out the virgins. Avoid old pros who claim they can carry the county. They're liars. They've also been in too many campaigns, with the scars and enemies to prove it. They talk a far better game than they play. They also want more than they're worth for their support. The virgins do it for love. They have no better sense than to follow instructions and speak right out loud for you in public. That's support.

A friendly pat on the head and nothing more is what you give important people who "can't say anything publicly" but promise, "I'll help you quietly."

What that means is they're going to help you like they do your opponents — not at all. They *pretend* being for everyone, "quietly."

"How much will you contribute?" is your only sensible question for these people.

If you look like a possible winner, they'll buy a little insurance by making a small donation. Then they'll be first on your doorstep when you're elected, telling how they shouted your praises to the rooftops and demanding your choicest appointment. Architects, contractors and lawyers comprise much of this group.

Believe me, nobody ever got elected by quiet supporters.

Don't waste time on elected officials either. They, too, will sing you a siren's song and deliver nothing. An elected official who supports another candidate for something has rocks in his head. Best way I know to get beat next election.

I hear a lot of talk about the need for "more positive campaigns." Editorial writers put out this line a time or two during every election. It fills space but don't believe it. Voters are aginers. They empty their bile in the voting booth.

If your opponent has shortcomings or a voting record (always bad), for heaven's sake don't keep it secret. It's only a smear when they criticize you. Best strategy is to let others make your opponent's failings public first. I'm not talking about making up things. When you criticize, be sure it's true.

If they prove you a liar once, you're finished.

But you're not apt to get elected without confronting your opponents. How else can people decide how to vote? You let your main opponent get by without criticism and chances are you've elected him.

The dictionary says politics is "competition between interest groups or individuals for power and leadership." And competition is "a contest between rivals." You're in the wrong ball game if you dislike rivalry.

If you're smart you don't attack an opponent's personal life or family. But pointing out differences on issues and reading the provable record on him is what campaigning is all about.

I'm not much for slogans or jingles. You need a campaign theme but that's different. The ancient Harrigan song, which Howard Edmondson gave new words when elected governor of Oklahoma, is a catchy tune to which Bill Hyden put a special lilt. It's the rare exception of a campaign song I might use. Most ad agencies think they're selling soda pop and adore jingles of their own amateur creation. They locate a bistro or church choir quartet, put a drab combo behind 'em and produce a jingle of gibberish that cheapens your campaign.

Voters consider politics and elections serious business, not the Saturday night dance. Besides, slogans can always be used against you. In 1980, I used a mean-eyed eagle as the symbol for Norma Eagleton's Corporation Commission campaign.

"Keep an eagle eye on your utility rates. Vote Eagleton," a stern voice proclaimed behind our eagle soaring into view, eyes flashing, to close out the commercial.

"Don't be surprised if that eagle comes back to haunt you," I told Norma.

Sure enough, after she and Hamp Baker outvoted Bill Dawson and granted several sizeable rate hikes, Attorney General Jan Cartwright, among others, began suggesting the Corporation Commission needed a hawk eye instead of an eagle with bad eyesight on the commission. Norma just sneaked in by a hair her second time, against a candidate with no money. Slogans can hurt as well as help.

Winning campaigns are big on committees, committees all over the landscape. Committees with as many chiefs as Indians. They cost nothing. They make newspaper stories, showing campaign strength. They flatter people and tie them to you. Once a committee is appointed and members' names published in the local paper, you have solid workers. The committee goes down if you do. Their egos are involved. So they'll fight to elect you. You can count on it.

What kind of committees to appoint? All kinds. If you're a Democrat, first thing you need is a committee of Republicans. From there you cover the waterfront—doctors, lawyers, wheat growers, preachers, veterans, and all the rest.

Besides the publicity and workers committees provide, you learn a lot while forming them. Most important, you learn who the liars are.

"Will you serve on a committee for the candidate and can we put your name in the paper?" is a question separating sheep from shearers. You hear from those who "want to help quietly" when you ask this question. Those who say "I'll help" are the only ones worth having.

Warning. Never let committees have anything to do with actually running the campaign. Be generous with titles but let no one speak for the candidate. Those calling the shots should be a tiny handful or less.

A camel, you know, is a horse created by a committee. Most campaigns have what I call The Camel Committee. Its members cause the campaign to degenerate into a lumpy, awkwardly-moving camel when you run decisions through this constipated digestive system. Each committee member feels obligated to demonstrate his brilliance by deflating everyone else's recommendations, while blowing up his own. The result is constant argument, bad feelings, disjointed action.

Beware Camel Committees full of geniuses. Smart candidates and campaign managers listen carefully to all suggestions. They seek out sound advice. But they take action on their own.

Nobody should be a candidate who depends mainly on the wisdom of others to elect him. Sometimes a multimillionaire gets elected that way but it's not the usual thing. These days you better know what you're doing. I'll take mainly virgins for campaign workers, with pros on top—pros without political ambition of their own.

Ten intelligent people, devoting all their energies and working without jealousy, can elect a governor or U. S. Senator any day of the week. I've seen it done with five in the hard core.

Finally, shoot on sight anyone who suggests changing the candidate into something better than he is. I urge every candidate, cling fast to the personality God gave you. You'll never find one better.

Remember what happened to the former president of Oklahoma State University, Bob Kamm, when he ran for the Senate in '78? Some media marvels changed him in TV spots from a learned professor to a strange cowboy out on the range before a fire. After watching Kamm's TV spots, voters wouldn't have elected him chuck wagon helper, much less their U. S. Senator.

Do you think a TV expert could make Henry Bellmon a better candidate by giving him speech lessons? No way. Henry's charm is his hayseed personality, masking one of the shrewdest political minds you'll ever find. He comes through as country smart and sincere, which beats your standard too-many-teeth political grin all hollow. Folks like Henry's honest answers and courage in taking an unpopular stand.

Your best campaign weapon is truth. Truth and leadership are in demand. Truth in politics is an honest opinion, backed by logic and facts. It may not be popular but, if it's true, you can sell it.

If instead you want to take a poll to learn what you think, you lack the other winning quality needed. I'm talking about leadership. Leadership is five parts courage and decisiveness, three parts common sense and two parts personality. Political courage is willingness to take a firm stand on an issue or two you firmly believe in, even though many people, maybe most, disagree. Controversial issues are *winning* issues *if your logic matches your courage in presenting them.*

Many now in high public office are hanging on because they have unlimited taxpayer money for campaigning year 'round. Half their staffs are mainly full-time political workers posing as bureaucrats.

People are looking for something better than these poll-taking fence-straddlers. But you need a snappier program than they're dishing out if you hope to replace one of them. You must stand for something. You need a thick skin and tough turkey neck so you won't back away from attacks that will surely be made against you. Above all, you must peddle something specific that's better than what we've been getting from the office you seek.

If you meet these modest requirements and can raise a car-load of money to spend with the media, no reason you can't hold high public office and become famous.

Those dumb voters out there have been flim-flammed so many times they're now getting smarter than the media marvels doing it to them. So now is the time for all good men and women to come to the aid of their party, city, county, state and nation.

I recommend starting near the top. It's as easy to win there as at the bottom and a lot more rewarding.

CAMPAIGNING, 1950 STYLE...

Mike Monroney and Mary Ellen and buddy Jay Perry and wife, Henry Ione Perry, pose in front of their avant-garde 1950 campaign wagons on the lawn of the Overholser mansion in Oklahoma City where the campaign was hatched. Although a real "poor boy" campaign by today's standards, it was largely conducted from the Perry's home, now an Oklahoma tourist attraction originally owned by Mrs. Perry's parents. Those loudspeakers were the main weapon used in defeating Sen. Elmer Thomas.

3

NEVER SWEAT THE SMALL STUFF

Don't get any on you.

Law of restrained involvement

Politics is a social disease you catch while having fun in your first campaign.

The fun and joy fade as you become jaded. But you'll never shake the disease. Whenever a new campaign season rolls around, you remember the good times, forget the hate and sadness.

Each campaign is different, teaching something new. Although involved countless times, I find myself woefully ignorant in some area every new time around. So I listen and watch a lot, picking up helpful pointers for next time. This chapter is for edification of "innocents" on some lesser known techniques I've learned, sneaky and otherwise.

CARL ALBERT'S FORMULA

I talked to Speaker Carl Albert about door-to-dooring it. He offers an angle:

"During my early years in Congress," he stated, "I'd make every town in the district, see nearly everyone in all the small towns. Went down street after street, house after house. Down one side, up the other.

"Then I'd come back to the car and—this is important—leave immediately. Never give anyone a second chance. You go back and somebody is sure to think up something to complain about. Give them another chance, you'll always get an argument from somebody."

Carl treated bankers gingerly.

"Down in my country banks and bankers aren't too popular," he told me. "So I made a point of never going to any bank as a special mission. Never let voters see you paying tribute to the mighty.

"I'd start my campaigning at least a couple blocks away and gradually work to the bank, stay only a short time, then on to the next business. That way they can't accuse you of being in the banker's pocket."

FUNERAL ETIQUETTE

For politicians there's one right way and a lot of wrong ways to make your presence known at funerals. I learned this from a legislator who served nearly 30 years, during the course of which time he and I attended many of the same funerals. His attention to even tiny funeral details explains why nobody ever beat him.

Like most politicians, our hero was present at nearly every funeral, out of respect for the deceased and surviving relatives who could still vote.

I noticed he'd always arrive just as the service was starting, taking a seat in the last pew at the rear. Thus everyone saw him passing the casket when the service was over, noting this fact appreciatively. At the same time, he escaped mourners on the outside who were apt to ask a favor or give him hell about something.

"These sad occasions are for meditation, not pontification," he once explained to me his wise last-in, first-out funeral technique.

NEWSPAPER ADS

I never buy a full page ad for political candidates. The cost is tremendous and it's too garish, showing excessive spending. You get better readership with a two-thirds page ad, since there is reading matter above it. Many readers instantly thumb away full page ads because there's nothing above or beside them to attract attention.

Over the long haul, smaller ads give you most for your money. Ads 2-col.x5" usually get placed above a larger ad and next to printed material. You often get better readership with this smaller ad because makeup men stack smaller ads on top of larger ones. It's the only way they get a newspaper page looking properly artistic.

And it's sure to save you money.

TV DEBATES

Today finalists in all major races are stuck with debating their opponents. This is fairer for some than others. Lawyers, especially former prosecutors, have an advantage. But there are ways to slow down bumptious barristers who will, if you let 'em, take up all the time asking you embarrassing questions, interrupting continuously.

When George Nigh ran against Attorney General Larry Derryberry in 1978, their first major debate was scheduled for Channel 2 in Tulsa, at request of news director Jack Morris. I was Nigh's second, handling arrangements.

The agreement I had with Morris was for a formal debate, the only way to go for a non-lawyer. It's also the only way to conduct a fair debate. Each speaker was to get 20 minutes extolling his own virtues, nine minutes to tear down his opponent's arguments.

But when we go to the studio, a hot-shot producer from back east somewhere insisted he would change the rules. Morris seated himself as far away from me as he could, acting as though we were just then going to make the rules and letting the hot-shot producer do the talking.

"It'll be a lot more interesting for viewers, Marty," Mr. Hot-Shot said, "to let the candidates go head to head, asking questions and answering back. That's how we've decided to do the show."

"The hell you beller," I interrupted. "We came here for a formal debate and that's what we're having. Or nothing."

"The show starts in 15 minutes," he sniffed. "What are you going to do about that, walk out and let everyone think your guy's afraid?"

"Walk out is exactly what we'll do," I shot back, reddening and rising from my chair. "On the way out we'll call a press conference. Several newspaper people are outside the door. We'll just hold ourselves a press conference and let the world know what you guys are trying to pull."

As I turned to go, wondering if I were stupid, Jack Morris held up his hand.

"Uh, Marty and I did sorta have an agreement," he admitted. "Maybe we should go on that basis rather than cancel."

Which we did. Except they let Derryberry horn in a few times on Nigh's time, with pointing finger and prosecutorial tone, asking questions and changing the subject.

A week or so later Nigh was in another debate on Channel 9 in Oklahoma City. Ed Turner, back from Washington and Metromedia, was KWTV news director. We made the same agreement for a formal debate as with Channel 2, except this time I told Ed how they tried to change the rules on us in Tulsa.

"I won't let it happen," Ed promised.

He lived up to his word. Midway of Nigh's remarks, Derryberry raised himself, began interrupting with a pointed question. George ignored him a few seconds. Derryberry's questioning became more insistent.

"Mr. Derryberry," Turner stepped in, "you know, I'm sure, rules of this debate don't allow you questioning your opponent on his time. If you question Mr. Nigh, you must do it on your time, not his."

Derryberry came off looking not so hot.

News people like blood on the floor. It's what you get from no-holds-barred argument between two candidates, billed as a debate. But if one debater is a gentleman and the other a gut fighter, the gut fighter will leave the gentleman dead on the floor.

Since my candidates are always gentlemen and ladies, I insist on a fair-to-both formal debate or nothing. Unless, of course, my candidate overrules me, in which case he's probably a lawyer.

HOW TO GET DRAFTED

Be a reluctant dragon when becoming a candidate. Use the technique girls did when I was young.

"How will I know you really love me if we don't get married first?"

Only sensible answer to that question is a slyly administered double martini. Girls who kept 'em begging and refused the martini until the engagement notice was in the paper, I observed, got married first.

I recommend this scarcity technique for political candidates. Don't hop in bed the first time someone says, "I love you." It might be only careless flattery. Play hard to get. Insist on the ring, which in politics means campaign funding.

If friends urging you to run are serious, they'll gladly form a Draft Jim Jones Committee. Should they first hang back from this suggestion, which they likely will, it's up to you to take them onto the mountain and reveal the lush valley below where they can stake a claim once you're elected. Nothing unsavory. Perhaps no more than a brief recitation of the choice patronage plums available to a governor or U.S. Senator, which you intend passing out to your true friends.

First you need a bell cow, somebody known and respected around the state. This individual should publicly anounce at a press conference he will, "for the future welfare of our great state," head the Draft Jim Jones for Governor Committee. It's all right to add, if he likes, "Jones is not a politician and that's what we need for a change."

He'll be lying, of course, but you have to say something. It's *always* time for a change when you're on the outside looking in.

Once you start running for public office, you're a politician in the public's eye. So never use that "I'm not a politician" baloney yourself on the stump. Smart people will vote against you. And don't forget, smart people influence the not-so-smart.

With some effort, you can get draft-me committees set up throughout the state. Each is good for a press release advertising your name, along with some flattering words about how lucky we are to have you.

Voters definitely want something different than they've

been getting, especially in Congress. They also know most people with sense won't consider running for office because of the constant beating elected officials take. So they'll believe there's no way to get someone worthy except by drafting you.

Getting reluctantly drafted gives you a nice head start over candidates who just come out of the woodwork at election time, unknown and unloved.

HOW TO APPEAR FASCINATED

On the campaign trail every candidate hears many twice told tales. Yet you must appear fascinated with a voter's every remark, just as you trust he will be with your gems of wisdom. It isn't easy. Best technique for appearing charmed I know was developed by State Senator H. L. Richardson of California, explained in his book, *What Makes You Think We Read The Bills?*

"Over the years," says Richardson, "I developed the belt-buckle-level stare. I fix my gaze at the belt-buckle level, then turn so I'm looking directly at my listener. I put one hand to my mouth and hold my elbow with the other. I try to appear as a standing replica of the statue, *The Thinker*.

"Whenever I strike the standing Thinker pose I wait for appropriate times to "humph." An occasional humph properly punctuates the other person's conversation and definitely shows you are listening intently. It is important to become an expert humpher. People appreciate the attention."

This is an excellent way to make a voter think you are hanging intently onto his every word, while avoiding danger of developing a tic from staring 500 people in the eye each day.

"The trouble with the dead-in-the-eye technique," explains Richardson, "is that most people become distracted . . . very nervous. If you stare at a person's nose, it isn't long before he wonders if he has a blemish ... I tried the hair routine for awhile but noticed it was only moments before the person with whom I was conversing started rolling his eyes upward and patting himself around the head as if looking for some foreign object."

Yes, democracy is the best available form of government. In totalitarian countries nobody in authority bothers learning the belt-buckle listening technique. Our politicians at least give the impression of listening while campaigning, no matter how quickly they ignore your wishes once elected.

BE THE UNDERDOG

Best thing to be in any campaign is underdog. Not just any old underdog — but a courageous, fighting underdog.

Never become a *too far under* underdog. Such underdogs are losers.

You become a courageous, fighting underdog by being loud and clearly specific on one or two hot issues on which you can get 51 per cent of the people to take your side. Pitch your fight against got-it-made groups like utilities or those with special tax loopholes. If you're sincere and have that $600,000 minimum campaign chest, your chance of winning is outstanding.

Avoid being an early front-runner. That's for the birds. The entire trailing pack of candidates will howl against you. You're also number one on the media's embarrassing questions list.

Nicest place to be three or four weeks before the vote is hiding in second place behind the front runner all other candidates are trying to cut down.

Concentrate on the leader at the end. Make it a two-person race. Many voters prefer "not to lose my vote." They're looking for a substitute when their candidate falters. You can be him. Not because they love you but because they hate the front-runner who bounced their hero out of the race. You will get their vote if you seem most likely to beat that front-runner rascal.

Early front-runners win a few golf tournaments but not many elections.

DON'T EXPECT MUCH

It's foolish to expect much from volunteer campaign workers.

A few are world beaters and will make their presence known. The rest are socialites seeking reflection on themselves from spotlights shining on the candidate. They'll do a little work if you don't overload them. Ask a lot and they'll do nothing.

If you let 'em, your supporters will waste tons of costly campaign materials. Make no material available to volunteers until *you decide* the time is right. Volunteers get eager and ambitious to start an August Primary campaign in March and April. Keep stalling them until June, when you'll need them.

Never give people as much campaign material as they demand. You won't have enough money left for media ads if you do. Volunteers seek to impress with their dedication. Many ask for a gross of every campaign item, boasting loudly how they intend to blanket their county.

Liars.

"Sorry, this is a poor boy campaign," you must insist. "We're buying materials bit by bit, as we get the money. To cover everyone, we're forced to limit what any one person can get. But we'll have new stuff when you get this passed out."

Most of these eager beavers never ask for more.

I wish I had all the money spent just for bumper stickers never passed out in the many campaigns I've worked. It would buy me a six-figure treasury bond. At this writing, small bumper stickers cost eight cents apiece. When you give someone a hundred, a small handful, you're handing him eight-dollars.

It's a rare worker indeed who will get as many as 12 friends to use your bumper stickers. Pass them out sparingly.

At least half a candidate's campaign materials are wasted. You'll find this true if you check your volunteers' car trunks and garages election night.

BEWARE CHISELERS

Never spend money for distribution of materials unless you, or someone you trust, has had agreeable prior experience with those you're hiring.

Some of the worst cheaters are commercial houses offering door-to-door delivery service. I helped a city council candidate lose an election once by hiring the wrong outfit for such work. I suspect there is no entirely right company.

Winos are the staple of their work force. The best of these winos deliver some and hide some in culverts and handy garbage cans. The worst cover a block or two, then dump the rest of their material and rest up until time to collect their pay.

This is bad enough. But when the guy you hire to cover half a city with your candidate's last-minute handbills is also dishonest, it's tragic. I was a little suspicious, so called friends at various points in the district the night before election and *nobody* had gotten my candidate's handbill.

I raised some loud hell next day with the dude I paid $1,500 for this chore. He gave me the hard, steely eye excuse, "I check-ed myself and I know most of your handbills were delivered. Sure, some of my people miss a house or two. I guess those just happened to be where your friends live."

I thought of punching the guy in the nose but restrained myself. He was big and looked like a brawler who wouldn't be fussy about fighting fair. When I finally threatened to sue, he relaxed, saying, "Go ahead." I finally slunk away muttering to myself, a knot in my stomach as big as your fist, temples throb-bing and mouth so dry I couldn't spit. I wanted to cry but wouldn't give that thief the satisfaction.

This bastard saved even the wino charges and we lost the election, $1,500 up front and even more in cost of materials thrown away.

He's not alone. The woods are full of 'em.

So be grateful for the postal service. They make every door and you can sleep nights with them in charge of your campaign material.

YOU NEED A "NO" GUY

I'm usually the "No" and "Hell, no!" guy in campaigns. You can go broke fast without a "No" expert.

There's not enough money in Ft. Knox to buy everything people try to sell a political candidate. Unfortunately, the can-didate, if you leave it to him, will buy anything for sale. He figures there's always at least one vote in it. Which tells you how far from reality candidates get.

Most of these peddlers don't vote. They're too busy swin-dling candidates to even register.

The candidate and all other key personnel *must* refer every salesman to your "No" man. Otherwise you'll be driven insane

Never Sweat The Small Stuff

and the campaign will be bankrupt halfway through.

Every lodge has some bulletin in which ads are for sale. Every denomination of church has a paper or skimpy magazine God told them to fill with political ads. All printers in town, naturally, are "for your guy." Every rag-tag paper and magazine, you may be sure, will put out a special election edition. You'll hear from people with out-of-the-way billboards they are willing to sacrifice. Also people with brilliant campaign ideas they are willing to sell at a handsome figure only because, again, they're "for your guy."

"Your idea and product are great," I encourage each of these deadbeats. "I'd buy in a minute if I could. But every expenditure has to pass our finance committee. I'm sure gonna recommend it highly to 'em."

Naturally, your finance committee members are forever nameless because they usually don't exist. In my case, of course, they do and you're a liar if you say otherwise. Either way, you need this skinflint committee to blame for idiotic decisions turning down all those glorious bargains.

"Those nitwits wouldn't buy it," I explain when our would-be benefactors call back. "I know they're short of dough but I personally think you've got a hell of a deal and they're stupid to pass it up."

They usually mutter something about "your campaign's going nowhere," then hang up. Not perfect but it beats letting them pester the candidate and is better than saying, "Maybe later." Say maybe and this horde of grafters will call you day and night for a definite answer.

Some won't take no gracefully even from the finance committee. In that case, I never hesitate to present them my "Hell, no!" followed by "I flat don't give a damn." The latter remark in response to their threats of bad-mouthing my candidate among their many friends and the populace at large.

I laugh at 'em when it gets to this point. First I remind them they don't have any friends. "What's more," I add, "having you badmouthing my candidate is like a pat on the back from anyone else."

Were it up to me, I'd have cards printed with the names, addresses and phone numbers of all other candidates to pass out to these hustlers, with the suggestion, "Go see these candidates. I hope they buy your scam."

You won't lose a vote. Might gain a few. People are smart enough to know there's a lot of good in any candidate these grafters are knocking. A candidate smart enough to bypass them could make a good public official.

DON'T SWEAT THE SMALL STUFF

Never get stuck on the defensive.

Which means ignore the daily two-bit charges hurled against all strong candidates. Nothing is older than yesterday's paper. Radio-TV newscasts vanish into thin air. Most political charges disappear with the day's garbage.

If you've committed no crimes, this will be evident as the campaign proceeds. Your accusers will be losers. Thin-skinned candidates who answer every question and accusation help make voters believe such little puffs of harmless smoke are really raging fires.

Even the media want something to hang their hats on after you've been accused twice. If no proof is presented, they'll quit writing about it. The same with criticism of your actions in some prior political office.

Don't sweat this small stuff. Explain only major and vital

issues. Most accusations have short lives if you let them die a natural death. Respond to everything said and you make yourself look to the public like a crook trying to explain away his shady past.

Keep your mouth shut and most voters won't know tomorrow an accusation was made yesterday. You only help circulate and make lies bigger by replying.

On that rare occasion when an accusation catches the media's fancy and they won't let up, you must answer. But be in no hurry. Let the opposition howl awhile. The less you say, the more confident they become and the wilder their statements. You want to be able, when you finally turn and fight, to call them a liar and prove it.

When you answer, swing a meat axe ferociously against "this gutter smear on my good name." Show your accuser wrong on a single point, you've made him a liar for the rest of the campaign.

Talk positive, stay on the offensive and never let up on an opponent's weak point. Forget about his strength. You can reduce his strength only by showing his weaknesses. And once you answer that rare charge which must be replied to, forget it.

"I've already answered his smear and proved it wrong," is your stock reply.

You'll be answering until doomsday, and lose the election, if you reply more than once trying to explain every detail.

MAKE 'EM READ IT

Direct mail is vital. You need regular bulletins to keep your workers enthused. Show your happy candidate surrounded by large crowds. Print the polls when they favor your candidate. Reprint portions of glowing editorials.

Onward To Victory!

Direct mail to voters is equally important, especially for special interest groups. They include everyone — doctors, lawyers, merchants, chiefs, teachers, union members and all the rest.

First, you gotta make 'em open your envelope. So put something in large letters on the outside to arouse their curiosity. Some examples:

HE'LL SAVE YOU MONEY

Inside you tell about the candidate's tax-cutting plan.

HERE'S HELP FOR YOU

The message will appeal to greed of teachers or other special interest groups. I like to make these special interest letters or flyers a message from the head of the organization. The candidate's statement, also included, should be high-flown and nonspecific but the organization leader must get down to brass tacks and tell, "how he's going to help us."

FIVE GOOD REASONS
FIVE GOOD REASONS
FIVE GOOD REASONS
FIVE GOOD REASONS
FIVE GOOD REASONS

I've used this a couple time with good results. Just about everyone will look inside to see what the five good reasons are. They turn out to be five good reasons why you should vote for my candidate.

You can dream up a hundred variations of these teasers to suit whatever message you're trying to put across. We're all tribesmen. Other things equal, Catholics vote for Catholics, Protestants for Protestants, and everyone for whoever they think will put something in their pocket. That's the way it is. It's also why the government's going broke and breaking you and me, too.

But I'm talking about getting elected, not salvation. Be aware, however, demand for salvation is growing. President Reagan isn't the last to get elected by putting take-it-away ahead of gimme.

When you talk take-it-away from some, you're promising more to others. So the appeal isn't really different, even when preaching hell-fire and salvation.

SAVE YOUR MONEY

Nowhere is money wasted so recklessly as in political campaigns. Early in a campaign, candidates all want to go first class with everything. Losing poker.

George Nigh, in his campaigns for Lt. Governor and Governor, used the colors black and white exclusively. Makes sense.

Black and white is one color, black on white paper. It's much cheaper than two, three or four colors. Also more distinctive. Black on white is the strongest color in the spectrum.

In George's last Lt. Governor and Governor races, we used billboard paper saying only NIGH. You could read it a mile away. What's more, he saved money and didn't look extravagant. He also stood out as a special personality among all the red, white and blue billboards, fence straddlers and literature other candidates were using.

I don't know why so many candidates insist on posing as super-patriots by using red, white and blue. It's a mistake. When you do, voters can't tell when they drive by whether it's you or the 12 other candidates running. Nigh is the only statewide candidate I recall who used black and white on all his out-door materials. Whenever you saw his plain Jane black on white, you knew it was good ol' George. Which didn't hurt him.

Another way to have enough money at the end of a campaign, when it's desperately needed, is to ask people for donations continually. When you send out a letter or flyer, put a box in one corner urging donations and telling where to send them. The same with your newspaper ads. I sometimes even do it on radio. You won't pay for the ads but will raise some money. With every donation you get a firmer supporter than you had before, plus money you'll be grateful for ere long.

HOW TO BUY

All media are important but in different ways. You need newspapers for the long haul, radio-TV for a shorter period and billboards in limited quantity and time.

You can't write a book on a billboard. Anything more than the candidate's name, plus six words, is too much. I never buy more than half a showing of billboards. Otherwise you look like a big money candidate. People suspect those big spenders.

It's also a waste of money you can't afford. Billboards have gotten expensive because they're often monopoly operations. The spring rains and wind tear your paper. Keep billboard paper up more than 60 days and your candidate's picture on the poster looks like a rag picker.

You need newspapers for publicity more than advertising but you better buy the advertising or you'll get little publicity. You need newspaper advertising too, and I recommend starting it a week or two ahead of radio-TV. About five weeks out is a good time to begin your main newspaper ads.

Publishers, like preachers, yearn to see something in the

collection plate. So let 'em know early you're planning to buy a full schedule from them. Don't be bashful about adding that you're starting with them ahead of radio-TV. Little green monsters appear before publishers' eyes every time they think of hated TV, where more and more advertising dollars are going.

There is no better buy than weekly newspapers. They are most thoroughly read, sorta like one of the family. The Home Town Bugle is where you need publicity as well as advertising. A show of support in all these little towns adds up to the margin of victory in most campaigns.

Do not buy what I call weekly "dogs." These are weeklies owned by monopoly dailies in the same town. They are printed only to keep other possible weekly competitors out. Their limited circulation resides mostly out of state. Buy them and you throw money down a rathole.

In many ways radio is your best buy, although there are some stations only overly rich campaigns can afford. Their rates are high, ratings nil. You must know the territory when buying radio.

Stations with strong news departments are a must. Voters are readers, listeners and watchers of news. For the money, radio in early morning and evening drive times is your best buy.

Much the same is true of TV. I'm not crazy about highly rated TV comedy and musical shows. Half the viewers of these shows are ignoramuses who won't vote. For years I bought *Meet the Press* and other news talk shows for little or nothing. Nobody wanted them because of their low ratings. But I bought 'em whenever I could because every viewer is a voter.

I don't get fancy with TV spots. No fake cowboys before a

fire for me. This medium is one on one, your candidate eye to eye with each viewer. A lot of hoopla in TV spots is distracting. Sincerity and getting to the point quickly in each message is the way to go. Voting is serious business for most who indulge. You don't need to sing 'em a song or show pretty pictures.

In radio-TV, I start my advertising campaign seriously about three weeks out, starting slow and building to a crescendo the last few days. You need a variety of spots so voters don't get bored by two or three.

In all media, brevity works best. Long-winded details on issues will be neither read nor heard. Anything longer than a 60-second spot on radio-TV should be a special program put on for a special reason, such as to answer charges crucial to the campaign.

Sad to say, we voters aren't interested in the gory details. Just hit the high spots but be sure you get the guts into 30-seconds. Which leaves no time for corny jingles.

GET THAT MIDDLE 20 PER CENT

The key to every campaign is that 20 per cent of voters in the middle who make up their minds last. Since the name of the game is 51 per cent, you must have more than half these key swing voters election day.

They're hard to convince. They tend to be moderates, liberal in some things, conservative in others. They're Democrats, Republicans and Independents. Unless you have a landslide going, put some bait out toward the end this group will nibble at. Campaigns get strident. Lots of yelling and wild statements.

When campaign noise reaches its peak, moderate your statements. Tone down your radio-TV spots and newspaper ads. Paint yourself as Steady Eddie, serene above the strife. Those late bloomer moderates will warm to such strategy and they pick the winner nine times out of ten.

Anything over a five per cent margin is a landslide victory. In most two-person races, both candidates have a point or two above or below 40 per cent going into the final couple weeks. One may be as much as ten per cent ahead but still lose if he antagonizes that 20 per cent still undecided.

So don't get carried away by what a poll tells you. Polls tell a little about what was going on a week or two ago. Things have changed since then and are changing now. This change will favor you as these thoughtful, hesitant voters at last make their choice if you keep your cool and lower your voice.

Hey, diddle diddle, that group in the middle, they'll help you jump over the moon. Or bury you. It all happens the last ten days, when you must tread lightly and carefully.

All the polls you took won't help you then. And it's too late to take another. The time has come to use your common sense.

Speak softly and carry no sticks.

4

IMPEACH THE BASTARD!

The meek shall inherit the earth, but not the mineral rights.

Anonymous

Impeaching governors was common as electing them in Oklahoma's early days.

Not long after Jack Walton took office as governor in 1923, all hell broke loose.

An Oklahoma City policeman early in his life, "Iron Jack" could swing a stick or his fists effectively and did both often. He became Oklahoma City police chief in 1919. Then as now, police chiefs were largely political, beholden to the city council.

Walton took a liking to politics and four years later he was governor. But not for long.

The former lawman governor developed a sudden tender heart for imprisoned convicts. During his short term, Walton used his executive power to free an average of one convict per day. The public and legislature took a dim view of the soft bleeding heart tough Jack Walton suddenly developed.

"Impeach Iron Jack!" became the cry everywhere. The legislature met in September, 1923, its express purpose to do just that. But anyone out to cook Jack Walton's goose found him tough to get into the oven.

"Not by a damn sight!" declared the irascible governor. "I hereby declare martial law!"

While the legislature was preparing to meet and draw up impeachment charges, Walton sent his soldiers in and flat ran legislators out of the capitol. Citizens were ordered to keep off the streets of Oklahoma City after midnight. Firearms were forbidden for all but Walton's handpicked gunslingers.

The former police chief took several of his toughest trusted police officers with him when he became governor. He ordered them to set up machine guns at the city and county jails. Women, children and most men peered timidly from behind curtains when Walton's curfew hour struck.

This was the terrifying situation when crusty Adjutant General Charles F. Barrett and his aide, young Jay Perry, went to the governor's mansion with an ultimatum for Governor Walton.

General Barrett was tough as Walton and Perry was a tall, handsome young man about town, polo player athlete and aviation enthusiast. Also best friend of Mike Monroney, later Congressman and U. S. Senator.

"We went in to see Gov. Walton and General Barrett put it on him pretty heavy," Perry remembers.

"I'm here to warn you to end this damn fool martial law of yours and let the legislature meet as the law provides," the Adjutant General told Gov. Walton. "If you don't, I guarantee your impeachment is assured."

"Walton got a little red in the face but didn't even move," said Perry. "He just raised one hand and motioned to a couple of his gunslingers."

"Throw their asses out," ordered Walton.

"General Barrett huffed and puffed some but in 30-seconds we were gone," recalls Perry. "We had the law on our side, so the general kept telling me, but the law wasn't popular that day."

A week later, however, Judge George W. Clark issued an order restraining Walton from interfering with the legislature.

Only reason the judge's opinion stood up was due to a

smart and courageous sheriff, Tom Cavnar. Knowing Walton, Sheriff Cavnar took the wise precaution of deputizing a brigade of 4,000 deputies to protect the people's rights.

Then he sent word to Gov. Walton, "Come take over the courthouse, Jack, if you think you're big enough."

After that the legislature met without interference. It was October 11, 1923 when the legislature began considering impeachment. Twelve days later they announced Lt. Gov. M. E. Trapp was being promoted. Iron Jack and his armed thugs got the same treatment they had been so happily dishing out to others.

And "Iron Jack" was impeached.

Jay Perry was also in on another governor's impeachment, this one not so justified as Jack Walton's.

Henry S. Johnston of Perry, Oklahoma — tall, gentle and Lincolnesque in looks and temperament — was elected Governor in 1926. He was impeached for no greater crime than loyalty to his chief aide, Mrs. O. O. Hammonds, a lady with considerable knowledge of and little respect for many of the most powerful members of the Oklahoma legislature.

Mrs. Hammonds, dubbed the "Ewe Lamb" by her legislative detractors, guarded gentle Gov. Johnston's welfare with an iron hand sheathed in a white glove. If she disliked a legislator, that fellow played hell getting in to see Gov. Johnston.

She was also influential in the governor's decisions. He held her in high esteem, strictly for her ability and loyalty. There was no hanky panky but Gov. Johnston defended his ewe lamb to the last. This loyalty cost him impeachment and disgrace.

The disgrace, however, was short lived. Now, some 60 years later, history decrees Henry S. Johnston took a bum rap from a group of State Senators who weren't big enough to handle one little ewe lamb.

"We'll impeach the bastard if he doesn't get rid of that bossy female," legislators threatened daily.

Delegations were sent to the governor's office, demanding removal of this upstart woman. Gov. Johnston turned away their wrath gently but wouldn't budge from his defense of Mrs. Hammonds and her right to hold her job. The more pressure applied, the more determined Gov. Johnston became to keep her.

So one fine day Gov. Johnston indeed found himself impeached. Lt. Gov. W. J. Bill Holloway, gentleman and scholar if ever God made one, smelled the impeachment coming and left the state for a visit to Texas until the deed was done. Like the governor he succeeded, Holloway had no stomach for unfair tactics, not even when they were to his own benefit.

Upon hearing of Johnston's impeachment, Holloway put in a call to crusty Adjutant General Charles F. Barrett.

"Now that I'm governor," he stated, "I'll be obliged if you will tell Gov. Johnston that I'll be back from Texas in a few days and I'd like to move into the mansion as soon as possible and get settled."

Henry Johnston in temperament was the exact opposite of Jack Walton. Nobody would fear to approach him on any mission. So General Barrett didn't feel it necessary to go himself and deliver Gov. Holloway's eviction message. He gave that small task to his young aide, Jay Perry.

"I went over to the mansion that very afternoon," Perry told me. "I told Gov. Johnston, 'Gov. Holloway just called and asked General Barrett to advise you he's on his way home. He'd like to move into the mansion in a few days so he can get settled. Lots of things been piling up on him lately.' "

"Yes, I know, and I'd like to oblige," Gov. Johnston replied politely, "but it's simply impossible for us to move now. Why, our children are still in school. It would break their little hearts to leave in mid-semester. Tell him we just can't do that to them."

"But Holloway says. . ." Jay protested.

"Surely he'll understand I have too many things to attend to here," replied the impeached governor, "I couldn't possibly just pick up and leave now."

"He was so darn nice and so sad," said Perry. "I didn't have the heart to get tough with him. I went back and told General Barrett about Gov. Johnston's kids being in school and all that. He blew up in my face."

"You listen to me and listen good," shouted General Barrett. "I told you to tell that old man to get out of the mansion pronto. Now you go back there and explain to him that I, Adjutant General Barrett, says, "It's too bad about your kids being in school, Governor, but your goddamn kids are impeached too!' "

"I softened up the General's message some in translation," said Jay, "but insisting to that fine gentleman, Gov. Johnston, that he really had to pack and leave immediately was one of my toughest assignments ever. When I finally got through to him there could be no delay, he quietly nodded. I can still see the hurt in his kind eyes."

Politics is too often cruel and unjust to the gentle.

FIRST AIRBORNE CAMPAIGNERS

Jay Perry and Mike Monroney in the '40's and '50's were the first Oklahoma politicians to use the convenience of flying almost exclusively. Here they are shown at dedication of the Western Hills State Park airstrip. Pictured (l. to r.) are Rex Presley, then park superintendent and later a Sen. Bob Kerr choice to become U. S. Marshall; Perry, the pilot; Grace Hudlin, longtime Democratic Party co-chairman, and Sen. Mike Monroney.

5

POLITRICKS UNIVERSITY

We'll double-cross that bridge when we come to it.

Anonymous

It started so innocently that blustery February day in 1972. The Oklahoma Capitol Improvement Authority voted to receive plans for twin 5-story tax and education buildings from its planning coordinator — Hudgins, Thompson and Ball, Big Daddy of Oklahoma political contractors and architects.

HTB's fee was a modest $175,000 for these first plans. Everything routine, in the slick ol' groove.

But before those buildings went up, contractor and sub-contractor blood was running in the streets. Grand juries were called in Oklahoma City and Tulsa. Every word of testimony was leaked daily to the media — fact, fiction, gossip, the works. They were out to do in Gov. David Hall.

They pounded plenty nails into Hall's coffin, softening him up for the later kill.

In many ways David Hall is the most remarkable governor in Oklahoma history. If you went to central casting searching for an actor to play governor or even president, never would you find another fitting the part so perfectly as David Hall. He looked and acted governor, from the toe of his highly polished shoes to the sky-blue eyes and premature silver-gray hair topping his 6'2" lithe, athletic body.

Hall's easy, winning smile was his headlight showing the way. He pressed the flesh warmly, affectionately on the campaign trail.

Highly intelligent, Hall mastered the strange political art of remembering thousands of names. If he met you once, 50-50 he'd call your name right next time. If he met you twice, the third time he'd say, "How's your wife Helen, Marty?" He was that good.

Speaker J. D. McCarty, who also took a fall and went to prison, possessed some of these same David Hall qualities. So did Big Bob Kerr, most feared man in the U. S. Senate.

But neither McCarty nor Kerr could carry David Hall's briefcase when it came to looks or mastery of the politician's main art, blowing charm and flattery over every living thing.

Yet with all those talents, Hall was a tortured governor from the day he took office. His basic problem, a bad case of the shorts: never enough money to cover elections and gracious living.

Remember this as you read on and are tempted to chastize Gov. Hall too severely. He came up the hard way. Worked his way through school, yet won all scholastic honors.

At 17, Hall got Outstanding Student Award at Classen High School in Oklahoma City. He then knew the names of 1,800 fellow students. He became student council president, got Best Citizen and History awards, made National Honorary Society, was forward on the Class A state championship basketball team of '48.

"My ambition," he said then, "is to go into politics."

Hall graduated from Oklahoma University in 1952 with a BA in government and history. Next Harvard Law School, then Tulsa Law School, where he got his degree in 1959. Seven years later he made his first race for governor. Scared 'em to death but lost.

In college he waited tables, worked in a clothing store and as a tutor. Paid all his own way the last three years yet made

Phi Beta Kappa, President's Honor Roll, was national scholarship winner as a Harvard freshman law student, outstanding junior and senior law student at Tulsa University Law School, and more.

This All-American Boy married the All-American Girl, Jo Evans of Morrilton, Arkansas. Jo is a part-Cherokee lovely who became Beauty Queen at Arkansas State Teachers College. She bore David three lovely children. She bore her political burdens with grace, courage and outward calm. She looked the devil himself in the eye and spit in his face many times for David Hall.

Jo and David Hall's love was forged in the fierce fires and white heat of Oklahoma politricks, producing a union stronger than hardest steel. They are that rarest of creations, a couple in fine tune who will, I'm convinced, remain so.

Sadly, our All American Boy had not accumulated the fortune he needed to go with his personality. That was his downfall.

I hear tell it is hard for a camel to enter the eye of a needle; even harder for a rich man to enter the kingdom of heaven. I believe it, Oral Roberts to the contrary notwithstanding.

There is something even more difficult. That is for a poor man to remain unobligated in politics if he hopes to win. Even in Hall's day it took a minimum $500,000 to be elected governor. This money doesn't come from heaven or the good fairy but from people with wants.

Hall had a pile of campaign debts left from his first unsuccessful race for governor. This pile of debts had grown mountain size by the time he was elected.

Most who contributed to Hall's campaign had no unethical wants in mind. There are 300 boards and commissions to which a governor can appoint people. Unless a flat idiot, he appoints his friends. That's the honest way to pay off campaign debts.

Hall's first problem was he had one hell of a deficit, at least $300,000. Problem No. 2, he didn't keep close track of who collected money and how. Biggest problem of all was Gov. Hall took on the most powerful people in Oklahoma and beat 'em. They never forgive you for that.

In the spring of '71, Gov. Hall, twisting arms fiercely, forced through the legislature tax reform legislation adjusting gross production and state income taxes. Made the wealthiest pay a more equitable share. Some dogfight.

At the showdown, one legislator was brought to the chamber by ambulance. Gov. Hall kept the vote open six hours in the House to gain his final one-vote victory.

Along with this victory Hall acquired the most cunning and cruel enemies one can have in Oklahoma. Folks like Eddie Gaylord, the big banks, Big Oil and many others whose lips drip with fat from the high side of the hog.

It was a rare day thereafter when the metropolitan press, *Daily Oklahoman* in particular, wasn't on Hall's case bitterly over something real or imagined.

Since David Hall went to prison, I often think how nice it would be for someone to remember him now and then with a kind word. Like members of legislatures who followed him and, most especially, teacher organizations always screaming for higher pay. Hall first cut teachers in big on that pie.

Had David Hall not been a man of courage and ability, that treasury at the state capitol which has been filled to overflowing in recent years would be flat busted and needing new taxes much worse than it does.

I sometimes go to the capitol and sit in the peanut galleries listening to the hollow, self-serving ramblings drifting upward. I strain in vain to hear a kind word of praise for the man most responsible for the largesse those now in power are handing out. I have yet to hear praise of Hall for benefit of the media and public by today's statesmen, who would be steering the ship of state in much angrier waters except for forgotten David Hall.

But I come to bury Caesar, not to praise him. The evil men do still lives after them, the good too oft interred with their bones. So was it with Hall.

Nobody wanted worse to be governor. Hall maybe wanted it too much. A dynamo, when he got to the top of the mountain he wouldn't stop climbing. Always another crag to mount. Finally soaring into the clouds.

In 1972, Hall's big thing was a giant road bond issue. Let me tell you about road bond issues. I have worked closely with and for three Oklahoma governors and known all others who served the past 35 years. Except for George Nigh, every damn one got sold on the idea of a giant bond issue for roads and highways somewhere along the way.

Where does each governor get this identical brilliant idea? From road contractors, of course. Road contractors give generously to political campaigns, especially governor races. They have the odd notion there is a connection between who becomes low bidder on state road projects and who backs the winner for governor.

Of course this is not true, according to all laws, rules and regulations. Still, road contractors persist in their campaign generosity. Read on. There shall be light.

In Hall's case, the pressure was on to submit a $250-million bond issue for roads. A way for road contractors to get more work and thus pay for their help in Hall's campaign. The people, in a rare flash of wisdom, turned 'em down, 3 to 1.

HALL'S ROAD BONDS LOSE

screamed the *Daily Oklahoman's* next day headline. It was Hall's first big setback and hurt. But the wound was minor compared to what came later. Grand juries met, Republican prosecutors schemed and rats in the hold of Hall's sinking ship of state scampered topside, hanging briefly by their tails from the ship's mooring rope before one by one jumping off.

Gov. Hall had both the FBI and Republican U.S. Attorney William Burkett on his tail. They were investigating political contributions from state contractors to Hall, "with an eye toward a possible extortion indictment," screamed the Hall-hating *Daily Oklahoman*.

Ace investigative reporter Jack Taylor of the Oklahoman was on Hall's case like a blood-sucking leech, trying to find something, anything, incriminating the governor. He came up with wind, smoke, allegations and plain country gossip by the carload. Various prosecutors seeking indictments allowed nearly every word uttered during the "secret" grand jury proceedings to leak to the press.

Grand juries investigated Hall and friends both in Tulsa and Oklahoma City during November and December, 1973. Several indictments resulted but David Hall's name was not among them. They couldn't lay a glove on Hall except through insinuations, more plentiful than stinkweed in a wet spring during Hall's last two years in office.

Not to say there was no suspicion. There was plenty. Clouds of question marks hung over Hall's head. They were dark, demanding clouds, the kind that used to follow Joe

Btfstk, that weird Li'l Abner character who left earth-shaking disasters behind wherever he trod.

Gov. Hall was no easy mark. He'd been around the block a few times. An attorney, he was a one-time able Tulsa prosecutor. He knew tricks of that trade. Having run twice for governor, he was an honors graduate of Politricks University.

Hall knew he was being bugged and spied upon. His sworn enemies were the most powerful and ruthless individuals in Oklahoma. So Gov. Hall walked softly but brandished no sticks. He followed the wisest maxim for any politician: They can't hold against you what you don't say.

When warning devices started going off in the governor's office, indicating bugging equipment at work, Hall became wary and scary. His tax specialist lawyer, Richard Frank McDivitt, hired flamboyant, fast-talking former legislator Robert O. "Bob" Cunningham to do some investigating for Hall on the other side of the street where Hall's enemies were.

"We've been told to dig out the truth," Cunningham told reporters. "Let the cards fall the way they're going to fall. The only thing I'm interested in and the only thing Gov. Hall is interested in . . . is that, hopefully, the truth of all transactions can be verified."

It seems clear Cunningham planned for his private detectives to go over much of the same ground as the two grand juries. Whether Cunningham's people helped or hurt Hall's cause is a hard question. Gov. Hall's top aide, Joe Carter, was indicted for perjury by a Tulsa County grand jury.

Carter's indictment was based on a flimsy allegation he lied to the grand jury when he testified he didn't hear all of a conversation between another Hall aide, A. W. "Sunny" Jenkins, and Gov. Hall's private eye, Bob Cunningham. During the conversation in question, Jenkins allegedly admitted delivering $120,000 to one Carl Ballew, fund-raiser for Gov. Hall.

Joe Carter was later cleared of all charges but it cost him money, his job in the governor's office and much pain and anguish for self and family. Grand juries are supposed to be secret but I have never known one in Oklahoma that didn't get front-page coverage with every rumor and piece of unfounded gossip presented.

I personally believe grand juries should be abolished. Rarely does one come up with an indictment that sticks. Yet they commonly destroy innocent peoples' reputations for political purposes.

Let's go inside the grand jury in Oklahoma City investigating contractors and sub-contractors who had the "lowest and best bids" for constructing office buildings in the state capitol complex under Gov. Hall. That something was amiss I'm sure you'll agree. But all the grand jury accomplished was to grant a lot of people involved immunity and create sensational headlines aimed at toppling Hall.

Had evidence submitted to the grand jury been put in the hands of a prosecutor willing to file charges, by-passing the grand jury, I'm convinced there would have been convictions. But politricks reared its head, baring forked tongue and slyly winking eye.

Those holding trump cards in this grand jury investigation were after Gov. Hall, not justice. That's how it is with grand juries. So I say, if you have evidence of wrongdoing, Mr. Prosecutor, file charges and give the accused his guaranteed fair and speedy trial. If you lack sufficient evidence, by what right do you smear reputations through trial by the media via grand jury leaks from the prosecution?

A popular lawyer for political figures called before grand juries in Oklahoma is James W. "Bill" Berry of Oklahoma City. He's handled many big ones, including J. D. McCarty and top figures involved in the proceedings I'm about to relate to you.

Berry is big on getting clients immunity. A former Oklahoma County prosecutor, Berry knows grand juries can be manipulated. If he can't get his client immunity, it's a good bet he'll take the Fifth.

"There are no deaf and dumb people in the penitentiary," Berry explains, "but you'll find lots of good talkers."

Berry appeared before the grand jury with his client, contractor Carl G. Ballew, December 5, 1973. Ballew was talking. He had immunity from prosecution, which makes talking easier.

I don't personally know Carl Ballew but from what he told the grand jury, he's gotta have a heart big as all outdoors. He was David Hall's main man for money who never faltered, even at the risk of going broke.

"I contributed about $5,000 . . . ran that up to about $9,000 by the time he (Hall) was actually elected governor," Ballew testified. "We were asked to put an employee on our payroll and we did that, at request of David Hall. She stayed on the payroll 10 months."

Ballew estimated for the grand jury that David Hall carried $300,000 in campaign debts with him into the governor's office.

"That's a lot of money," he understated, which it sure was in '69 and '70. No way the governor is going to pay it off from his salary.

So Ballew entered into an agreement whereby he helped raise additional funds for Hall.

"The reason a larger amount was needed . . . was that the

mansion fund was going to be approximately $5,000 short of actual needs," Ballew stated, "so I agreed to fund this money every month, up to the tune of approximately $50,000."

Some babe in arms! Ballew soon found out the more money he raised, the more was needed. Normal in politics.

"As months went by, requests for money got bigger," he testified. "Last amount I furnished was $10,000 . . . and we had run up approximately $80,000 worth of expenditures during that time."

Ballew testified he had nearly $500,000 worth of his own collateral up to guarantee his loans to Gov. Hall. Where did the money go? Here, there and yon. Such things as Dan Rambo, Hall's legal counsel, "signed for some," claimed Ballew.

"We paid the moving bill of Joe Carter, the press agent, from Washington, D.C. down here," said Ballew. "We paid money to a black man in charge of some sort of public relations in the governor's office so he could go to the funeral, I believe, of Martin Luther King."

Such things, I assure you, seem essential when a new governor rides proudly into office with his victorious entourage feeling their oats. The world is their apple and they never. suspect worms until they've swallowed one.

Ballew made clear monies he furnished Gov. Hall were understood by Hall as loans to be repaid. But repayments came slow, requests for more money frequent. Ballew couldn't keep up with his big shot beggars.

"It was astronomical, the amounts needed," he declared. "I just couldn't finance it. Not much was going on at that time . . . no work being let. I'm not insinuating work had to be let for me to be paid," he added lamely, "but there wasn't much going on."

Ballew was a worried man when Lynn "Buddy" Hall, dark-haired, jovial and slightly heavy set but a cheerfully smiling hail-fellow-well-met decided to pay Ballew a visit. This Hall, no relation, was Gov. Hall's chairman of the State Board of Affairs. Ballew explained Buddy Hall's potential for becoming his saviour. Buddy Hall was the state's chief buyer.

"He's in position," Ballew advised the jury, "to at least be part of the final say on who would be awarded contracts . . . So he would have some influence, with that kind of purchasing power."

Yes, Virginia, there is a Santa Claus. You just need to know his many disguises.

Ballew said he visited with Gov. Hall several times about the money owed him before Board of Affairs Chairman Buddy Hall came to see him.

"I am told that . . . we're supposed to help you with anything we can," Ballew quoted Buddy Hall. "In the conversation, Mr. Buddy Hall told me he could get some money . . . by invoicing a man by the name of David Vaughn for some work."

Vaughn was identified as an Oklahoma City contractor. Ballew explained how the deal was to work.

"If I would give an invoice to this man; we didn't do any work but still we got paid. That was handled by Buddy Hall. He brought the invoices. Then he carried the invoices to Mr. Vaughn, picked up a check and brought the money back . . . We put the money in the bank, put the invoice on our books and declared it income."

You see why Ballew's attorney, Bill Berry, is a believer in getting immunity for his clients before they testify? Assistant District Attorney Marti Hirst had some pointed questions for Ballew at this point:

Q. It's a phony invoice? You didn't do the work but you got

paid for it from some contractor?

A. Right.

Q. The first phony invoice was with ... Tankersly Construction Co.?

A. Right.

Q. And it was Buddy Hall's idea. Is that correct?

A. Right.

Q. And you knew you weren't going to do the work, is that right?

A. Yes, before we invoiced the man we knew we weren't.

Q. What was the amount?

A. $6,800.

Q. OK, what was the next one?

A. The next one was with Vaughn Construction Co. for $4,900. I believe.

Q. All right, were there any others?

A. To Jack Cook Construction Co., or J. J. Cook Construction Co., and ...

Q. Are all these Oklahoma City construction companies?

A. Yes, right. And then W. and W. Steel Co.

Tell us about the one to J. J. Cook Construction Co.

A. Well, that was in the latter part of '72, before we had gotten any money back at all, other than the $50,000 from Jenkins (A. W. Sunny Jenkins, Gov. Hall's chief aide). So we invoiced J. J. Cook Construction Co. for one invoice of $5,700 and one for $20,000. We were paid ... the $5,700 and we were paid $15,000 on the $20,000 account ... and then we invoiced W. and W. Steel Co. for one invoice of $2,200 and one invoice of $10,000 and those were paid."

These payments helped ease Ballew's pain but not entirely. He was holding the sack for more, and no snipe in sight. But on a cold December day, Ballew related, he got a call from Gov. Hall's dollar-a-year aide, A. W. Sunny Jenkins.

"I was called by Mr. Jenkins to meet him at his motel room," explained Ballew. "He said, 'We are going to get you paid the money we owe you.' I said, 'Fine' ... In the meeting, with him came Allen Cowen from Shawnee (chief contractor on the capitol complex office buildings) ... Mr. Cowen informed me we were going to have to invoice for this money. There wouldn't be any payment unless we did. My main concern ... was the taxes that would be due ... We were going to invoice $122,000 worth of business ... So I said, 'It looks to me like that someone is going to owe $60,000 more money.' They wanted me to take the total $122,000 ... We would report it as income and we would then have to pay the tax."

Who likes to pay taxes? Nobody. Wise contractors do so anyway. Ballew admitted an understanding that he was to write phony invoices to get his money. He was to go to Shawnee and be told how much to bill on what jobs.

"So I went to Shawnee next morning and met with their (Cowen's) accountant," Ballew testified. "He had a list prepared for me to bring back to Oklahoma City and type the invoices and then I was requested to deliver them back. I understand now why I was requested to deliver them back ... because there is a penalty for mail fraud."

Indeed there is. You can go to jail.

Ballew admitted delivering the invoices. A week passed, the plot thickening.

"I got another call from Mr. Jenkins," Ballew stated. "He said, 'Meet me at the same place, my room. We are going to get you paid.' "

"Well, fine," a surprised Ballew responded.

"There's been a change ... We'll pay you in cash," Ballew quoted Jenkins.

"So then I got to thinking about the possibilities," mused a confused Ballew. "The meeting was to be at 6:00 p.m. That was a strange time. He called me about 3:00, and at 6:00 in the evening there aren't any drive-in banks open. What am I going to do with $80,000?

"I was concerned enough about it, I called a member of the Highway Patrol, David Hall's ex-security chief. I was going to ask him to accompany me to the Habana Inn (Where Jenkins was staying), but he was out of town. So I asked my secretary and her husband to meet me there ... I didn't like the idea of that much money to keep overnight ... *I was concerned I might not get to keep it.*

"When I went to the club ... Mr. Jenkins came to the top of the stairs, motioned me to come upstairs. We went upstairs and he gave me $80,000. When he opened the suitcase he had, I think, three packets of money ... The packet I received was an $80,000 bundle of brand new twenty-dollar bills. They were wrapped and bound with a wood end (and) had a metal binder on two sides. They were signed out of some kind of Federal Reserve system."

Ballew added that Jenkins left the $80,000 for him inside Jenkins' suitcase.

"Then I gave it to my secretary and her husband and they took it home that night and delivered it to the office next morning."

During that day, Carl Ballew testified, he "took Mr. Jenkins from the bank to the bottom entrance of the capitol office building and on the way over he (Jenkins) showed me he was wearing a gun. He asked me what I was going to do with that $80,000.

"I said, 'Well, I'm going to put it in the bank.'

"He said, 'I wouldn't do that if I were you.'

"Why?"

" 'Well, you may not have to pay tax on it.'

"So I split the money up, put part of it in the bank and part in a safety deposit box ... By doing that, if I did have to pay tax on it, I'd have $40,000 in one year, $40,000 in another."

At this point Ballew put in an unsolicited testimonial for Gov. David Hall, even though the governor's needs apparently had gotten Ballew into all this hot water.

"I want to make this plain," said Ballew. "I instructed David Hall that anything we did, that I did for him, we were going to leave records, tracks. He acknowledged this and said I should keep records and destroy them after 12 months. So he was sure I was keeping records. He was also aware I may have to pay some taxes. He had agreed to pay those taxes."

$80,000 in cold cash twenties is a pretty good bundle but it didn't cure all money-man Ballew's wounds. He said he wound up owing $120,000 on a three-year balloon type note with ABC bank. The former bank president he dealt with had left, Ballew alleged, and the bank wouldn't renew his note.

"When they called the note, I visited with the governor and then I did make some more payments," said Ballew. "The chairman of the board extended the note one time (but) the new president made a threat that if I didn't pay that note he wanted my farm and the real estate my business is on. I refused to give him my farm because it was about a $180,000 item. So then he sued me immediately."

At this point, Ballew testified, "I went ... to see David Hall. He called Mr. Jenkins in and says, 'Do we still owe you any money?'

"I said, 'I can't answer that because we still have a tax problem and if it's decided taxes must be paid on these invoices, then you owe me a considerable amount of money.'

"Then Jenkins says, 'I can guarantee you we are not going to use those invoices.'

"The governor stood up and said, 'I want this man helped.' In other words, 'I want this thing out of that bank so we don't have any depositions and no problems with it.' "

Ballew estimated he incurred indebtedness of "over $200,000" while fiercely flapping his wings to stay airborne as Gov. Hall's financial angel. Yet after the crash he took his lumps philosophically.

"I don't feel any deep animosity toward the governor," he declared. "I have learned a good lesson but I was 21 years old when I went into this."

Thus wisdom is acquired in our wicked world.

GOVERNOR CANDIDATES . . .

This crew of hearties were all candidates for governor in the spring of 1958, assembled together for the Democratic Party's Jefferson-Jackson Day Dinner, whose featured speaker was a young Senator who talked funny, John F. Kennedy. Front row (l. to r.) are Herbert Hope, W. P. Bill Atkinson, Wilburn Cartwright, Tom Payne and Waldo Stephens. Back row includes (l. to r.) Bill Harkey, J. Howard Edmondson, Jim Rinehart, Bill Doenges and George Miskovsky. Barely visible upper left are (l. to r.) Senator Bob Kerr, Gov. Raymond Gary and Senator Kennedy. Payne and Stephens from this group failed to file but the rest did, along with R. V. Samples, Joe Barber, William O. Coe, Andrew Wilcoxen and A. B. McDonald.

BEFORE TRAGEDY STRUCK...

In front of a backdrop of the party faithful manning phones, Gov. David Hall and I make our Oklahoma pitch for funds during a national Democratic Party telethon shortly before David's world started falling apart in the early '70's. I never knew a better political fund-raiser than Gov. Hall but when his time of trouble came, lawyer fees were high, donors to his defense fund few. In politics, next question after "What have you done for me lately?" is "What can you do for me next?"

6

LOWEST AND BEST BIDDER

POLITICAL GUARANTEE: If it breaks in two before you get home, we'll give you both parts.

Carl Ballew had big trouble getting back the money he loaned Gov. Hall because of complications involved in complementary bidding.

Complementary bidding is the exact opposite of competitive bidding. The low bid is always higher than it should be under complementary bidding. That's because the contractor ticketed to get the "lowest and best bid" has good buddies bidding even higher than his high bid. The predetermined winner of the contract usually tells the others how much to bid.

Into this thicket the grand jury headed.

Complementary bidding, Oklahoma style, was explained to attentive jurors in December, 1973. Two of the central figures were contractors E.A. Cowen II of Shawnee and Walter Nashert, Jr., Oklahoma City.

Cowen was awarded the prime contract for the state capitol complex office buildings, let during Hall's administration. After sounding out a few folks, Nashert decided to submit a complementary bid instead of the serious bid he said he initially planned.

But shed no tears for Nashert. He wound up with a nice contract of his own.

By promising to be truthful, Nashert was granted immunity from prosecution. Cowen got no such chance to be truthful without risk. Makes a big difference. When political contractors get immunity, they speak right up against the less fortunate buddies they're testifying against, who cringe, cuss and take the Fifth.

"Did you intend to perform the work as you submitted the (complementary) bid?" they asked Nashert.

"No," he replied, "we did not."

"Did you ever intend to perform the work?"

"No."

Nashert testified to getting a call about it from Robert Berry of Cowen Construction Company, Shawnee.

"I told Mr. Berry I would consider submitting a complementary bid for him," Nashert admitted. ". . .Complementary bidding is not uncommon in the construction industry."

Indeed not. Such bids always turn a fine profit for someone.

"A complementary bid," explained Nashert, hitting it on the head, "is one in which a contractor submits, at the request of another contractor, (a bid) that is generally understood will be higher than the bid the other contractor would turn in."

Assistant Oklahoma County District Attorney Marti Hirst broke in to inquire if this practice is common on state projects.

"It is common to the extent it is an accepted practice," replied Nashert.

There is one slight problem with the "accepted practice." It is unlawful.

Nashert submitted a complementary bid for Cowen, and Cowen got the main contract. But Nashert got a contract of his own from Gov. David Hall's Democratic administration. Not because he was a loyal Democrat. Fact is, Nashert confessed to being Republican.

"Through complementary bids," is how Republican

Nashert explained his luck in getting his big state contract.

There was tunnel work to be done on the capitol complex projects. Nashert's company enjoyed digging tunnels.

"We were pursuing this (tunnel work) and had a couple contractors call and say, 'I'm not particularly interested. Would you give me a complementary bid to turn in?' We said we would . . . I contacted all the bidders and said, 'We would like to give you a complementary bid to turn in *so we will, in fact, be low bidder.*' "

That is how Nashert's company came to submit "the lowest and best bid" on tunnel work. As fate would have it, Cowen Construction Co. was among those returning a favor by this time submitting a complementary bid on Nashert's behalf. Nashert got an $829,000 contract.

My interest in tunnels is minimal. When you've seen one, you've seen 'em all. Round things with a hole at each end. But when I go into contracting, I'm specializing in complementary bidding. That's where the money is.

The number of immunity shots given witnesses by County Attorney Curtis Harris made the 1973 grand jury proceedings resemble a clinic more than a courtroom. For Scout's honor promises of truthful disclosure, Harris let off the hook Don Lippert, Edgar Blount, R. C. Cunningham and several other contractors.

Contractor Cunningham bid on the State Library Building. He admitted he would "probably have to say yes" when asked if his was a complementary bid.

General contractor Don Lippert testified Lippert Brothers bid on the Tax and Education Building. He told of calling Bob Berry of Cowen Construction because he heard they were bidding the job "real hard."

"It doesn't look like I'm going to be able to get a bid together," he claims he told Berry, "and I would like for you to give me a figure or indicate what the job might be worth." Then he added, "I used the figures he gave me . . . to establish figures that I wrote down."

Blount came right out and admitted submitting a complementary bid on the Library and Education Building.

"We do it all the time," he declared.

J. J. Cook's company also got a contract on the State Library and Education Building. Asked about complementary bidding, Cook stated, "It is just like they say . . . you scratch my back, I'll scratch yours."

Cook testified he paid $12,000 to W. & W. Steel Company "to get delivery we needed" on materials. He also explained why he allegedly paid $20,000 to Interstate Painting Company at request of Board of Affairs member Buddy Hall.

"I just felt like somebody possibly . . . might have given me a bad time before the job was over if I didn't," he stated.

Pressed as to why he dished out that kind of money from his own pocket, Cook gave this tolerant answer:

"We found it better in some cases to go ahead and give them what they want, whether it is right or wrong. That is the way we have been doing business for years."

When Gov. Hall's aide, Arthur Warren "Sunny" Jenkins took the stand, he did so at considerable risk. He had no immunity nor had he taken the Fifth.

But some things were weighing heavy on his heart, such as the fact he was about to be indicted. So Jenkins unburdened himself.

Jenkins said one of his duties with Gov. Hall was to "furnish funds as requested" to pay the governor's expenses. He added that he gave the money to Hall or his secretary and it was "generally speaking, cash, at the governor's request ... He (Gov. Hall) felt it would be in his best interest not to have names thrown around."

You understand why cash was wanted. Checks carry names. Names become live witnesses.

Jenkins unfolded a lurid tale of intrigue and mystery. He declared he kept a "complete set of records: showing who he gave money to." But a sad thing happened. In fact, two sad things.

"The records were taken from my office," Jenkins lamented.

But wiley Sunny Jenkins had still another set of these same records. Kept 'em at his house.

"My house was broken into and these copies were also taken," Jenkins complained.

Jenkins swore he kept the records to show, if asked, where every dime had gone.

"I didn't want to take chances of anyone saying I kept any money whatever for my own benefit," Jenkins said, "because I didn't need any money of my own ... I've got plenty money to last me the rest of my life ... I wanted to know how state government worked and, believe you me, I found out."

Jenkins' story may sound unlikely to you, but I've heard stranger tales in Oklahoma politics that are absolutely true.

Jenkins told of getting $122,000 from contractor Allen Cowen, "in an attache case, in twenty-dollar bills."

Jenkins said he counted it to make sure the amount was correct.

He admitted having a loaded gun the day he paid contractor Ballew $80,000. He also told of collecting money from H. E. Bailey, then Oklahoma's toll road czar. In cash, he said, because that was the governor's standard directive.

"I have handled hundreds of thousands of dollars," declared Jenkins.

"Sunny" exactly describes Jenkins. Slender, of medium height, Jenkins could use an equalizer if confronted. His laughing blue eyes and modest physique bespeak gentleness. Few men would cower before Sunny Jenkins unless facing a loaded gun. Being involved with so much cash money, and with many people knowing it, Jenkins was wise to let word filter out he was carrying a rod.

Jenkins and Allen Cowen, who got the prime contract on the state office buildings, were close friends. Cowen is an opposite of Jenkins. Sturdy and strong, he wore the long, full sideburns then favored by macho young men.

Jenkins admitted specifications for the job, later awarded Cowen, didn't contain an anti-collusion provision. Asked if he did anything to help his good friend Cowen get the job, Jenkins stated:

"Not any more than I would anyone else if they called me to help them get these jobs within the money . . . My concern was saving the state money, not gypping the state out of money."

Questioned further about the $122,000 cash he picked up in an attache case from his friend Cowen, the following dialogue took place between Jenkins and the district attorney:

"Kind of unusual to deal in that kind of money in the way it was dealt with, isn't it?" Jenkins was asked.

"Yes, it is."

"Did you think there was something wrong with that?"

"Well, when you are acting under directions of someone else . . . that was the best way I knew how to do it. . . ."

"You thought something was wrong with it, didn't you?"

"...No, I didn't think anything was wrong with it. The governor wanted the money...."

"Wasn't it a most unusual thing, to deal in that money in cash that way and carry it around in an attache case?"

"Very unusual, yes ... as a matter of fact, my eyes bugged out. *I never saw so many twenty-dollar bills in my life.*"

"Was the governor aware of your plans with Mr. Cowen to borrow the money?"

"Yes."

"Did you tell him Mr. Cowen borrowed the money?"

"I told the governor I borrowed $122,000 from Allen Cowen ... I didn't know how much plainer to put it."

"Did you give Mr. Cowen any money from campaign funds to pay that debt back over at the bank?"

"No, I didn't give him anything."

"Where do you suppose he got the money to pay the loan back in 30 days?"

"Well, from what I have heard — I've heard he got it from subcontractors. That's all I know."

Before Jenkins gave this testimony, there was newspaper speculation he was about to be indicted. His last-minute grand jury appearance didn't save him. Jenkins was indicted along with four others.

On land or sea, big fish eat little fish. So it is with contractors. Jimmy Lee Clay, head of Comet Mechanical Contractors, at one point thought he had a lock on one $2-million subcontract for the State Tax and Education Building. Somebody broke his lock.

"I did make the statement to Allen Cowen himself," Clay told the grand jury, "that if we bid this project we weren't going to put in any kickback money."

Asked why he told Cowen that, Clay said it was "because of general knowledge and rumors that there was a kickback in it."

According to Clay's further testimoney, you better be on the inside during a contract letting if you hope to prosper. Things change fast, up to the final minute before a bid is let.

Clay told of getting a suite at Lincoln Plaza in Oklahoma City the night before the letting, directly above Allen Cowen's suite. He thought he was an insider.

"They had just come out with this addendum, a change in specifications, that evening," he declared. "We knew what was going to be on it the day before. No other contractor had this information. . . ."

Clay said he didn't get the addendum until that evening at the Lincoln Plaza.

"It had just been printed," he stated. "One of the changes made was reduction in size of the equipment."

"Reduction in size of equipment" and other last minute changes nobody else knows about can really help the bidder ticketed to get the job.

Yet even when you think you're on the inside, you can wind up on the outside, as Clay learned. Change in signals from "the Big Man."

"A subcontractor, only thing he's got to go on is the word of the general contractor," Clay woefully advised the grand jury, "because your bid is not submitted in a written form . . . You're depending strictly upon the general contractor."

Clay's downfall on this particular contract began when competitor Ted Wolfe allegedly came to him "trying to make a deal." Clay bore Wolfe no ill will but felt he had this fish fried for himself and wasn't about to cut Wolfe in.

"I wouldn't go for no deal," testified Clay, "because at the time I thought we were pretty well assured of the contract . . . Ted is a good competitor. If he could pull some strings and get the job, then as far as I was concerned, that's a competitor. I would probably do the same thing to Ted and go out and drink a beer together later. That's not, in the construction business, considered to be cheating."

You gotta go some in the construction business to be considered cheating. Clay was nonetheless sorely disappointed to learn pressure was apparently applied to produce a complete reversal on "his" contract within two hours.

"They said they had gotten the word from the Big Man," he said. "Hall was very definitely who they were referring to."

Clay claimed Bob Berry of Cowen Construction called and wanted him to come to his office in Shawnee and talk about the job.

"So Stan Anthony (working with Clay) and I went down Saturday . . . They said they were hit up. Said there had been some new political debts come up and they had to come up with another $100,000. He was wanting the whole thing from us and I told him we didn't have that kind of money in the job."

So Clay's fish flopped back into the water, to be caught by competitor Ted Wolfe. Wolfe assured jurors there was no politics involved. Then he was asked about Cowen allegedly wanting a kickback.

"Well, I would have to say yes, although they didn't call it that," replied Wolfe. "Allen Cowen asked me if I had any objection to putting $50,000 on my contract, adding it to my contract."

Turned out they wanted cash. It was "funds involving politics" as best Wolfe knew.

Subcontractors don't get all the gory details. But Wolfe did get the contract.

Had he known getting it would bring him before this grand jury, he might have taken his friendly competitor, Jimmy Clay, out for a beer and let Clay have the contract instead. He could have made money losing that particular contract.

The grand jury called to the stand H. Harber Lampl, president of American National Bank, Shawnee. Lampl leveled about $125,000 cold cash borrowed from his bank by Allen Cowen. He agreed a $125,000 cash loan was unusual.

"We had to go to the Federal Reserve Bank," Lampl said. "There was $100,000 checked out from the Federal Reserve . . . the majority of it in $20 bills."

Banker Lampl also told of something else fairly common in Oklahoma politics. A real estate deal involving Lampl and others on a state highway interchange. Although it pays a pittance, the most sought after post in state government is that of highway commissioner. Read on and learn why.

Lampl said the real estate deal involved 154 acres. He confirmed the "joint venture" involved Allen Cowen, 30 per cent; banker Harber Lampl, 30 per cent; Sunny Jenkins, 30 per cent; and Shawnee attorney Richard M. Steed, 10 per cent. The land was a choice location on Interstate 40 and Kickapoo Street in Shawnee.

"We loaned the money to Allen Cowen to purchase his portion," said Lampl.

"Is Sunny Jenkins paying his part?" asked the district attorney.

"I, I really don't know," Lampl stuttered. "I know Mr. Cowen, you know, handled that portion of it. I don't know whether he's paying his part or not. I mean, you know, I don't know what the arrangements are."

"Well, Sunny Jenkins isn't paying your bank anything on this loan?"

"No, sir; no, sir, he's not paying me. I'm looking straight to Mr. Cowen."

"When did you enter into this contract?"

". . . In May of this year."

"And you knew Mr. Jenkins was going to be part owner, did you not?"

"It was my understanding Mr. Cowen was offering him an interest in it, yes."

Questioning then turned to the $125,000 loan granted Cowen by banker Lampl, who said he got his money back the way he gave it to Cowen — in cold cash.

"In cash?" repeated surprised Assistant District Attorney Marti Hirst.

"Yes."

"Paid back in cash?"

"Yes, ma'am."

"$125,000?"

"Yes, ma'am."

"And who made the payments?"

"I don't know who made the payments . . . I do know people down at Mr. Cowen's office — on the first payment I remember in particular — somebody down at the office called and said, you know, 'I want to make a payment on that note.' "

You may wonder why a banker can't remember who makes payments, in cash, on a most unusual $125,000 loan.

Please understand it is quite informal when cash, politics and state contracts mix. A man's word is everything. You go around asking for checks and receipts, good buddies think you don't trust 'em. A handshake, stuffed envelope and safety deposit box are your basic tools.

Take the money and run. The suspicious IRS gets picky about large cash transactions. So things like who paid off $125,000 in cash are best forgotten.

I have handled large media buys and managed many state-wide political races over the past 30 years. Far more cash was used 20 years ago than today. When Gov. Turner and Senator Kerr had their head-knocking battles over Kerr's senate seat in '54, it did more for the state's economy than a bumper wheat crop.

Some claimed banks closed one day a week during that famous campaign to let the candidates replenish their supplies of "frog hair," the term Turner's campaign manager, "Coach" McNeil, used in referring to folding money.

One reason cash still turns up frequently is Republican businessmen don't like the world to know when they're donating to the friendly enemy, Democrats.

But they do and it's necessary. Otherwise, where would we poor Democrats get our campaign money? From our loyal friends on welfare?

Democrats and Republicans are interchangeable when it comes to business in politics. Republican governors and U. S. Senators get plenty long-green from Democrats, too.

Maybe you're wondering what Marty Hauan does with cash money when he gets it. I'll tell you. A natural craven coward, I deposit it to my business account.

Many years back the high-minded founding fathers of Oklahoma City, including top bankers and oil people, called on me to help elect a couple city councilmen. When the race was over and we won, they paid me off in cash, about $10,000.

I ran to my bank with this cash fast as my legs would carry

me. You see, I got to know those dudes during the campaign. I wouldn't trust one of 'em an inch. Had I skimmed off a dime of cash and not reported it they would have known. Easy for them to check your bank account.

They are not to be trusted with such information. They won't hesitate to blackmail you with it anytime it might help them.

Keeping track of such closet information is how they keep control of City Haul and make sure their real estate holdings get special assessments, zoning, roads and other blessings not available to you and me.

There are many reasons why honesty with the IRS, however, is a wise policy. Particularly when dealing with politicians, contractors and business tycoons.

I don't recommend paying more tax than you owe. Nor do I think you'll go to hell or jail for stretching a point in your favor here and there. Chiseling in business is more common than the common cold.

I've been a close observer of politicians sweating out grand juries. Also of criminal trials for political activity that wouldn't lift an eyebrow if it were businessmen involved. Believe me, the smallest step off the straight and narrow will destroy a politician.

Politicians with sense know it. So politics is more honest than business. Complementary bids come from businessmen, not politicians. Anytime you find one crooked politician, you'll generally find a gang of merchants, lawyers and business leaders in the same bed.

Did you report every dollar on your income tax return last year? I thought not. Most politicians come close to doing so. Some, like Ed Edmondson, have revealed their income tax returns publicly over 20 years or more.

But show me 100 merchants and I'll show you 99 who are skimming off cash here and there to avoid taxes. Then there's the growing practice of trading out — the dentist fixes your teeth and you take care of his plumbing. So don't tell me how bad politicians are.

Of course the dishonesty of speaking with forked tongue is something else. That's what we need a law against, if it could only be enforced.

When you talk about money deals in politics, you're talking about cash on the barrelhead. The grand jury investigating contracts on the state capitol office buildings found money tracks everywhere. All it takes is a smart lawyer like Bill Berry, seeking immunity for his clients, and the beans are spilled.

David L. Harter, president of Harter Concrete Products, got his name in the paper and himself on the witness stand for no greater crime than unselfishly donating to the Democratic Party of Oklahoma.

Harter furnished outside wall panel for the Tax and Education Building. He also furnished $4,000 to the Democratic Party. Harter testified Sunny Jenkins asked him for the money to help pay off Democratic Party debts.

So he gave it, in cash, against the wishes of his Republican father.

"I wasn't about to write him checks," said Harter.

District Attorneys gotta have a little fun, too. The D.A. asked Harter if he got a receipt for his $4,000.

"No, I did not," said Harter, frowning.

Nobody gives receipts for cash. Such a practice would halt half the nation's business activity.

Electrical contractor John W. Shawver also told the grand

jury about cash donations.

"They needed some money to pay off campaign expenses," said Shawver. "It was to . . . repay some of David's (Hall's) campaign debts . . . They just asked me if I could, you know, sorta like the United Appeal . . . see if I could get some money from some of the electrical contractors."

Shawver was asked how much he tried to get from each contractor.

"Well, they asked if I could get a thousand dollars," he replied. "They said they could take all they could use, all they could get."

Honest testimony. Never in my 30 years in Oklahoma politics have I seen a time they couldn't use "all they could get." Like Shawver says, "sorta like the United Appeal." A kind of charity.

Shawver said he told those he contacted the money was needed to get the Democratic Party out of debt. It flustered Shawver, the next question. He was asked what *his* political affiliation was.

"Am I supposed to answer that?" he asked. "Is it public record or not? I'm a Republican by registration, if it makes any difference," he finally confessed.

Makes no difference what you are, John. For 15 years the Democratic Party of Oklahoma was a Hauan Agency account. During those years, nobody gave more freely to the Democratic Party than the Republican oil gentry from Bartlesville's Phillips Petroleum Company. I bet they had more members on LBJ's President's Club ($1,000 minimum) than any Oklahoma group.

Our poor Democratic Party would have gone broke except for help from a host of Republicans besides Mr. Shawver. If you think Democrats aren't pitching into the Republican pot today, go look in the pot.

This money buys special privilege and special honors. Nothing wrong with the honors. Do you expect a governor or president to appoint his enemies?

If you donate to a politician hoping to get some appointive honor, it's no different than some fine Oklahoma lady buying herself an ankle length mink coat. You think she buys it because she's cold? No, she wants to lord it over those who can't afford mink.

Folks savor political appointments for the same reason. When people get more money than they need, most don't know what to do with it. I remember going to a golf tournament near Ardmore years ago, sponsored by oil millionaire Waco Turner. Waco wasn't suave but he spread his money around and liked to have golf pros near and get his name in the paper. So he personally financed an annual golf tournament, complete with lush cash prizes.

My wife and I attended one of Waco's soirees, where fun and laughter continued through the night until tee-time next morning. As we were leaving after the tournament, I noticed several slightly used Cadillacs parked off the roadway at different points around Waco's property.

"What are those Cadillacs doing off in the bushes?" I asked Gerald "Curly" Smith, our host.

"Haven't you heard the story?" Curly laughed. "They claim ol' Waco never changes oil. Just drives his Cadillacs until they stop, then pushes 'em off into the bushes and buys a new one."

After a lifetime grunting, grinding, lying and cheating to stock up a pile, folks suddenly discover all they can get for their money is envy. So that's what they buy.

Money won't even improve your sex life, more's the pity. You can buy more sex than you can handle for not very much. A terrible thing to discover late in life, when you're finally rich. That's why rich people try for kicks in politics. When your "go" horse days are over, you still can become a "show" horse.

Which is beside the point of the Oklahoma County grand jury I was telling you about. Except the brass ring most of those appearing before that grand jury were reaching for was coin of the realm, in big bundles. Some of 'em got it.

Five also got indicted on 25 counts of "conspiracy to defraud the State of Oklahoma." Named in the indictments were A. W. "Sunny" Jenkins, Lynn Dewayn "Buddy" Hall, Walter Akins, Robert A. Berry and E. A. Allen Cowen II.

While all this was going on, day after day the *Daily Oklahoman* ran stories seeking to link Gov. David Hall to the conspiracy. After indictments were handed down, even some of those indicted made noises indicating maybe the main culprit had been overlooked, Gov. Hall.

District Attorney Curtis Harris and his assistant, Marti Hirst, who conducted the grand jury, stoutly defended Hall. Harris pointed out all the five indicted except Jenkins took the Fifth Amendment.

"These people had plenty opportunity to tell all they know about the governor," Harris declared. "Every person indicted and every other witness was given the chance to name not only the governor but anybody else connected with it.

"That's what I was looking for when I asked the district court to call the grand jury. I was seeking evidence that would stand up in court and Jenkins and the others sure didn't testify to anything (involving Hall)."

Harris chided those indicted for, after their indictments,

"squealing like a pig when it's caught.

"They won't talk under oath," he added. "Why don't they submit affidavits and present them to me? Why don't they swear to what they're saying? They had every opportunity to swear to what they know.

"The story this grand jury is protecting the governor is pure bunk," Harris added.

I agree. If Hall was involved, he covered his tracks well. They couldn't pin anything on him. Lord knows they tried. Republicans and Democrats alike.

Attorney General Larry Derryberry was then considered a prime candidate for governor to run against Hall. Derryberry urged the House of Representatives to investigate Gov. Hall's campaign financing when the grand jury findings hit the press. He was highly critical of Hall and state contractors. After his call for an investigation, Derryberry told the press of getting phone calls threatening his "political funeral."

"I know political power in the State of Oklahoma has been in the hands of contractors for years," declared Derryberry.

"I've been told they are planning my political funeral. Well, I'm going to let them just get at it. Today I'm serving notice that the State of Oklahoma and the attorney general will no longer tolerate this kind of activity.

"I think the people of Oklahoma deserve better and as long as I'm attorney general I will see they get it."

Brave words. But he wasn't able to put them into action. I agree with Derryberry there were grounds aplenty, however.

Gov. Hall was incensed by Derryberry's posturing, felt he was hitting a guy when he's down. He turned loose one of his rare displays of temper against the Attorney General, although I think Larry Derryberry had a good point.

"He's a Democratic turncoat, a modern day Quisling and a Benedict Arnold," fumed Hall.

For Hall, slow to anger and still slower to vent his anger upon another, those were words brimming with bitterness and hate.

"He has tried to use the Oklahoma Legislature as a political tool to further his own ambitions.

"Let me make this crystal clear," Hall snapped, "I have never received any kickbacks during the time I have been governor. I have never solicited any. I have never authorized anyone to accept one on my behalf. I have never participated in any way, form or action for any kickbacks in this administration."

As you can tell from the grand jury proceedings, it looked ominously dark for the Hall administration and a bunch of contractors snitching on each other about complementary bids and kickbacks. On the surface it seemed a gut cinch for someone to benefit politically if ambitious for higher office. Derryberry was the logical beneficiary.

But Derryberry's balloon, well gassed and ready to go, never got off the ground. One reason was Gov. Hall started raising questions about $43,000 in campaign contributions to Derryberry, which the Attorney General failed to list as coming to him from a group with the high-flown title, Independent Citizens for Good Government.

The House of Representatives was less than lukewarm about Derryberry's efforts to impeach Gov. Hall. An investigating committee took a look and concluded there was insufficient evidence.

"Probably the best forum to decide the issue is in the courts of Oklahoma," said investigating committee chairman Rep.

Don Davis, Lawton.

During this time, Derryberry was working closely with Republican Federal District Attorney Bill Burkett. Burkett allegedly gave Derryberry a transcript of the grand jury proceedings but said Hall "has no right" to the same transcript.

Which made it appear Gov. Hall was playing in a poker game with marked cards and a house dealer with soft hands.

When his balloon against Hall failed to rise, Derryberry decided against running for governor in the next election. Instead, he waited four years and took on George Nigh, who defeated him. The wind was in Derryberry's face all the way running against the popular Nigh.

Some Hall people's memories are long. Those living by the sword still die by it in politics. You better believe Hall lovers were for Nigh over Derryberry.

As for the five alleged conspirators on state building contracts indicted by the grand jury, delays were asked for and much time went by. Costly lawyers working their magic, maybe helped by someone with power in Washington. Ultimately charges were dismissed. Standard procedure in Oklahoma then.

Grand juries are mainly for political benefit and the news media. When half the culprits investigated are granted immunity and the other half take the Fifth, God alone can prove who are liars and where truth, if any, lies.

They failed to convict Gov. Hall this time, although all major power forces in the state were whaling away at him unmercifully.

Hall took his big fall later. He tripped himself up, with a little help from his friends.

Oklahoma's political graveyard overflows with such

corpses, buried alive by their best buddies.

The ghosts of these buried corpses are rising now as I write this in the hot July of 1983. A new set of contractors is sweating the federal heat from indulging in the age-old game of complementary bidding.

REST IN PEACE...

Its rooms rocked with laughter of winners, sorrowed watching the tears of losers, and the halls held a million political-shenanigan secrets in the '50's and '60's when the old Biltmore Hotel was Oklahoma political headquarters. This classiest grand dame of all structures in downtown Oklahoma City, good for another 100 years, was sentenced to death by dynamiting, a senseless and heartless sacrifice to the bumbling blight of urban renewal. (Johnny Melton photo)

7

THE OLD BILTMORE

The great advantage of a hotel is that it's a refuge from home life.

George Bernard Shaw

It's March 25, 1983 and I just got back from "Johnnie" Johnson's funeral. During much of my heyday in Oklahoma politics, Johnnie managed with style and grace the Biltmore Hotel in downtown Oklahoma City, political headquarters.

Didn't see any of Johnnie's old city ledger boys at his service but guess most are gone by now. They did whoop it up those days, so no wonder. But a little knot of Johnnie's old bellmen and I exchanged happy reminiscenses in the church foyer, recalling the '50's and '60's when our juices were running strongest.

Present were smiling Chris Sarras and Ralph and Mickey McGuire, all at one time bellmen, later assistant managers of the Biltmore. Other former bellmen who came to mind were Jack Buchanan, sharp as a tack; Carl Murphy, rare bellman who never took a drink and whose morals outdid any preacher's and Hal Crippen, who managed several hotels himself, kind and decent a man as you'll ever know. These were good people, yet wise enough to know you can't stop the world from turning in its natural way.

If that old Biltmore could talk, it would scandalize more than the Huckins Hotel, its predecessor as repository for Oklahoma's most salacious political secrets. Bellmen mentioned here know more about certain political matters than most governors.

In the beginning (1953), I officed in 830, Democratic Headquarters was 800 and road contractors held forth in 1100 with their shrewd and affable leader, T-Bone McDonald.

Ben Blackstock and his troops were on the 24th (top) floor for many years. Ben trained more capable state press association executive directors than anyone in America. He has a talent for hiring smart, modest, hard-working people, then providing them with so many projects they don't have time for mischief. If you don't believe me, ask Bill Boykin, Lyndell Williams, Connie Logan, Jean Daniel and Jim Swain. They got the job done with a smile.

The press association moved into the Biltmore when it opened in 1932, with Ray Dyer, one of God's chosen, as executive director. Ben Blackstock told me about Ray's special training for the job.

"Everyone took ice then," Ben reminded, "and Ray Dyer was executive secretary for Oklahoma's ice plants. His main chore was tracking down horse thieves who were making off with horses trained for ice-wagon work.

"Dyer always claimed those horses could read. They'd stop automatically in front of any house with an ice card in the window but I didn't believe his boast they told the driver whether a house wanted 25 or 50 pounds.

"They were valuable horses. Took years to train 'em right, so horse thieves had a ready market for these animals."

When Ray Dyer bought the El Reno *Tribune,* he was succeeded at Oklahoma Press Association by Vernon Sanford, who served 14 years, then went to Texas. Morris Moore from the *Oklahoman* came next, followed by Tom Rucker, from KMBC radio in Kansas City and a big Bob Kerr man. Blackstock was Rucker's assistant and took over in '53.

Ben reminded me of the Variety Club, organization for entertainers, which was also on the Biltmore's top floor. Poker and gin rummy games for money flourished throughout the hotel but only the Variety Club had slot machines. Made money for their charities.

Periodically the *Oklahoman,* usually during the dull summer, would start another campaign against sin. Word would be sent to the Variety Club that gambling raids were scheduled on a certain day. The reporter due to write the story might well be having a drink at the Variety Club when this warning came.

"Those slot machines weren't bothering anyone," Blackstock laughed, "but the law wanted to be able to tell the *Oklahoman* reporter they checked the Variety Club and found nothing. So these slots were kept on rollers. Whenever a raid was on, we could hear 'em rolling those one-arm bandits down the hall to the freight elevator for transport to a different floor."

For years this system worked well, for the Variety Club and others with the means to convince vice raiders it is in the nature of man to savor sex, gambling and a drop of the grape. The day did come, though, when the sheriff's office called with a different message: "The heat's too hot this time from 4th and Broadway. Get rid of your machines or we'll have to pick 'em up."

This sad event and the beginning of the end of the Biltmore's influence occurred almost simultaneously. Hard for a place as politically powerful as the Biltmore to hold its head high again after being denied the small favor of operating a few slot machines.

For more than 30 years, the Biltmore turf was its own. The hotel largely made its own law and policed itself and guests. They had people who could do it. Anyone working at the Biltmore was the best at what he did, including 11th floor maids Jeffrey and Jean, parking garage managers Chuck DeBoer and Cecil Pearson—whose son was an outstanding OU fullback—and those wonderful gals, Gladys and Ruby, who ran the coffee shop. You could trust them with any secret.

Bellmen had their biggest day and night of the month when road contractors came to town to find out who got which contracts. They worked harder, for less money, when we Democrats were holding functions and candidates for office kept their hospitality suites open all night. Also when the legislature was in session and the weightiest matters were decided at night (behind closed doors) that would become law next day.

H. P. (Johnnie) Johnson was a long, skinny and happy guy from Springfield, Missouri who started hopping bells when he was 17 and played basketball for money on the side.

I promise you he got better than a college education working the Biltmore. He later taught Sociology I to his bellmen.

When the wind was right those days, you could elect a new governor or U. S. Senator without ever leaving the Biltmore. The money was at 1100 (contractors), party machinations at 800 (Democratic Headquarters), advertising at 830 (Hauan Agency) and publicity on the top floor (Blackstock, Boykin, et al).

We also had Fisher Muldrow (Truckers Assn.) and Ted Knoop (Retail Merchants Assn.), both of whom dealt heavily in politics. You wanted them on your side.

Ambitious politicians spent much time and money at the Biltmore.

Johnnie Johnson helped open the Biltmore as a bellman March 8, 1932. He resigned as managing director in 1959. During Johnnie's reign, the Biltmore was a sturdier, classier structure than any you'll find anywhere in downtown Oklahoma City today, except maybe the Skirvin.

Johnnie knew most of Oklahoma's important political people. He saw them with their guards down, learned the extracurricular sex habits of many and knew what really made those people tick.

"Holloway was governor when I started in '38," Johnnie told me shortly before he died. "Ted Knoop was his secretary. In bellman lingo, I was a gunsel, a greenhorn who didn't know the score.

"Bellmen then took pride in their profession. You paid for the privilege of working, 50-cents a day. We had some characters but they were pros who took care of guests like you never see today."

Most bellmen had a nickname and Johnnie remembered some. "There was 'Boxcar Tommy' Walton, 'Lockerroom' McFarland, 'Salad' Durkee, 'Dinnerbucket' Downing, 'Preacher' Sisk, 'Jew' Brownie and 'Jumpin Joe' Higgs," Johnnie recalled.

"Boxcar Tommy" rode the rails into town. "Lockerroom" spent all his time in the lockerroom bellyaching about how bad business was, "Preacher" was always on his soapbox telling how to handle things, "Jumpin Joe" was so nervous he'd jump to do everything and "Dinnerbucket" was a little square, brought his own lunch.

These bellmen used a foreign language all their own.

Money was a half-check (quarter), check (50-cents), ace (dollar), fin ($5), sawbuck ($10), double saw ($20) and C ($100).

Johnnie gave me some other examples of bellman talk:

"Put the bees and honey on the near-and-far, Joe Goss is looking at Jack and Jill." Translation: Put the money up, the boss is watching the cash register.

"Jew Brownie is coming to work and he's double breasted this time." Meaning, he has two broads working for him.

Those days many bellhops had an old lady (girl friend) who doubled as prostitute. Some had two, providing at least one wasn't in love. The bellman's cut on this activity was a major part of his income.

"Here's how they'd describe their activities," Johnnie explained: "A guy would say, 'My twist (old lady) turned three double-saw ($20) tricks. She's gone to the shovel and broom (room or apartment), put her ones and twos (shoes) under the roses-red (bed) to lay her lead (head) on the weeping willow (pillow). I'm going to the joint across the street where I'll ask the fried potato (waiter) working the near-and-far (bar) to bring a couple suds (beers) to my achin' tooth (booth). Later my old lady's comin' by and we'll cut the turkey (slice up the money).'

"Lots of bellmen traveled then, like some prostitutes do, usually with a for-sale old lady. We called these bellmen "rodeos" because they made a circuit. You had to be a real pro to get and keep a job. Hell, bellmen dressed better than the manager. A lot of 'em made more money. An exciting life."

As we all do in life and love, Johnnie learned the bellman's lingo and lessons the hard way.

The Old Biltmore

"When I first went to work in Tulsa, I learned fast," said Johnnie, "why bellmen have their own language. Smoking on the job was forbidden but we'd sneak a smoke regularly when the boss, Henry Ketchem, wasn't around.

"Three of us sneaked off to huddle beside a plant and smoke in the lobby when Henry walked in one day. 'Time for the heel and toe, a big weed just walked in,' one of my buddies whispered and then took off. I stood there like a nut, holding my cigarette and trying to digest what was said. Ketchem walked up and grabbed me by the neck. Fired me on the spot.

"I sadly told the head bellman what happened. He gave the other guys hell for not warning me. 'We did,' they protested. 'The dummy can't understand English.'

"But it worked out. 'Go on home for a couple days, then come back and stay out of Ketchum's way for a week and he won't know the difference,' the bell captain told me. So that's what I did and when I came back I studied hotel language seriously."

Johnnie was then a kid and green. He had more lessons to learn and older bellmen were happy to teach him.

"My uncle, who drove an armored car, got me my first job in Tulsa. Other bellmen resented this use of influence," said Johnnie, "mainly because an ignorant gunsel can mean trouble, especially when dealing in broads and whiskey during those prohibition days.

"My first day on the job, 'Jumpin Joe' Higgs comes over and warns me about the house detective. He says the house Dick won't stand for traffic in broads and booze except in unusual circumstances.

" 'Anyone asks you about those two items,' he says, 'you

tell 'em, "I'll see about it," then come straight to me. I'll check it out with our detective. It will put you in good with him and won't bring the cops down on us.'

"Until somebody wised me up, I spent most of my time hunting up Higgs so I could turn over to him all my most lucrative business. I was starving to death while he was grabbing money with both hands."

Times were double tough in 1932 when the elegant Biltmore opened in downtown Oklahoma City. Families were living on five dollars a week and plenty people ate out of garbage cans. But we had oil in Oklahoma those days, too, and there was a high side to the hog where you'd find mainly wild oil tycoons plus politicians setting up a new state and themselves. Some were not so principled as the greatest Oklahoman of them all, Alfalfa Bill Murray.

The Biltmore was one grand place. For a price you could get anyting on the planet. Those with access to buyers, like alert and agile bellmen, were envied.

"A part of what you touch is yours to keep" was their motto. Believe me, lots of college graduates were standing in line to take your bellman job if you made the slightest mistake.

"Everyone working at the Biltmore then was immaculate and savvy," Johnnie reminisced. "Bellmen wore white gloves and fancy tight pants. Waiters were in tuxedos at all times and desk clerks wore them evenings. A former symphony orchestra conductor, Victor Alexander, played piano at night.

"Whatever sports were around those depression days wound up at the Biltmore. I felt a little snobbish having a job there. Considered myself lucky, which I was."

You could do whatever you were big enough to handle at

The Old Biltmore

the Biltmore, providing your bankroll could pay the freight. When money does the talking and it's playtime, things can get out of hand.

"I remember E. W. Marland as a dignified gentleman people were always freeloading on," Johnnie said. "Then we had a drilling company owner from Tulsa and the head of one of Enid's main plants who made things interesting.

"Those birds were competitive over who was the biggest big shot. When both went on a binge at the same time, Biltmore chandeliers rattled. They tried to outnoise each other.

"I called the Enid guy one time and told him, 'Hey, calm 'em down, you're disturbing everyone on the floor.'

" 'Then move 'em to another floor,' he says, 'I'll take this floor myself.' 'Can't do that,' I told him. 'Can if I pay enough' he shouts back, which was the damn truth."

Johnnie told me about a time when Mr. Enid and Mr. Tulsa checked in the same day and went on a binge together.

"He later quit but Mr. Tulsa was drinking pretty good then," Johnnie related. "He was a match for Enid.

"On the second day, crazy Enid went out and bought up a band, bringing all those musicians into the hotel. They had one floor to themselves and put on a concert. Of course you could hear 'em one floor up and down. Word quickly spread throughout the hotel. It was early evening, so most people got a kick out of it.

"But then Mr. Tulsa went into his act. He's a little oiled so thinks it's a brilliant idea to rent *him* a band, which he does and brings 'em in after midnight. They were tooting away coming in and ran half the people out of the hotel before we could stop 'em.

"After that we had one guy tried to register with a cow but I drew the line there."

There were many characters, mainly new-rich oilmen. Johnnie himself was in on one oil deal with a guy who is memorable. I won't use his name because my editor wife says he, although dead, may have a wife or daughter who would be embarrassed. I go along to get along too but feel guilty omitting such names. Johnnie and I agreed these dudes would proudly acknowledge they were sports who had fun openly and paid the bill. Even when it hurt, which it did in the case of Johnnie's oil partner.

"He was a fabulous man, pure promoter," Johnnie laughed. "Once he got a deal promoted, that was it for him. Someone else worried about the details.

"His phone bill could run $3,000 before he paid, other things in proportion. Once he was living in a $100 suite, when I went on a Florida vacation. When I got back, I asked Lil Holman, our auditor, to check and see how much my oil partner owed.

" 'Bring the accounts and let me take a look,' I told her. She was apologetic handing them over. I nearly fainted when I saw the total — $22,000.

" 'I can't owe that much,' my partner protested. 'Haven't been here that long.' "

Johnnie went over all the accounts with his friend, who finally agreed that when you're having fun money sure gets away. He wasn't in shape to settle up but had a solution.

" 'I'm in serious trouble with my directors over this,' I warned him," Johnnie recalled. " 'You've gotta get your bill paid.' "

" 'Don't worry, Johnnie' he told me, 'I got it all worked out. I'll just move to a cheaper suite.'

"That was his solution, $22,000 in debt to the hotel and

The Old Biltmore

he's solving it by moving to a cheaper suite, on the cuff. I nearly fell on the floor laughing, although it was no laughing matter. After I quit laughing I wanted to jump out the window but it was the 15th floor.

"I helped him along with the solution and he finally paid up. We had to sell the oil property we owned together to do it.

"But I always had faith in that guy, although his mind worked in strange ways. No matter how big the problem, he'd come up with a small, easy solution like, 'I'll move to a cheaper suite.' He was a little guy with the biggest ideas you ever heard. Enough of his ideas worked, for him, to keep him solvent in spite of wildly spendthrift ways."

Now I must tell you about the famous city ledger. Some of Oklahoma City's most noted "blue ribbon" leaders had secret city ledger accounts. I could tell you who some are but if I did they might dream up some lie to tell on me.

Johnnie started the city ledger when he became manager at the Biltmore. For the afternoon trade, male and female. Brought in a lot of badly needed extra business.

If you qualified for city ledger credit, an account was set up under an assumed name. Smart guys paid off in cash. That way no one could prove anything.

"Of course we had to have people handling such transactions who were trusted completely to keep their mouths shut," Johnnie said, "otherwise our credit ledger business would vanish. Many downtown businessmen used it, a few women, too. Some are still alive who, I believe, have fond memories they'd like to brag about concerning things they can't do anymore."

Most special city ledger clients were people prominent in

business, politics or the professions. When they got an itch, discretion dictated they not scratch publicly.

"Sad Sam" Jones was one customer, head of a major Oklahoma City company. His ledger alias was "Sad Sam" because he always looked like he was going to cry when required to pay with cash instead of a deductible company check.

"The way it worked," Johnnie explained, "was a guy like Sad Sam would call my room clerk and say, 'This is Jackson Jones, city ledger. Get me a number.' The clerk gives him a number. Then a bellman immediately takes the room key corresponding to that number and places it in the door's keyhole.

"Sad Sam soon appears in the lobby, looks around to see if he knows anyone, then heads for the elevator. Not long after, you could bet on it, some lady appears and repeats the process.

"Best thing about the system, not even the room clerk knew, providing you really wanted to keep such matters strictly private. I was the only one who knew. Of course, if you ordered anything from room service, which most did, you had to confront a bellman. Usually nothing to worry about. No bellman in his right mind would purposely endanger this profitable afternoon business. These were good tippers. A guy with a guilty conscience is *always* a good tipper and good tippers were protected."

Naturally, city ledger regulars did become known to hotel people. They knew their secrets were safe with them, although once in a while there would be a slight slipup.

"A guy came in all hot and bothered one day," said Johnnie. "His alias was John Seal. Good friend of mine. We played golf together.

" 'One of your bellmen saw me on the street with some people awhile ago,' Seal complained. 'The dumb-ass says, "Hello, Mr. Seal." You tell him who the hell I am so he won't pull that trick again.' "

Even a few ladies heard about the Biltmore's special city ledger and started using it. Johnnie was surprised to learn there were women, not completely satisfied at home, bold enough to sneak out on their own that way.

"Some guy would bring them but they made the arrangements," Johnnie said. "One ol' gal, a party from out of town, liked one of my bellmen. He charged a small fee and she gladly paid.

"Our city ledger got started when times were tough. It's a good piece of business, a turnover, being mainly an afternoon thing.

"But you couldn't do it without discreet employees. Guests must have complete confidence. A good hotel man sees everything, divulges nothing. Our guests knew they would be protected."

I asked Johnnie how the hotel handled the law where liquor was concerned, especially during prohibition, and afterward, when booze wasn't legal in Oklahoma.

"Moonshine was a problem in the early days because you had to strain the gnats and flies out before serving," Johnnie chuckled. "When nearly everyone else had legal booze but Oklahoma didn't, it was hauled in from Joplin and other places.

"Things were organized, taken care of. If you bought right, saw the right people, no problem.

"Bootleggers gave me a list of 'safe numbers' to call but I said, 'To hell with you. I'll make my own arrangements.' Which I did.

"For a while those bootleggers nearly wore me out but I had good arrangements. Such things are easy to hide in a hotel anyway. A lot of vice-squad guys couldn't track a bear with bloody paws in the snow."

My personal recollection of those days, vice-squads had their own list of "safe numbers," just like customers. They made regular arrests of independent bootleggers who didn't have the fix in. They also knew who *not* to arrest. The vice-squad operated sorta like the Corporation Commission today, a price-fixing agency that set spacing and allowables for bootleggers.

Johnnie and I got to talking about newspapers and I asked if he was ever caught up in one of the *Oklahoman's* anti-sin campaigns.

"Never," he laughed, "because I wet-nursed a lot of their boys. Used to play poker with the leaders—Otis Sullivant, Ray Parr, Arch Dixon, Bruce Palmer—that bunch. Otis used to laugh about the legislator who made a big speech about it when Sullivant got thrown by a horse and broke his leg. The guy shouted, 'Why did it have to be Otis' leg? Why couldn't it be his writing arm?'

"I furnished quarters for writing the gridiron each year, so I guess I've hidden more drunk newspapermen from Gaylord than anyone in town. One guy in particular used to upchuck over everything and we'd have to clean up him and the room both before we could send him home.

"The top bunch were class guys but newspapermen to a great extent were pure moochers. Never a problem with moochers if you let 'em freeload.

"Walter Harrison was hated by some people, as all *Oklahoman* managing editors are, because he could be tough. But nobody honest would tell you that, deep inside, Walter was ever knowingly unfair.

"I used to play golf with Walter. He had a wit sharp as his pen. One day a legislator jumps him on the golf course over something he'd written. 'I resent you calling me a goat,' the fella told Walter.

" 'I didn't say you were a goat at all,' Walter replied with a big smile but eyes hardening, 'I just said you *smelled* like a goat.'

" 'Well, OK then,' the guy mumbles, 'I just wanted your apology.' "

The Biltmore was political headquarters, especially for Bob Kerr's crowd. Aubrey Kerr, who was chief cook and bottlewasher for much of the Kerr operation, spent most of his time in a nice suite he kept there.

"Besides Aub, there was J. D. McCarty and Bill Harkey," Johnnie recalled. "And there was the guy big in national politics, even international, Patrick Hurley. He had *some* dignity about him. Would have made one hell of a maitre de.

"I also remember Harkey brought Raymond Gary around, saying they were running him for governor. I told him, 'No way. You're outa your mind.' But Raymond got himself elected and Harkey was made Speaker.

"J. D. was pure politician. Trained by experts and strong. He and I went to Ada and visited Roy Turner and Bill Likens at the Flying L Ranch when Bob Kerr was running for governor.

"Travis Kerr used to stay at the Biltmore, too, the one who had that great race horse. A delightful man with a great sense of humor. Kirksey Nix, Mead Norton and Henry Brown also were part of the Kerr bunch.

"They used to have card games. Bob Kerr and Bill Kerr were both great gin players and Bob an excellent bridge player. There was a prominent preacher who attended those sessions. Would gamble higher than any preacher you'll ever see.

"Kirksey Nix, Jack Conn and Don Baldwin were my all-time favorites. They and J. D. did a lot of behind the scenes work for Bob and Aub. Kirksey was brilliant but it almost killed him when his son went to prison.

"I always felt comfortable dealing with these people. You knew where they were coming from. They wouldn't hassle you without a special reason."

Back 30 years, when legislators made only $100 a month while in session, it was important for certain poor boys to get room-rent sponsors. Some top politicians with money and ambition for higher office picked up a few such tabs and the Biltmore "gave free rent to certain people," as Johnnie put it. Just as today, nice discounts were available to a legislator in a top power position. Back scratching is not yet a lost art.

"What amused me," Johnnie recalled, "was those legislators would decide something in the hotel at night, then go out to the capitol and just debate hell out of it next day. A show for the folks. I guess Kirksey was maybe the greatest orator, even when he knew the majority was already convinced.

"We'd have 60 to 80 legislators staying at the Biltmore," Johnnie added, "so they could get most things figured out at night. I don't say that's bad, maybe good. Better than going out to the capitol cold and watching some dummies mess things up."

I questioned Johnnie closely on free rent for legislators.

"At the beginning of a session," Johnnie replied, "for starters I'd give a party for new members. Free booze and buffet, that sorta thing. That's when the money would be brought down in a bag and given to me (for room rentals).

"There were instructions. 'This one gets a free ride, so-and-so 50 per cent off,' like that. It wasn't my business who put up the money, so I didn't ask anything. I stayed out of the politics personally and didn't ask favors."

What happened, as I'm sure Johnnie knew, was people with wants put something in the room-rent pot for a handshake receipt and maybe a favor down the road.

My black hair is now gray, turning white. Some of those kid Biltmore bellmen, I notice, are getting a little stooped. But we have proud memories of hotels before the chains took over, when the customer got as much consideration as the balance sheet.

"All real hotel managers came up through the ranks, the best starting as bellmen," Johnnie insisted. "Now they grind 'em out fast from those hotel schools. They get a manager's job, an office to go with it, after which they rarely come out to meet a guest.

"In my time the guest was special. Every morning at 8:00 o'clock, I'd be in front of those heavy bronze Biltmore elevator doors, smiling and passing out the *Daily Oklahoman*.

" 'Good morning, Mr. Jones,' I'd say. 'Have a morning paper?' If I didn't know you, I'd introduce myself, ask if you had a good night's sleep. Spent at least an hour each day doing this. If there were complaints, I heard them first.

"I had one main rule: Give the guest whatever he wants that you can get without going to jail or burning down the hotel. Today when you enter a chain operation, they slap a key in your hand, maybe without looking up, and say, 'You're in 937.' Nobody speaks to you again until they give you the bad news at the checkout cash register.

"I allowed no soliciting for booze or women. That was grounds for firing. I'd also fire you for failing to give a guest who asked for it the very best of such commodities.

"Girls working good hotels like the Biltmore then were immacuately clean, not dopies. If you did business with them and my bellmen, you could drink too much, leave money and jewelry around, and next morning it would still be there.

"We tried to make a friend of every guest. We didn't tempt sinners nor try to reform them. We catered to their wants, protected confidences. My theory is there's some sinner in everyone. There was in everyone I ever met worth knowing."

They've dynamited the old Biltmore, Johnnie died and I've seen better days myself. But I wouldn't trade what I saw and enjoyed during those happy Biltmore days for the same amount of time up ahead.

Out of respect for my kidneys, I moved out of the old Biltmore the day after they turned off the water. Except for that, plus the fact they blew the place up to celebrate the glories of urban renewal, I'd be there still.

I learned more at the Biltmore than from two colleges and eight years with governors Murray and Gary. Besides, it was fun.

Those who wish may leave their hearts in San Francisco. Mine is with the old Biltmore—wherever warm, loving and tolerant old hotels go when they die.

8

THOMAS JEFFERSON STEED

Young men think old men fools; old men know young men are fools.
George Chapman (1659-1734)

Many a modern political hotshot loaded up his peashooter trying to beat oldtimer Tom Steed at different times when Tom was in trouble for being too honest with voters of Oklahoma's 4th district.

A couple times the Republican Party sent its best brains, bitterest bloodletters and bulging bankrolls after Tom. There were also special backup troops guaranteeing to carry the day—media magicians, special organizers and pollsters.

Old-fashioned Tom Steed has heard of such folk but never associated with 'em.

"Tom Steed is ripe for pickin'," they said, "because he doesn't use up-to-date campaign techniques."

All these experts found Tom too tough a nut to crack. He just voted his conscience, spoke his mind and helped people with legitimate need for help. This outdated system was good enough to keep him in Congress 32 straight years.

Tom's a big talker. Ask him a question and you better get ready to lean back and listen. He doesn't choose words carefully but comes right out with what he thinks. Unusual in politics and refreshing.

That's how Tom operated on the campaign trail.

"Don't be scared. Tell the truth as you see it. That's the best way," advises Tom. "Always worked for me."

Indeed it did. Tom set the record for length of service in Congress by an Oklahoman. He never needed today's costly self-confessed political geniuses. He believes their departure from political campaigns and the halls of Congress would benefit the democratic process.

When Tom retired in 1980, it marked the end of three glorious decades when Oklahoma held preferred position at the public trough. Anytime our Oklahoma delegation dug in its snout, it came up with acorns aplenty. Spurred on by cheers from such unselfish groups as the Oklahoma City Chamber of Commerce, Oklahoma became the nation's log-rolling and pork-barrel champ.

"The year I was elected to Congress, 1948, Oklahoma's seniority and power started taking hold," says Tom Steed. "Later, with Bob Kerr in the Senate and Carl Albert, Ed Edmondson, Page Belcher and myself in the House, Oklahoma took a permanent seat at the head table."

The feast lasted until Speaker Albert, Steed and Sen. Henry Bellmon retired.

Bellmon became a power on the Republican side during his second term and Tom controlled purse strings in the House. Bellmon took Page Belcher's place as lead dog for Oklahoma when a bone was needed from a White House occupied by Republicans.

"During those peak years, Oklahoma's six Congressmen boasted the largest per capita seniority of any state in the union," Steed recalls proudly. "Our power grew and flourished under leadership of Bob Kerr. It became even greater when Carl Albert became, in order, House Democratic Whip, Majority Leader and Speaker.

Oklahoma had this top seniority in Congress when it made the difference. Steed and Bellmon were the last of our practiced log-rollers from the old school, an era dating back to before the

Great Depression of the '30's. Elmer Thomas helped start it, serving 28 years before being toppled by Mike Monroney, who acquired great influence in his own right. Speaker Albert served 30 years; Page Belcher, 22; Ed Edmondson and Jed Johnson, Sr. 20 each and John Jarman, the Democrat who voted Republican and finally became one, 26 years.

Bob Kerr was the Oklahoma delegation's undisputed leader. His friendship with Lyndon Johnson, aggressive intelligence and pragmatic philosophy of being "agin' any deal I ain't in on" made the Oklahoma delegation feared and respected.

Those boys brought home the bacon, everything from our Arkansas River outlet to the sea to a fat 20,000-people payroll at Tinker Field in Midwest City. After Kerr's death, Tom Steed, Carl Albert and Ed Edmondson carried the burden of getting projects funded for Oklahoma. Although outside their districts, distress calls came to them most frequently from Oklahoma City.

"If it weren't for its federal government installations, Oklahoma City wouldn't even make a good suburb of Tulsa," Tom told me.

"Oklahoma City had more federal money lavished upon it per capita than almost any other city the last three decades. A Congressman can never quit scratching out federal dollars because folks back home, mostly in organized groups, keep up an unending demand for them.

"Almost all local problems now first get the test: 'Can we get the federal government to do it for us?'"

Our red-blooded Oklahoma leaders are anxious to expand their military installations, improve flood control and water conservation projects, lower freight and barge rates, and get ever more money for urban renewal and other welfare-for-the-wealthy projects.

"They demand their Congressman get these things done for them," says Tom, smiling, "while at the same time being well-practiced in the good old American custom of bellyaching about government waste. Oklahoma City is especially talented in the art of complaining about shameful wasting of federal dollars."

Thank-yous from recipients of this largesse are few for a Congressman like Tom Steed.

"The value and production power of these vast federal expenditures are seldom mentioned or remembered," he grins. "It would detract from their fun of bellyaching."

I asked Tom about the Oklahoma City Chamber of Commerce.

"Well run," he responded, "but has the misfortune that certain members' attitudes and activities prevent its being universally popular.

"My favorite manager was Paul Strasbaugh, who suffered in silence and did all he could to keep the record balanced with our Oklahoma congressional delegation. But if there is no rain until the Oklahoma City Chamber of Commerce becomes known for its gratitude for service, we are in for one helluva dust storm."

Politics has changed greatly since Tom Steed first went to Congress. He was elected the year Harry Truman fooled everyone and Tom rode with President Truman when his campaign train passed through Oklahoma. Truman and Steed were a matched set—blunt and unafraid.

Steed is the last of Oklahoma's elected-by-newspapers politicians. Mike Monroney is in the same category but was deserted at last and defeated by the *Daily Oklahoman* and Oklahoma City Chamber of Commerce, whom he helped more than anyone.

Has politics changed? Harken to the story of Tom Steed's career and you'll see how much.

Tom Steed was born March 4, 1904 to Walter and Sallie Johnson Steed on a scrub farm situated between Rising Star and Okra in Eastland County, Texas. The family moved by covered wagon just after statehood to a farm they rented from a Seminole Indian north of Konawa, Oklahoma.

Tom was the sixth son and seventh child in a family of eleven. Living on a rented Oklahoma farm with 11 kids didn't spell affluence.

Tom Steed's first important honor came on graduation from the eighth grade at Konawa Public School. He was named valedictorian in 1919 after compiling the highest composite grade for 14 subjects.

That same year he attended summer school and part of the fall session in the high school division of East Central University, Ada. This was his whole formal education. Yet he emerged from those eight years of "schooling in the basics" better equipped to face the real world than are many college graduates accepting bogus degrees today.

Tom's first job was apprentice printer at the *Ada Evening News*. Not exactly starting at the top.

"I was proud when the paper began publishing a column I wrote, with pencil, about our Ada Boy Scout troop," said Tom. "I was senior patrol leader. Attorney Orel Busby, later a member of the Oklahoma Supreme Court, took the lead in forming a Boy Scout Council which I also wrote about."

Due to the scouting stories, they soon advanced Tom from

apprentice printer to apprentice reporter. He was flattered and they didn't cut his pay.

"I was untrained, couldn't type and had no experience," recalls Tom, "so editor Marvin Brown created a crude journalism school for me. He made me copy the front page of the *Daily Oklahoman* every day for three months."

No better way to teach Journalism I. If you possess curiosity, plus ability to spell and punctuate, that's all the formal training needed to become a competent reporter.

Tom's newspapering career included three stints with the *Oklahoman*, plus work on the *Bartlesville Examiner, McAlester News-Capital* and *Shawnee News-Star.* He became managing editor of the *News-Star* in 1939.

Just before World War II, Tom attained such prominence he was named to the Pottawatomie County Draft Board.

"When war broke out, I resigned as editor and from the draft board to join the U.S. Army as a buck private at the over-ripe age of 38," recalled Tom. "I was trained to fly radio-controlled target airplanes and promoted to 2nd Lieutenant but lost my job when the army decided I was overage in grade and released me."

Then as now, newspapering wasn't the road to riches. The most one could aspire to from Shawnee was becoming an *Oklahoman* slave and Tom learned, as I did later working for Gaylord's WKY-TV, that E.K. Gaylord didn't become a multi-millionaire overpaying guys like us.

Released from the army, Tom was ambitious to step up from newspapering, so he returned to Shawnee and opened an auto agency. But cars were scarce "and questionable sales ability soured me on this enterprise, so I started looking elsewhere."

What Tom finally settled on was politics. He had worked in

Thomas Jefferson Steed

Washington from 1935 to '38 as secretary to Congressmen P. L. Gassaway, Gomer Smith and R. P. Hill.

Some said Tom was going from bad to worse—reporter to car salesman to Congressional candidate. But when he settled in as Congressman, Steed found his niche. Nobody served his constituents more faithfully.

As with most things in life, Tom becoming Oklahoma's 4th District Congressman was an accident. He happened to be available when the power structure in his district was seeking a replacement for Congressman Glen Johnson.

"I don't really know when my name got mentioned but there was disenchantment with Johnson, who had defeated 10-year veteran Lyle Boren in 1946, and friends started urging me to run for Congress. I thought I'd had all I wanted of Washington," Tom remembered, "but after about four months being talked to I got interested. Congressman Johnson, meanwhile, developed a desire to run for the U.S. Senate and Bob Kerr eliminated him.

"It's hard to explain," Tom concluded, "but to this day I honestly don't know when or why I agreed to run."

It had something to do with the caliber of folks buttering him up. People like Ross Porter, then manager of radio station KGFF; Elmer Harber, banker; Link Cowen, contractor; John Tubbs, Shawnee News-Star advertising manager; Merle Chapman, attorney; Orel Busby, attorney and later State Supreme Court Justice; Tom and Milt Phillips, Lou Allard and George Hill, newspaper publishers; Tol Foster, banker; Bob Blackstock, attorney and Don Powers and Lavern Fishel, who became district judges.

Nobody paid Tom's way into Congress. He spent less than $15,000 in the primary, runoff and general elections. That amount wouldn't qualify you for an interview with most of today's media consultants.

"My biggest donation was $100," Tom remembers. "A few friends in Shawnee passed the hat and I cashed some saving bonds to pay for printed materials, some advertising and direct mail letters.

"Newspapers, especially the weeklies, got most of my advertising money. TV wasn't yet a factor but radio proved useful and was inexpensive.

"My most influential support came from newspapers. I enjoyed strong free news column advantages as well as favorable editorials. The editors were my friends."

As you know, newspapers are always impartial in their news stories. Like Tom, however, I always like trusting my fate to an impartial friend rather than an impartial enemy. Somehow it works out better, even with impartial editors.

Before Steed's time, from the back of a pickup or wagon was the standard way of campaigning, setting up on Main Street or in the park and haranguing a crowd. Tom popularized using caravans, a type of campaigning used most effectively by George Nigh and his Good Guy white hat brigade in 1978. Steed's caravans consisted of a couple dozen friends in their cars, going from town to town, honking to attract attention and passing out Tom's literature.

Fellow newspapermen printed a lot of impartial pictures of Tom and family, with details about his fine character and personal record. His opponents never seemed to have any decent pictures. The big issue in his first race was "difficulty people had getting to talk to their Congressman."

"So I made a firm commitment everywhere that I would be fully accessible," said Tom. "Promised to make at least one trip a year to each community and meet any and all who wanted to see me. I kept this promise and it proved so popular all our Congressmen now do the same.

"I had no paid workers, wrote my own speeches and ads and spoke no words of abuse about my opponents. My experience as a newsman and writer for Office of War Information, the propaganda agency, proved valuable and effective."

Tom blames TV for most of the skyrocketing costs of campaigning but he got elected for 32 years and used TV most sparingly of any candidate I've known.

"Thank God TV can be harmful as well as effective, which reduces the advantage a rich man has," Tom noted.

The payoff for Tom from his newspapering career was election to Congress. He got into the runoff with Lyle Boren (David's dad), trying a comeback, and Tom got most of the vote from supporters of six eliminated candidates.

"The almost solid support I had from newspapers counted most," Tom says. "That and the wives of union members hauling voters for me election day."

Tom beat a bunch of guys who spent a bundle on TV, were handsome and half his age.

"I never quit shaking the bushes is why," Tom explains. "Never lost touch with my home folks. They knew I made up my own mind and respected that enough to keep electing me."

Tom Steed has some salty comment for today's media.

"Radio stations and country newspapers have improved and become more effective," he told me. "The metropolitan press has gone to more propaganda in its news columns, hence they're less influential. TV loses its clout by chasing ratings, no matter what kind of bilge required to lure listeners.

Thomas Jefferson Steed   133

"The Washington media is worst. It has lost a lot of its greatness since television. There the press corps includes many free-lancers who barely make a living. They'll grab at anything, or even concoct something, to "expose" someone for a story they can peddle. Legitimate pros in the media worry some about this but don't know how to stop it.

"Speaker Carl Albert had his media problems. He came under *Daily Oklahoman* sniping because he didn't kowtow to its Washington bureau as expected. Mr. Albert never learned to trust any of the Washington press.

"Chain store news we have today scares me most. It says the dollar is more important than the truth. Thus it lends itself to manipulators seeking to guide and control public opinion.

"As for TV, I go only live. I like the print because you can't put an inflection in it, just plain black and white. With TV it's, 'Have you quit beating your wife?' with 10 seconds to answer.

"I only had one enemy, Eddie Gaylord. I don't think he has the capacity to like anybody his dad, E. K., did. E. K. was a progressive conservative, the younger Gaylord a reactionary conservative.

"In Oklahoma City, Eddie Gaylord runs things, so Tulsa is getting ahead. He's a definite liability."

Tom always speaks his mind. He did as a Congressman and does today.

Al Cromley, whom I've know and liked since we both were at the state capitol during the Johnston Murray days, told of Tom's reaction in 1954 when Congress voted to raise its salaries from $12,500 to $22,500 a year.

"He called an impromptu press conference just off the

House floor," Cromley related. Then he announced, 'I voted to give myself a raise because I'm a greedy sonofabitch.'

"Other members looked shocked. Steed looked pleased, having again used his secret weapon with reporters — overwhelm them with candor and take the offensive."

Steed campaigned the same way. Not being afraid to say what he thought helped him beat what should have been one of his toughest opponents, Jay Wilkinson, Bud's son. The Wilkinsons are jinxed in politics.

One problem Jay Wilkinson faced was Tom's considerable influence in Washington. It was 1970 and Bud Wilkinson was a Nixon aide.

"A White House colleague of Wilkinson's was sent to a Republican campaign rally in Chickasha," Cromley wrote. "To Steed it looked as if the administration had taken a personal interest in his race. Steed was chairman of the Appropriations Subcommittee which had jurisdiction of funds for the White House staff.

"Steed told a reporter, 'After we take a look at the White House budget, they're just liable to find themselves minus some of their staff.' This word got around and presidential aides sent down orders . . . to stay out of Steed's campaign."

What really put young Wilkinson away, however, was Tom's crusty offhand remark about one of Jay's TV spots.

Jay Wilkinson had slick TV ads, designed to be pretty, I guess, and make viewers feel good. One showed Wilkinson walking happily and carefree through a pasture, head held high, gazing at the blue sky above.

"Anyone ambitious to be a Congressman ought to have sense enough to look down instead of up at the sky when walking through an Oklahoma cow pasture," Tom snorted.

This comment was printed widely and didn't help Wilkinson.

Tom now speaks highly of Henry Bellmon. I remember a campaign or two where Tom and I had different thoughts. Since then, Tom and Henry have both gone through hellfire and damnation for supporting the Panama Canal treaty.

Steed's toughest campaign was against Bellmon's fellow Republican, Truman Branscom, whom he barely beat by a scared-to-death 364 votes. Tom gave Henry considerable angry credit for Branscum's near miss.

"Henry's self-appointed halo," Tom threatened at the time, "will be irreparably broken and his blight on Oklahoma erased when he runs for the Senate."

Well, nobody makes good on all predictions, especially about Bellmon, who's just as independent as Tom Steed. Because of his independence, I believe Henry Bellmon would get more Democratic than Republican votes today.

I guess most people have Tom Steed figured as a former ultra-liberal Congressman, same as they pegged Ed Edmondson. Not quite true. I asked Tom about how Congress has changed.

"Congress," he replied, "is a very true reflection of the nation's citizenship in quality, honesty, courage, morals and citizenship, or lack thereof. 'What's in it for me?' has replaced 'Is it right and can we afford it?' in this nation.

"New Deal-Great Society programs created too much bureaucracy. No effective way to curb this bureaucratic growth has been found.

"People are joining up into too many gangs to assault the public treasury. This evil has grown in almost exact proportion to decline in the percentage of those who cop out by not voting.

"A fantastic growth of one-issue lobby groups swarming the capitol has occurred . . . promoters, shysters, self-servers and do-gooders. American greed, properly stimulated, seems adequate to continue this curse indefinitely.

"I don't see a balanced budget in the foreseeable future. Politicians voting enough taxes or reducing spending sufficiently to cause a balanced budget will be wiped out at the next election. Everyone wants the other guy's program cut and for him to pay the taxes."

I suspect Tom sees some of these problems more clearly now than when *he* was being beseiged by the "gimme" crowd. He reminded me socialists have always predicted death of capitalism through greed and bankruptcy.

"Public greed constantly increases the national debt," Tom lamented. "If continued, all experts agree, national bankruptcy is going to follow. A wise Congressman once said, 'We made our first mistake when we gave away the first sack of flour.' 'Can we afford it?' is rarely heard in Congress these days.

"Washington is a cesspool of one-issue pressure groups. It's essential Congressmen get away from that pressure, come home and walk Main Street to clear their heads. I voted against revenue sharing from the first," Tom put in. "We have no revenue to share.

"The record shows those who receive the money aren't being required to face the taxpayers who fork it up. They use it to avoid responsibility that belongs at home."

Staying in is the one great dedication of today's Congressmen. To this effort they and their staffs devote 90 per cent of their energies.

"A Congressman wears four hats," according to Steed.

"He's a lawmaker, errand boy, employment agency and chamber of commerce. Only his lawmaking role will determine whether he deserves a place in history.

"Congressional voting machines have only three buttons—Yes, No and Present. There is no 'Maybe.' Oldtimers learn to live with this constant threat while newcomers lose sleep.

"I was always pained watching grown men in the cloakroom cry over a vote they knew to be right but might cost them political support. It's distressing that our system contains punishment for honesty and integrity.

"Lawyers in legislative jobs also concern me. They swear allegiance to the judicial branch of government, which weakens their ability to be completely loyal to the legislative branch. Some think a decrease in the number of attorneys would be an improvement.

"Increase in women members has been beneficial but not the great loss of farm Congressmen. Once in a healthy majority, this group has dwindled to less than one-fourth of the membership. Farm Congressmen are fewer, while younger, more cynical members have increased."

E. F. Hutton stole Tom Steed's slogan. When Tom talks, people listen. He laughed about why he gives longer answers to a question than even most Congressmen.

"Because I know more about it," Tom replied.

Tom does know more about nearly everything than most people. He sees no need to keep what he knows secret and is glad to tell you about it. He likes to reminisce about the greats he knew.

"I believe Presidents Truman and Nixon will command more attention in American history than others I served with—Truman for the right reasons, Nixon for the wrong.

"Eisenhower was most polished, Lyndon Johnson was my closest friend, Jerry Ford my friend and classmate. I started my Congressional career on a committee with Nixon and Jack Kennedy.

"Carter was the poorest of the lot. I don't think President Carter was a competent judge of America's true character. He had his chance and muffed it. If he had called me for advice, I would have suggested he go back to peanut farming.

"My personal favorite politican was LBJ. Knew him longer and had closest association with him.

"President Johnson carried a heavy load with courage and determination. I met him in 1935 when he was House doorkeeper and I was secretary to Congressman P. L. Gassaway. I was a campaign manager when LBJ was elected to the "Little Congress," our employee association.

"Johnson liked to play devil's advocate and show his humor at times. I remember once when the Oklahoma and Arkansas delegations met with President Johnson, wanting his signature on a bill boosting spending for our Arkansas River project. LBJ brought up every objection he could think of and it was looking dark. Sounded like he wouldn't sign it. Senators Kerr and McClellan were stunned.

"Finally, after he had us sweating hard for a long time, the President opens a drawer and pulls out the order, already signed.

" 'Why all this gabbing if you were already convinced?' Senator Kerr asked. Johnson replied: 'Just wanted to see if you raiders of the treasury know what the hell you're talking about.' "

Looking back, Steed has some words of wisdom and caution for those ambitious to follow in his footsteps.

"The main three pieces of advice I give a freshman Congressman," Tom stated, "is: Be patient. Be patient. Be patient. Congress will break the spirit of eager beavers wanting speed.

"Then remember, no Congressman was ever defeated for something he did *not* say. Your voice is the not the sweetest music on the House floor. Use it sparingly.

"Finally, knowledge is power. You gain knowledge by burning the midnight oil."

Tom Steed's boyhood heroes were Tom Jefferson and Abe Lincoln. He went to Congress with more ideals than ambition, feeling honor bound to do what he believed right.

We, the people, would like to hasten the day when members of Congress could again bear the thought of defeat better than rising above principle to vote against conscience. With nearly every voter part of some special interest group hollering for help, Congress has largely abdicated its duty.

Our hope for something better rests with that 20 per cent of swing voters in the middle who decide elections today. They are looking for some Tom Steeds willing to vote against the Gallup poll if that's the right vote.

These conscientious voters are learning who the poll-watchers are and marking them for extinction. They've nailed a few already. Tom Steed and I will be glad to see more go.

They give the honest pork-barrel of old a bad name.

9

SEX IN THE U. S. SENATE RACE

I never knew any man in my life who could not bear another's misfortune perfectly, like a Christian.

Alexander Pope

No campaign ever bubbled with so much heat from sin, sex, unrewarded virtue and snarling hatchet men of press and politics as the 1978 Oklahoma U. S. Senate race.

Featured actors in this melodrama were Gov. David Boren, old political warhorse George Miskovsky, and a very strange man who filed for the Senate under the pseudonym Anthony Points.

I'm personally not concerned about sexual habits of David Boren or any politician. For campaign purposes, my ideal candidate publicly drips with sex appeal but is actually a closet eunuch. Eunuchs can't get into bedroom trouble.

The '78 Oklahoma Senate race was utter Dullsville until two things happened to open folks' eyes and set 'em tattling and tittering.

Gene Stipe entered the race at the last minute, to everyone's surprise. So did an unknown "character" candidate, one of whose many aliases was Anthony Points. Can you imagine a guy running for office under an alias?

Stipe announced he was selling a large ranch, a mere bauble for the Prince of Darkness, to finance his campaign. But he didn't garner enough votes outside Little Dixie, which Stipe owns politically. He owns a bunch of it personally, too.

Nobody heard of Anthony Points until he accused Senate candidate Gov. David Boren of being homosexual. Points wouldn't have been heard of then had not ancient warrior George Miskovsky, his campaign shield dragging in the summer dust, shouted his last hurrah by picking up on Points' unfounded homosexual charge against Boren.

Miskovsky wanted to know: "Are you homosexual, Gov. Boren, as Mr. Points claims?"

Sort of a personal question, I thought. Especially when asked right out loud in public during the heat of a U. S. Senate race. Miskovsky, while piously claiming he only wanted to give Boren a chance to clear the air about Points' reckless charges, got the "Is-he-or-isn't-he-gay?" gossip about Boren really rolling.

This definitely was not Miskovsky's intention, you may believe, if you accept George's view of the matter. He had no idea it would result in so much controversial attention. So he claimed.

Although embarrassing, the homosexual issue probably wound up helping Boren.

Ever since Boren and his first wife were divorced suddenly and surprisingly while he was governor, rumors about Boren having a limp wrist circulated freely in political circles. Shortly before announcement of their divorce, the first Mrs. Boren was featured in a newspaper article telling how she enjoyed being first lady and "helping David."

Then suddenly Boren announced their divorce intentions, at the same time "accepting full responsibility" for splitting of the sheets. Gossip is what makes politics fun. So the statehouse immediately rang with rumors of Boren's alleged homosexuality. Nowhere louder than in the capitol press room. Soon John Q. Public was whispering, "Is he or isn't he?" in Oklahoma's classier watering holes.

Most felt such rumors were hurting Boren. Not me. Anyone who starts his campaign with the homosexual and bisexual vote locked in is not going to get skunked. That 15 per cent is a lot more than Miskovsky, Points and a couple other candidates got put together.

When Points and Miskovsky brought homosexuality into the open, Boren took his famous oath on the Bible before God and the TV cameras. He swore to adhering to the missionary position and tradition in all things sexual. He added he is quite clear on what homosexuality is but has no taste for it.

The Borens' divorce came like a bolt from the blue. Mrs. Boren always gave the appearance of a delighted First Lady. So the divorce, folks whispered, must have been caused by some abomination she accidentally discovered about David.

All eyes turned toward the governor's office, where several handsome young men, as is usual, worked.

"Look at that guy's pink cheeks," it was said of one.

"Isn't his voice kinda high?" they asked of another.

Such comment was common everywhere, including in editorial rooms of the Daily Oklahoman. Newsmen close to the scene probably speculated and gossiped more than anyone else about what Boren's bedroom habits might be.

Grossly unfair, but who ever said politics is fair?

Miskovsky, after the election, dropped another bombshell. He filed a $25-million libel suit against Oklahoma Publishing Company. Claimed he had been destroyed personally and politically simply for being a Good Samaritan to fellow candidate David Boren, the big winner.

The real question is: Was Miskovsky murdered by OPUB-CO or were George's wounds self-inflicted, a case of suicide? You be the judge.

In his petition seeking $25-million damages for libel, plaintiff Miskovsky, who ended a slow fifth in the seven-man race, talks touchingly of his reputation, children and grandchildren, and especially his deep concern for fellow U. S. Senate candidate David Boren.

George of the jutting jaw worrying so over an opponent's welfare seemed out of character for this former prizefighter. Much of the public, especially lawyers, laughed uproariously when George filed his suit. But he fooled 'em in court, thanks to two exceptional attorneys — Everett J. Sweeney and E. Joe Lankford.

Before it was over, even the Oklahoman's ace investigative reporter, Jack Taylor, who has dirtied up his share of politicians, found himself in contempt of court and sentenced to jail. Nobody in either the ivory towers or sweatshops at OPUBCO ever thought God would permit such an indignity done to one of His own, an investigative reporter.

It set Jack Taylor sorrowing in "Why hast Thou forsaken me?" fashion on the front page.

"What Do I Tell My Kids?" Taylor wanted to know.

He should instead have been worrying about what to tell Judge Preston Trimble. Trimble refused to be blown out by a snarling tirade of media criticism which followed his sentencing of Taylor for refusing to testify as ordered.

Reporters tend to work in packs, like wolves. Especially so when one of the pack is cornered. At such times the barking, baring of teeth and snarls from a united and enraged media are frightening.

Our drama begins August 9, 1978, a day starting out as a repetition of a hundred previous humdrum days leading up to it during this dull U. S. Senate campaign that suddenly exploded. The fire bomb went off in an unlikely place, the Ponderosa Restaurant, before, of all people, the Women's Democratic Club of Canadian County.

All U. S. Senate candidates were invited to this historic meeting but only three had the foresight to appear — George Miskovsky, Dean Bridges and Anthony Points. The three low men on the Senate race totem pole who could think of nothing better to do.

Points, it turned out, was really Anthony Flores Reyes, operating under an alias.

His changing names didn't help much. Points finished seventh. Since seventh was also last, Points couldn't have done worse with his regular name, Reyes. I personally feel he'd have been wiser filing under a third alias he used in placing an advertisement, Tony Determan.

But when you get right down to it, Points-Reyes-Determan would have lost running under all three names at once, even if allowed to total the votes from each. A guy seeking to hide his identity this way really has no business in a political race, although such unusual political modesty certainly deserves praise.

Miskovsky, David Boren, Eddie Gaylord and Jack Taylor grabbed most of the headlines. Yet Points deserves billing as top star. I intend now to give him his overdue due.

What I can't understand is why the media ignored an imaginative candidate like Points, whose platform I now reveal for the first time.

ANTHONY POINTS PLATFORM
The People's Voice

- "I am in favor of cutting the price of gas
  and electric bills in half."

Who knows how many votes this plank alone would have brought Points had we, the people, but known.

- "I am against Arabs entering the United
  States in exchange for the reduction of the
  price of oil."

I'll bet you didn't even know we were being offered such a deal.

- "Our last three presidential administrations have had Communist overtones,
  from the Panama Canal treaty through
  selling of arms to the Arabs."

If Eddie Gaylord had known he and Anthony Points saw eye to eye on the Panama Canal treaty, I don't see how Eddie could have ducked supporting him as successor to Henry Bellmon. Bellmon voted for the treaty and was excoriated by Gaylord's Daily Oklahoman.

- "When Nixon let the Arabs into the
  United States in 1970, a lot of plutonium
  started disappearing. Arabs are buying
  buildings across the United States and are
  always demanding plutonium for their
  country. What is to stop them from making nuclear explosives in these buildings
  and then going back to their own country?"

I bet you never thought of that before.

- "I am against the human baby being clon-
  ed."

You know anyone else willing to come out flat-footedly on a controversial issue like this?

Clearly Points was no one-issue candidate trying to get by on his many names and dark good looks. And we're only now coming to the hard core of his platform.

- "I am against homosexuals in the school system. They are a threat to our children. They are like vultures preying on our young.
- "I am against homosexuals or bisexuals in office or government. They are a threat to our national security. They are subject to being blackmailed and will give out a favor or leak information from the government in return for having their homosexual identity kept secret."

I've been wondering why all the leaks these days from the FBI, the CIA and a torrent of leaks from every other agency of government. Clearly our government is honeycombed with homosexuals known only to the media, a media which equally clearly must be in bed with them, so to speak.

And now we come to the juicy part of Anthony Points' platform, as recited to the horrified staid ladies of the Canadian County Women's Democratic Club.

- "There is a side to David Boren that is a known fact in legal and political circles, and that's the fact that David Boren frequents with homosexuals and I'm putting it lightly. I don't think that is what you want for a U. S. Senator.
- "It is this type of activity, homosexuals or bisexuals in office, along with U. S. Senators being blackmailed, that is send-

ing America down the tubes."

Not just down the tube, see, down the *tubes*. Pretty serious.

- "If elected," Points' platform concludes, "I
  will put these issues before the people of
  Oklahoma for a vote and, if passed, by
  God, that's the way it's gonna be. Then I'll
  carry these issues on a national level."

Points then listed two phone numbers and allowed as how he could use some help, an understatement in more ways than one.

The good ladies of Canadian County were aghast at Points' accusation against Boren. Could it be true?

But where, one wonders, was the usually sensation-seeking media? In Dullsville, off covering those they had decreed to be front-runners, ignoring completely Miskovsky and Points who were dealing with the red hot issues.

Points badly needed a press secretary but couldn't afford one. Boy, the publicity I could have gotten that guy!

Of course, there was a slight flaw in Points' platform. The only one Points had backing up his charge about Boren being homosexual was that elusive fellow, Everybody Says. We all hear from ol' Everybody Says a lot in politics and Points is quite correct, he was extremely active spreading gossip about Boren during the '78 campaign.

Trouble is, when you need the guy to prove a point you never can find him. Everybody Says is the most quoted person around yet will never appear in court as a witness.

Boren probably doesn't think so but again I say Points did him a favor. The homosexual vote surely went to him almost unanimously. Depending on the crowd you run with, estimates of how big that group is range from 10 to 20 per cent. Even higher if you include all occasional experimenters.

Everybody Says claims it's 20 per cent and I don't know any better authority who puts it under 10 per cent. Since most elections are won by five per cent or less, only a fool sticks out his tongue at the homosexual vote. In San Francisco, politicians get down on bended knees for that endorsement.

The only truly experienced politician who was fully aware of Points' gay platform was, of course, George Miskovsky. As George pointed out in his petition seeking $25-million libel damages from the Oklahoman, he was honor bound to notify a fellow candidate of such scurrilous charges. If George didn't, who do you suppose would? Maybe nobody.

"Do unto others," was Good Samaritan Miskovsky's stated motive, which somehow took people by surprise. Nonetheless George did his soldierly duty as he saw it, tipped off Boren as to what was being said about his alleged sexual proclivities.

Boren was busy campaigning and hard to contact. So George did the logical thing, wrote Boren a letter. Being also a firm believer in the First Amendment and the public's right to know, he gave copies of his letter to the media.

You'd think the media might appreciate this act of generosity. It was one hell of a story, as subsequent events proved. But to George's surprise and sorrow the media, especially Oklahoma Publishing Company and satellites it influences, really got down on ol' George.

They started biting the hand trying to feed 'em. In no time they devoured Miskovsky's entire carcass.

"Tell us, George," asked the *Oklahoma City Times*, "are *you* gay?"

A *Daily Oklahoman* editorial offered, "AN APOLOGY TO GEORGE: An editorial in last week's *Oklahoman* identified

George Miskovsky as a septuagenarian. Turns out George is only 68, which makes him, instead, a sexagenarian," they joked.

That's the thanks you get. Something to remember next time a reporter asks you to dish out a little off-the-record dirt.

Miskovsky "believed then and believes now," it says in his libel suit petition, "that it was not only appropriate to ask Gov. Boren to answer the charge but was his *duty* to call this to the attention of the governor and voters, to give the governor an *opportunity* to answer straightforward questions concerning the charge. To make certain there was no question about the rhetoric, the plaintiff (Miskovsky) communicated his questions in a typewritten letter and released copies to the press."

How noble.

"I am asking you to respond to the following questions:" Miskovsky stated in his letter to Boren.

"Do you know what a homosexual or bisexual is?

"Are you homosexual or bisexual?

"Have you ever been a homosexual or bisexual?

"Have you ever engaged in homosexual or bisexual activity?

"I believe it is the right of every citizen, if it can be ascertained," Miskovsky added, "to know if a candidate for the U. S. Senate is affiliated with this kind of abnormal behavior."

Once that letter reached the press, the roof caved in on George.

George complained, "OPUBCO's intent and purpose was to influence public opinion and hold plaintiff up to scorn, oblique, disrespect, ridicule; and to destroy plaintiff politically, professionally and personally, and as a basis for further editorializing affirmatively for OPUBCO's candidate, Boren."

There's no doubt the *Oklahoman* and *Times* pulled out all stops against Miskovsky. Boren also responded dramatically.

Before God, the world and all media, Boren placed one hand on his white Bible and swore, "I know what homosexual and bisexual is. I am not, have never been and never will be homosexual or bisexual."

The *Daily Oklahoman* printed a touching photo of Boren kissing his new wife, Molly. A picture is worth a thousand words. No way someone willing to kiss a woman in public, and have his picture made doing it, could possibly be homosexual. That was the unsubtle, unstated message.

Next my friend Ed Edmondson got into the act. Ed was about to go down for the third time in a Senate race and wanted some fun doing it. So Edmondson called himself a press conference to point up another rumor, that Boren was more Republican than Democrat. Edmondson also took a solemn oath before the TV cameras.

"I swear on this book about Harry Truman, *Plain Speaking* by Merle Miller," Edmondson mimicked Boren's more solemn ceremony, "that I know what a Democrat is. I also know what a Republican is and I swear on the sainted memory of that great Democrat, Harry Truman, that I am now, have always been and will forever remain a Democrat."

Later it turned out the only one they proved homosexuality on was the author of the book Edmondson swore his oath on. Actually, they didn't have to prove it. The fellow admitted it. Said he wouldn't have it any other way.

Edmondson, who got in the race late with a short financial stick, wasn't the only one washed onto a sandbar by the heavy sex waves being stirred up. George Miskovsky's nephew, Mike Miskovsky, was running at the same time for the State House of Representatives in District 91, south Oklahoma City. He learned Uncle George's "favor" to David Boren was no favor to him.

"As much as he likes his uncle," wrote Oklahoman reporter Paul Wenske, "Mike Miskovsky says he wants to make it known to prospective supporters that even though their last names are the same, he doesn't like what Uncle George said about the governor — in fact he's chagrined."

"I feel," Mike Miskovsky was quoted, "that such campaign tactics are both unnecessary and demeaning to the State of Oklahoma. I consider such statements based upon unfounded rumors and cheap gossip to show a complete lack of political responsibility. I have no ties whatever with George's campaign or anything he does, period."

The disavowal didn't help. Mike Miskovsky, 33, did better than Uncle George but must await another day to make it to the legislature.

We, the people, rallied to Gov. Boren while two Miskovskys bit the dust. So did Gene Stipe, Prince of Darkness from Little Dixie, in spite of his late hip-hip-hooray flurry. He got off to a fast start but tired in the stretch, due at least in part to indigestible TV commercials.

Lawyers are pretty persuasive people. It should be noted here that all main candidates in the '78 Oklahoma Senate race were lawyers — Boren, Edmondson, Stipe and Miskovsky. Even sadder to relate, 65 members of the U. S. Senate at that time were lawyers. Will we ever learn barristers are grossly overrepresented in public office?

Lawyer Boren, who also has certain preacher qualities to go with his legal talents, rose in his wrath and smote both Anthony Points and George Miskovsky roundly when advised of the charges made against him.

"I don't know Mr. Points," Boren said sternly, "but if he made such a statement he is a more vicious liar than anybody I would care to know. This is the kind of gutter politics that does not merit further comment.

"It is a shame a person has to be subjected to this personal attack in order to serve the public," Boren commented further. "This kind of tactic just makes it even clearer to people the contrast between the other campaigns and a clean, positive campaign that I intend to continue to run."

In the press, Boren's statements overrode completely statements by Miskovsky. Miskovsky became the immediate heavy. Points, who in fact made the accusations about Boren, was ignored. Everyone jumped on George, who found this hard to understand.

"Who, me?" George asked innocently.

The press asked Miskovsky, not Points, for substantiation of Points' allegations.

"That's not within the context of this press conference," Miskovsky huffed, when asked if he could prove Points' statements.

Lawyers like to split fine points. Reporters, however, paint with broad brushes dripping with the heavy juices of sensationalism.

10

WHAT DO I TELL MY KIDS?

Wad some power the giftie gie us
To see oursels as others see us!

Robert Burns

They didn't know it but the working press was sort of on trial, too, during the Miskovsky vs. OPUBCO libel trial. They did protest too much, seeking pity.

One of OPUBCO's stalwarts who lived by the sword, investigative reporter Jack Taylor, felt the rapier blade in his own side as this gay drama unfolded. Politicians throughout Oklahoma laughed gleefully at the headline, "Newsman Handed 30-day Contempt Term."

Jack Taylor was found in direct contempt of court and arrested for refusing to reveal the name of a news source. Judge Preston Trimble, unimpressed by OPUBCO's power, handed down the sentence, then released Taylor under his own recognizance.

Taylor admitted he was assigned to investigate U. S. Senate candidate Anthony Points. Judge Trimble ordered him to answer questions about the investigation and produce his notes.

"We have a right to determine the state of mind of the publisher (Edward L. Gaylord) at the time these (Taylor) articles were published, and the only way we can do it is to search these records and this witness," argued Miskovsky attorneys Sweeney and Lankford.

Judge Trimble agreed and ordered Taylor to speak up.

"I most respectfully decline to answer under my privilege

under the first amendment of the U. S. Constitution and the newsman's shield law, as I understand it as a layman," responded Taylor the martyr.

Then all hell broke loose in the hallowed halls where hallucinating journalists of Oklahoma pop their "protect the people" pills.

"It's high time Oklahomans get worried about what is happening to freedom of expression in our state because of the attitude of some judges," whined the *Daily Oklahoman*. "What if some politician didn't like an opinion you expressed and hauled you into court, forcing you to pay thousands of dollars in attorney's fees, and perhaps obtained a large judgment against you?"

As one who has been there, I'll take my chances in court any day ahead of my chances with the *Daily Oklahoman* for expressing an opinion *they* dislike during a political campaign. As a journalist myself, I have long known we who dish it out so heroically rarely take even the slightest criticism with the good grace we expect of ordinary mortals. Only we journalists are more pious than preachers and politicians.

An Oklahoman and Times reporter was assigned to search out reaction to the outrage against Jack Taylor. Predictably, he discovered the court committed a grave sin against God, flag, country and reporter Taylor.

"First Amendment watchdogs and journalism leaders reacted indignantly Friday to the contempt citation and jail sentence handed to Oklahoma City newsman Jack Taylor by Cleveland County District Judge Preston Trimble," the Oklahoman's not so even-handed story began.

"It's a damned outrage," said Jack Landau, director of the Reporters Committee for Freedom of the Press, headquartered

What Do I Tell My Kids?

in Washington, D.C.

"It doesn't seem to me Jack Taylor has any information that's related to the lawsuit," Landau in far away Washington, D.C. added, "This is a classic case of why the press is angry at the courts."

Now I ask you, how does this guy in the nation's capital know all the details of a complicated libel suit so well he can give such a firm off-hand opinion? You may find an answer in the fact this is a case of journalist defending journalist.

Taylor's boss, Oklahoman managing editor Jim Standard, also came to bat as impartial designated hitter on Taylor's team.

"It's an affront to a free society that reporters in Oklahoma must face prison for doing their jobs," moaned Standard.

"We will assist his legal defense in every way," Standard continued. "That this libel case is still in the courts after 14 months makes one suspicious that some judges have never read the First Amendment ... As a result, Oklahoma newspapers — more so than in any other state of the union — are susceptible to financial punishment or ruin for expressing opinions guaranteed by the Constitution of the United States."

Next up was Mike Hammer, billed as "deputy regional director for Oklahoma and Texas of the Society of Professional Journalists, Sigma Delta Chi." They forgot to mention Hammer is the *Daily Oklahoman's* political reporter covering the state capitol.

Like other Taylor defenders, Hammer's words were designed to make Judge Trimble tremble.

"Another example of a judge who is insensitive to the people's right to know and the First Amendment," Hammer hammered, "allowing attorneys to harass reporters and go on fishing expeditions for material unrelated to the lawsuit at issue.

"Surely this decision cannot be allowed to stand. Sigma Delta Chi will join the Oklahoman & Times in whatever legal steps must be taken to overturn the ruling."

You know, I sorta expected ol' Mike Hammer to defend his own paper.

Next to fume at Judge Trimble came the Oklahoma Broadcasters Association and Oklahoma Associated Press Broadcasters. Judging by what we read and heard from the media, the judge had not one defender in the world.

"The Oklahoma Broadcasters deplore the action," declared genial Tom Parrington, president of the association but not, to my knowledge, a reporter. "The press, which includes the electronic media," Tom continued, "has always contended that the people have a right to know and in order to meet this responsibility as professional journalists, the confidentiality of sources must remain protected."

George Tomek, handsome president of the Associated Press Broadcasters, said his group "wishes to express its support for Jack Taylor and regret that Taylor was forced to choose between his freedom and his principles."

It's interesting to note both Parrington and Tomek worked for Channel 4 in Oklahoma City, owned for more than 25 years by Oklahoma Publishing Co. and still with close ties to OPUBCO at the time of Taylor's tearful trials and tribulations.

The Oklahoma Press Association board of directors, many of whom can't stand Eddie Gaylord, Jack Taylor or OPUBCO, nonetheless voted to intervene in Taylor's court appeal. There was bad blood between Ben Blackstock, who so effectively runs the Oklahoma Press Association, and Eddie Gaylord,

What Do I Tell My Kids?

Oklahoman and Times publisher. But such hatreds wash away quickly in holy waters protecting the media's right to do and say what it damn well pleases.

Jack Landau, director of the Reporters Committee for Freedom of the Press, was heard from a second time. He said the nation's judiciary "frequently believes it is above the laws or the Constitution."

He added that there is a "certain judicial arrogance" not limited to the U. S. Supreme Court. "It is alive and well in Oklahoma," he sadly concluded.

Look at what pot is calling which kettle "arrogant"!

Media people are known for having one arm longer than the other, caused by patting themselves on the back so frequently.

Piece de resistance of this melodrama was an article written by No. 1 martyr, the eye-for-an-eye, tooth-for-a-tooth *Daily Oklahoman* journalist, none other than Jack Taylor himself. REPORTER WONDERS: WHAT DO I TELL MY KIDS? Thus cried the headline over Taylor's tear-jerker.

"Few people relish the limelight. No one wants to be a test case," Taylor began his wonderings.

I thought of so many given the cruel limelight of innuendo, gossip, and unproven grand jury leaks by this same Jack Taylor now crying in his beer.

"It might have left me a little cynical and more than a little depressed," Taylor confessed . . . "Although I was not involved in preparing any of the articles or cartoons at issue in Miskovsky's suit . . . Miskovsky thought I might have been.

"He wanted everything I had in my files and records on himself, Points and Boren. Quite obviously, no journalist can turn over such raw data any more than a lawyer such as

Miskovsky would willingly turn over his work papers.

"Such journalistic files, particularly involving political figures, *frequently contain more unsubstantiated gossip than fact.* Such files, if made public, could cause needless embarrassment to the principals, including Miskovsky."

How touching and noble. I never before realized what deep concern Taylor and OPUBCO have for Oklahoma political figures they routinely smear with the mud of unproven grand jury leaks, quotes from unknown "usually reliable sources" and downright damn lies in front page editorials.

"I'm no Thoreau," our hero continued, "but I do have principles and I was being asked to violate them and, by doing so, irreparably damage the integrity of my newspapers and profession. . . .

"What do I tell my six children in whom I and their mother have tried to instill respect for our democratic system and values, including the judiciary? . . . I sat in the witness box feeling awkward and out of place and wishing I were with my colleagues, the reporters, instead of the reported."

Ah, yes, don't we all! Whatever else may be said of Taylor and reporters generally, they do understand their own business. If you don't believe me, try interviewing one of *them* sometime. I've tried many times and rarely get one on the record. They know how dangerous it is to talk for publication.

The Sunday Oklahoman of February 17, 1980 printed nine letters to the editor in response to Taylor's article about himself. Eight of the letters upheld Taylor, one God-blessing him "for the fine, gentle person you are."

The ninth letter was unsigned but the Oklahoman printed it anyway, contrary to its standing journalistic rule not to print unsigned letters. In the interest of fairness and balance, I'm sure.

What Do I Tell My Kids?

"Why don't you tell your kids to call you the "SOB" that you are?" the dastardly unsigned letter stated. "An article of yours quoting reliable sources caused a fine wife to divorce me because she believed your writing rather than the truth. Why don't you try telling the truth or keep your mouth shut?"

Only this one cowardly unsigned voice in the wilderness upholding Judge Trimble and excoriating Taylor and the *Daily Oklahoman*. But I assure you this lone dissenting voice was echoed with titters a thousandfold throughout Oklahoma that Sabbath day.

". . . As that hearing droned on," lamented Taylor, "I felt a sickening loss of confidence in the judicial system and some of those values Americans hold in such esteem. I half-listened and I thought: I wish Miskovsky, who had forced me into the predicament, would show up.

"He didn't, and I excused him in my thoughts, mindful that he is a septuagenarian and probably was sleeping in."

What a generous, forgiving thought. Except Miskovsky was in his '60's, not '70's, as 'septuagenarian' implies. We all make mistakes, don't we? And sometimes on purpose.

It's nice once in a while to see with what grace those who dish it out so grandly can themselves take it, when their turn comes.

By May 7, 1980, Eddie Gaylord couldn't stand Miskovsky's needling libel suit any longer. He up and filed his own lawsuit against George, seeking $2.1-million while alleging Miskovsky *conspired to restrain OPUBCO from exercising its constitutional right to free speech.*

Some giggled at that one, especially we who remember being maligned untruthfully ourselves in front page *Daily Okla-*

homan editorials. We didn't realize the *Oklahoman,* with its huge fountains of black smearing ink, ever was denied the right to say anything it pleases about those the publisher dislikes.

According to OPUBCO, Miskovsky and his lawyers filed "a series of totally frivolous and vexatious libel suits against OPUBCO," They claimed Miskovsky tried to "influence plaintiff's editorial policy ... by bringing frivolous and bad-faith litigation." They declared they took after Miskovsky only "to support the integrity of Gov. Boren."

OPUBCO may have thought Miskovsky's suit frivolous but a Cleveland County jury thumbed its nose at the *Daily Oklahoman's* claim of being denied free speech. They did so loud and clear, awarding boreworm Miskovsky a fat $1-million award in his libel suit.

Some less than the $25-million George asked for but a million dollars more than a whole lot of people, including learned and costly lawyers for OPUBCO, thought he'd ever get. You could get 3 to 1 from any lawyer in town that Miskovsky's libel suit would be tossed out before ever reaching the jury.

Miskovsky was a gracious winner, taking his great court victory with not-always-characteristic modesty.

"It will have a purifying effect," Miskovsky sniffed, looking heavenward. "I have no ill will at all. I'm grateful to my lawyers. We're satisfied with the verdict."

Miskovsky's lawyers deserve their client's gratitude. Attorney Everett Sweeney and the rest performed a courtroom miracle. Miskovsky lawyer Carroll Gregg laid it on heavy for a jury well acquainted with OPUBCO's reputation for disemboweling political enemies.

"OPUBCO has been bullying Oklahoma for 100 years,"

Gregg shouted to the jury. "Today is OPUBCO's judgment day. Stand up and be remembered as the people who said to OPUBCO, 'You may own a U. S. Senator but you don't own me!' "

The jury said exactly that, to the tune of $1-million.

Immediately wounded wails, gnashing of teeth and claims of our republic's impending doom again echoed throughout Oklahoma's Fourth Estate. Even Ben Blackstock, Gaylord enemy of the first water, buried the hatchet and donned his white Oklahoma Press Association robes as executive vice-president to call the verdict "shocking and disappointing." Ben added the heavy judgment for Miskovsky would help destroy aggressive news coverage of political candidates.

"They deserve complete coverage, scrutiny and criticism," cried Ben.

Which of course is exactly what public officials get at all times, to a point these days many good people who would like to run for office won't. They don't want their reputations torn assunder by some miffed newspaper publisher. We have several in Oklahoma who use their printer's ink to gain personal political favors.

"Obviously," Blackstock's sermon continued, "those jurors neither understood the need for commentary and criticism of potential elected officials, nor did they understand the First Amendment and its importance to the public."

Ben's a good ol' boy and best press association manager in America. But I figure we, the people, understand the First Amendment and respect it more than publishers like Eddie Gaylord of the *Daily Oklahoman,* to name but one of Ben's fellow protectors of the True Faith. Ben knows that too, I believe, down where he lives.

A gang of others with titles as head of broadcasters, Sigma Delta Chi and other radio-TV and publishing groups also broke into print again, tearfully lamenting the Cleveland County jury's injustice in finding that great paragon of public virtue, the *Daily Oklahoman*, guilty of libel.

Other folks just snickered. Once in a while those who sit in daily judgment of others get a small taste of their own medicine. It always strangles 'em.

I couldn't resist asking some of these pontificators where they were when the Oklahoma City Fair Board, headed by Eddie Gaylord, refused to hold public meetings as required by law, although using gobs of taxpayer money.

"Hey, I'm worried about the First Amendment dying," I said, "and unless you guys keep me informed about what Gaylord's Fair Board is doing, the First Amendment may die."

They acted surprised, looking at me as though I were pissing in public. Their problem, you see, is that Gaylord for years has been the biggest customer of both wire services. He was also in position to personally fire half the heroes who were so courageously defending the First Amendment for us against all but certain publishers.

When OPUBCO announced appeal of the unfavorable verdict, George Miskovsky also erupted with prayerful words about the First Amendment, adding that the verdict "provides a chance to regain my reputation as a lawyer and as a person and to restore the name Miskovsky to my grandchildren.

"I have always prided myself as being one of the staunch supporters of a free press," said Miskovsky. "We must not abuse that right. It applies to all.

"Abuse is the thing that could destroy a free press. The verdict is one in favor of preservation of free speech and free press."

I am not among those trembling with fear for Miskovsky's right or ability to speak freely. George will never bleed to death from biting his tongue.

He and Eddie Gaylord have more traits in common than either likes to admit. If the deal were right, they still could end up as business partners somewhere.

You can bet on it being a profitable venture.

But the Miskovsky-Gaylord partnership probably won't be formed right away. Alack and alas, at this writing George's fat $1-million libel award has gone the way of his ill-fated campaign—"down the tubes" as Anthony Points would say.

The Oklahoma Supreme Court, only fearless Justice John B. Doolin of the one-man Doolin gang dissenting, voted to reverse the jury's award. The sizeable majority said, in effect, Judge Preston Trimble shouldn't have let the case go to trial.

The high court also absolved reporter Jack Taylor of any duty to answer questions in court like an ordinary mortal.

"We see a new sunrise," rejoiced Ben Blackstock, manager of the Oklahoma Press Association. "Oklahoma has the strongest reporter privilege law of any state...

"Justice Barnes in Miskovsky vs. OPUBCO wrote the most important anti-libel decision since statehood. By 8-1 Barnes said both public officials and public figures are subject to reporting, editorial and cartoon comment."

This was a murky case of libel at best, with very weak legs to stand on. But the reversal and decision absolving reporter Jack Taylor of any duty to testify means all ye who yearn to serve the republic in elective office better get ready to duck if the big publishers aren't your friends.

You're fair game for any slur and slander they choose to heap upon you. Which is as it should be and not an insurmountable mountain for unafraid political candidates. George Nigh won a landslide victory despite Eddie Gaylord's scurrilous attacks against him in 1982, carrying every county and becoming Oklahoma's first twice-elected governor.

Maybe the happy day has arrived when it's better to have OPUBCO against you than for you. But don't count on it unless you're blessed with untainted blood. For bleed you surely will when they throw knives your way.

Lonesome George Miskovsky appealed his reversal by the Oklahoma Supreme Court to the U.S. Supreme Court. In vain. On October 12, 1982, the nation's highest court turned thumbs down on Miskovsky, refusing to review his libel case.

End of the line on this one for George. But all hail to his tenacity. Anyone George takes on better get ready for a full 15-rounder, with some of Miskovsky's punches sure to land. Miskovsky's wildest swing hit OPUBCO flush in the face and made the *Daily Oklahoman & Times* a little better newspapers for having to wear Miskovsky's $1-million award eyepatch awhile.

OPUBCO is mightily miffed at Miskovsky but George doesn't worry. He has journalistic friends of his own to regularly cheer him as conquering hero. I refer to *Scoop* — editor, Khyle Goddard — not the best rag ever to be graced with printer's ink.

Scoop is properly named. A pure pooper-scooper newspaper. Alongside *Scoop,* the *National Enquirer* is a Christian catechism.

Thus doth our sacred First Amendment continue to be protected on all fronts. Eddie Gaylord and Khyle Goddard, fellow soldiers in arms fighting for the sacred right to excoriate whomever they please.

What Do I Tell My Kids?

When the nation's highest court tossed Miskovsky's appeal in the wastebasket, managing editor Jim Standard of the Daily Oklahoman lauded the court as proper, just and Christian.

"From the beginning, I felt it was a political lawsuit aimed at silencing criticism of Mr. Miskovsky in the press," Standard proudly stated. "All citizens, members of the press included, must always have the right to criticize public officials with vigor."

Ah, yes, but how sad it is that so few public figures dare use this same right of expression against the media at those times, and they are many, when the media so richly deserves it. They don't because newspapers have too much ink and radio-TV stations too much of both free and hot air.

So in spite of George Miskovsky's near-win, our hallowed 5th political commandment still reads:

Honor thy newspaper and radio-TV, and forgive them their sales taxes, so that it may be well with thee and thou mayest live long in office.

SO YOUNG WE WERE!

Happy Democratic primary winner celebrants the year of youth in Oklahoma politics, 1958, are (l. to r.) Herbert Wright, Jr., first district Congressional candidate who came within 3,600 votes of upsetting Page Belcher, Lt. Governor nominee George Nigh, Congressman Carl Albert, Congressman Ed Edmondson and the Big Red "E", governor nominee J. Howard Edmondson.

11

MR. SPEAKER

Great men never feel great; small men never feel small.
Chinese proverb

Oklahoma politicians of greatest power have been flamboyant wheeler-dealers. Except one.

This rare exception reached the highest pinnacle of political success attained by an Oklahoman. He became Mr. Speaker — No. 3 post in the nation's hierarchy, No. 2 in power.

When Vice-President Spiro Agnew was forced to resign and President Nixon himself fearfully waited in the wings to resign or be impeached, the presidency of the United States was this Oklahoma country boy's for the taking.

Carl Albert turned it down. He walked away from the most powerful position in the world out of respect for American tradition.

Can you imagine Bob Kerr or Lyndon Johnson doing that?

The most civilized man to emerge from Oklahoma's wild and wooly political warfare was in the larger than life Horatio Alger tradition of service before self. He came out of a two-room country school in the rugged mining country of southeast Oklahoma, a wide spot in the road called Bugtussle, near McAlester.

Politics there has always been a way of life and livelihood. Political schemers abound. Hard-driving gut fighters usually hold sway.

Yet mild-mannered Carl Albert — idealist, Rhodes Scholar, orator, statesman — outdid 'em all, on his rugged home grounds and away. Let me tell you how.

When he was six, Carl Albert embraced a dream that never left him. Half the dream came from his teacher, Mrs. Lottie Ross, who was still alive and well at 99 when Albert was a few years into retirement from his distinguished politcal career in 1980.

The other part of Carl Albert's dream was instilled by Congressman Charles D. Carter, Congressman from Albert's district, who was elected at statehood in 1907 and served until 1926 when Wilburn Cartwright, on his third try, beat Carter by 1,065 votes.

Mrs. Ross took a shine to Carl Albert, her smallest and brightest student. She talked to him about honor, industry, ambition.

"Very much a disciplinarian but in a kind way," Carl remembers. "She lighted in me a desire to do more than the usual.

"Always talking about me getting interested in government. She did fire my ambition in that direction. I would go hear a political speaker from the time I can remember."

Carl Albert became Mr. Speaker January 21, 1971, at which time he said, "I've gone as far as I want to. All I want to do now is serve the country. First comes my country, then my state and Congressional district."

Carl's first grade teacher, Lotti Ross, 89, was present on this historic day with her own memories of the Little Giant from Little Dixie. She recounted how, on the first day of school, Carl asked her to reread the story of *The Goat and the Troll* three times. After she had done so, Carl said to her, "Now I'll read it to you."

"He read it off word for word," she recalled proudly. "He

didn't know one word from another but memorized it while I was reading."

That was the day Mrs. Ross told Albert's mother, "Your boy is going to be a great man someday."

"But I'd always pictured Carl being great in an educational way," added Mrs. Ross. "Never thought of him being in politics. I thought he'd probably be a great teacher or president of some college."

I, too, am surprised Carl Albert chose the rough and tumble of politics. At the heart and soul of himself, Carl is pure scholar. Yet I guess we're lucky to get such a rare impartial intellect into government occasionally, so we don't forget the difference between a Carl Albert and the crowd of showhorses we too often elect.

One day Congressman Carter came to Carl Albert's school, a part of campaigning in that far away pie supper time. Carter, a Choctaw Indian, was born at Boggy Depot, west of Atoka.

"He was good looking, very impressive," said Carl. Had those Indian dark eyes and hair plus outstanding speaking voice with a southern accent. What impressed me most was him telling us kids about Washington.

"We had a picture of the capitol on the wall and he talked about Wilson, president at the time. About 1914 or '15, it was.

"Then he talked about Congress and what they did, and said, 'Any boy who wants to run for office can do it. *Maybe some boy right in this room.*'

"That hooked me. I thought hard about how wonderful it would be.

" 'I'm a Chickasaw Indian in a predominately white population,' the Congressman told us. 'I'm of humble parentage. But I studied hard and finally went to Congress.' Then he said again,

'Some boy in this very room could do the same.' It was kind of a dream but I hugged it to me and thought, *'He could mean me.'*"

From that day forward every step Carl Albert took led him to Congress, then on to become Mr. Speaker.

Love of country was born in Carl Albert, along with a fierce desire to study and learn. His parents were hard-working, loyal citizens but uneducated.

"I don't have a single ancestor whose forebearers weren't in this country before 1800," Albert told me. "Some fought in the Revolutionary War. They started coming out west in 1790."

Carl Albert's mother was from Gainesville, Texas, his dad from Granby, Missouri. Carl was their first child, born when Mrs. Albert was 22. Father Ernie Albert was a horse trader and farmer.

"He was completely uneducated. People could hardly get learning in the west then," Albert explained. "Although only 5'6", dad was physically strong. Solid as a rock, a he-man who could work circles around anybody I've seen. Loved to work, in coal mines and on the farm. Most of his farm is now under Lake Eufaula but I live on the rest of it still.

"Dad had a strong mind-me voice. He'd get mad, too, and · give you a lickin' if you needed it.

"Mother was pretty and deeply religious. Pentecostal. My father was a non-performing Southern Baptist. But his parents were extreme Baptists."

At home and in school, Albert was solidly grounded in love of country and his fellow man. His mother drilled him in religious teachings but Carl's religion is personal, not for public display.

The big fire burning inside young Albert was fueled by desire to go to Congress and "make great speeches." He began entering speaking contests in the '20's, his first when a high school sophomore. Carl won the local contest but lost out in the district finals at Ardmore.

The following year Carl again won the state and also the regional contests in Kansas City.

"This was the great event of my life then," Carl recalled. "I went to the finals in Washington and got a three-month trip to Europe. A girl won the American contest, a Mexican boy the International competition."

But Carl did get his first peek at the exciting big world out there and wanted to be an important part of it.

Next year Carl was enrolled at the University of Oklahoma. Still pursuing his dream, as a freshman Carl entered another speaking contest. This one was about the United States constitution. An elated Carl Albert took first place.

"The prize was $1,500 cash," recalled Carl, "a lot of money in 1928. Also a trip to Hawaii. I'd never been out of Oklahoma until I entered the speaking contest and now I went to both coasts and was getting a year in Europe, Hawaii and Mexico. It gave me a fine perspective of the world for a country boy.

"It was another big turning point in my life, like the day our Congressman talked to us at Bugtussle school. My dad gave me $20 when I first went to OU and I never had another cent from my family. So I felt rich after winning that speaking contest.

"Not only did I get the $1,500 prize, I also was paid honorariums for giving my winning speech to different groups in Hawaii. Came home with over $4,000. Made ten speeches for a total of $2,000 and they kept me on free at the Royal Hawaiian Hotel."

In tall cotton and only the start. After graduating from OU,

Carl was named a Rhodes Scholar. His international education began. He thrived on competition.

His most difficult course at Oxford was Latin. He studied it more carefully than anyone else so he could properly translate. Result: Highest grade in Roman Law . . . Carl Albert.

"They were strict when I was there," Carl mused. "Had to wear a hat and gown as an undergraduate. Couldn't be caught in a pub or down front in a movie where the common folk were. A bit of snobbery at old Oxford."

Another well-known American, Dean Rusk, was in Carl Albert's class at Oxford.

"Rusk always impressed me as a very decent man," I observed.

"He was indeed, and very low key."

"The opposite of LBJ, huh?"

"Completely opposite," Carl laughed. "Rusk never raised his voice, LBJ never lowered his."

Carl Albert learned tradition at Oxford and his eyes were opened to the entire world.

"The Oxford background was important in my election to Congress, vital to my service there," Carl stated. "Gave me a certain status in Congress. Particularly with easterners. Got me support most of the time from the Harvard crowd."

During his stay at Oxford, Carl couldn't fulfill training requirements so he had to give up the Second Lieutenant commission he earned through ROTC at the University of Oklahoma. When he returned to the states and wound up with a low draft number, the army drafted him as a Buck Private in June, 1941.

But Carl got his commission back in a hurry. Within a few months he was a Field Artillery sergeant. The commander of the Third Armored, Colonel Vincent Meyer, heard of this bright sergeant and brought him into headquarters.

"My battery was a sophisticated group of young Privates," recalled Carl. "Some 60 had just graduated from Iowa State University. We were in competition with old regular army soldiers, with about a fifth grade education, mostly from the south. So we younger soldiers soon took over."

One day Col. Meyer called Carl in and said, "You ought to be an officer."

Carl hesitated. This was before Pearl Harbor and Albert's hitch was supposed to be for only a year.

"I'm thinking about applying for OCS one of these days," he hedged, "maybe when basic training's over. I just have a year and might wait and see what that's like."

"You've got a war ahead of you, young fella," replied Col. Meyer, soon to be General Meyer. "You should be an officer and you don't need to go to Officer Candidate School."

Meyer called Washington to recommend appointment of Carl Albert to 2nd Lieutenant. He learned Albert, 5'4", was too short to meet the height requirement. So he sent Carl to his medical department for another measurement, called Washington again and Carl heard him say, "By God, I tell you he *is* tall enough. I want him an officer and that's all there is to that."

So Carl Albert became the shortest officer of World War II. Though short of stature, he shot up fast in rank. They put him in the Army Air Corps Judge Advocate General Department, since he was an eminently qualified lawyer plus being over age in grade for the Artillery.

In rapid strides he became assistant executive officer, assistant military affairs officer and finally head of the Military

Justice Department in Air Corps headquarters. Later he was shipped overseas as a Judge Advocate for the Eastern Air Command.

"I lacked only three weeks of serving five full years in the army," said Albert. "Started out doing all the menial things a GI does but I didn't mind. Good training for politics. Learned a lot about people."

Politics was Carl's first order of business on discharge from the army. It started out tough in little Dixie but not too tough for Carl Albert.

"I was barely back from World War II in March of '46 and filing was in April," Carl remembered. "I hadn't been around in a long time, what with Oxford, the war and working away from my home base."

Paul Stewart was sitting Congressman. He had some built-in opposition but would be hard to unseat, as incumbents using the power of their offices always are. Nonetheless, Carl went to work.

"Made a trip all over my district, calling on everyone I knew," explained Carl, "including Lloyd Noble in Ardmore, a Republican. I knew Noble well because we worked together on university activities. He was even then one of the biggest Oklahoma oilmen."

Carl concentrated on his classmates from high school and college.

"I had ten times more supporters among these groups," he said. "Had other strong support, too. My dad being a miner, later a farmer, his friends rallied to me. Every miner and farmer from Bugtussle to Ft. Smith knew and liked him. In fact, I was the only candidate with any labor identification, plus support from blacks."

Organized labor was strong in the McAlester area and could beat anyone in the upper eastern part of Albert's district. Its influence still lingers there.

"Gene Stipe's main support has been organized labor," Carl said. "Labor is a stubborn crowd which hangs in there politically."

Albert also got the black vote in his first race. They didn't trust Steger and were vigilant against Paul Stewart, whose campaign rhetoric urged "keeping Negroes in their place."

I was surprised to learn from Carl that blacks then voted as much as 50 per cent of their adult population, even though Jim Crow was robustly alive in Oklahoma.

Stewart's "Keep 'em in their place" attitude toward blacks was prevailing sentiment in the district but not Carl Albert's. Stewart reflected his district's beliefs and prejudices all up and down the line. He appeared a cinch for reelection. So Carl did a smart thing.

"I decided no use running against Paul Stewart," said Albert. "Instead, I went and told him, 'I want you to know I have no intention of running against you, Paul.' "

Which made Stewart an instant fast friend of Albert's.

Then Stewart had a heart attack. Like all public officials, he hated to leave the arena. Couldn't decide until the last day of filing whether to run. Finally, at noon of filing day, an ailing Stewart announced he would not toss his hat into the ring again.

"It was after noon when I accidentally found out," Carl related. "A friend of mine was one of Stewart's main supporters and he came running in exclaiming, 'Paul's not gonna run and he's mad as hell at Bill Steger.' "

Steger was odds-on favorite among the four announced

candidates who were already out campaigning — Steger, M.L. Misenheimer, Harold Moore and Bayless Irby. Albert was an unknown but not expected to win if he filed, which no one thought he would do at such a late hour.

"But a few of us got together and somebody said, 'Heck, let's file, Carl. I'll take you over to Oklahoma City.' That's just how it happened. I got to Oklahoma City barely under the filing deadline."

Largely unknown, Carl Albert had but 30 days to campaign in the primary. Nobody thought he had a prayer. It seemed foolish to jump in so late. But Carl's dream told him to try.

"If I don't win first time out, well, I'll try again," he vowed.

His main opponent, handsome Bill Steger, had been campaigning for months. He was well known — former county attorney and state senator, with a following of proven campaign workers.

Albert was better prepared to be Congressman but not to win the election. So said the wise men of Democratic politics.

They forgot Carl Albert had friends of his own. Fewer than Steger but more capable and dependable. Among them the wealthy Republican oilman from Ardmore, Lloyd Noble.

Walter Arnote, young attorney and close friend, managed Carl's campaign. He organized attorneys in the district, Carl's OU friends and many veterans, like Carl, just out of World War II khaki.

Money talks loud in Albert's district, did then and does now. Noble and others helped with finances but Steger got more and bigger donations. Not looking back, Carl dumped his life savings of $10,000 into the campaign pot.

He surprisingly made the runoff, although trailing Steger by a sizeable 3,922 votes.

"At the end of the primary I felt momentum coming to us," he recalled. "We were figured to finish third but came in second and some lucky things happened in the runoff."

One of those lucky things resulted from Carl's opponent freezing him out of campaigning at a rodeo in Atoka.

"I went to the rodeo hoping to speak but found I couldn't," Carl explained. "It was a hot July day and when I got there they were passing out fans with Bill Steger's picture on one side, the rodeo program on the other. I went up to the ticket taker and asked if I could hand out my cards.

" 'No chance,' he told me. 'Steger paid for this privilege, so you can't do it.' That really hurt. A big crowd there and Steger the only one introduced."

It was late afternoon, a day seemingly wasted, when glum Carl Albert left the rodeo and headed toward Antlers.

"I was driving along feeling blue," he related, "when I saw a little sign on a gravel road saying BENTLY. I drove down that road about eight miles. When I got to Bently, I found two stores and a post office."

Not much compared to Steger's huge rodeo crowd. Yet in the end it turned out to be more.

"First thing I saw in Bently was a young man sitting on a porch, his horse tied beside him. I introduced myself. He hadn't heard of me or the Congressional race and cared less. I couldn't arouse any interest until I asked if he was in the war."

"Yeah," he answered.

"Well, I was too," I told him.

"Pacific?" he asked.

"I was there. Ever hear of New Guinea?"

"Stationed there."

"Me too."

"That got him interested," Carl told me.

"I want to help you," he offered. "My dad's well known and I got an uncle by marriage who's Indian. Next box up north, Post Oaks. Lots of Choctaws there. Another uncle owns this store and I got an uncle who's postmaster. They're all up at the house. Let's go talk to 'em."

So Carl went and met the family. He told them he lived north of McAlester.

"Ever hear of Bugtussle?" asked the boy's father.

"Went to school there."

"Know Ed Mitchell?"

"He rented the farm adjoining ours."

"He's my brother-in-law. Whose son are you?"

"Ernie Albert's."

"We know your dad and we're going to work for you. I think we can carry these two precincts."

It turned out those two precincts did more for Carl Albert than the big Atoka rodeo crowd did for his opponent.

Steger was well known from serving in office before. But you make enemies as well as friends in office and Steger had a goodly portion of both, even in his home county. Among his enemies was judge Bob Williams, former governor, who came out strong for Albert.

"Former Gov. Williams and I were talking on Durant's Main Street one day when an oldtimer came up to him and said, 'Why you supporting Albert? Don't you know we have a Bryan County candidate? Bill Steger's lived here 30 years.'"

The brusque former governor eyed the man coldly, looking him up and down.

"On that basis," he snorted, "I oughta be supporting you. You been here 50 years. What does that prove?"

Some folks standing around laughed and word quickly spread that Durant's leading citizen was supporting Carl Albert. Steger carried his home county but Albert got an unexpected 1,500 votes there. Steger got only 800 in Albert's home Pittsburg County.

When they counted the runoff ballots, Albert beat Steger by 330 votes. In one of the two precincts where Carl met the Indian boy with his horse, Carl got 116 out of 120 votes cast. Got 80 per cent of the votes in the second precinct.

Won the race right there, while nursing his wounds over being barred from passing out his cards at the Atoka rodeo. Every once in a while justice prevails, even in politics.

Fortune also smiled on Carl Albert when he got to Congress. Mainly because he had sense enough, right after winning, to visit Sam Rayburn in Bonham, Texas. Went to see Sam again soon as he got to Washington.

"Felt a sorta kinship to him," said Albert. "Our districts joined at the Oklahoma-Texas border. Rayburn lived within just six miles of my district. Closer to my district, he was, than most of Texas. We were sort of alike many ways, too. LBJ used to tell me that."

The similarity was something LBJ liked because nobody he called on more during his wheeling-dealing career in the U.S. Senate and White House than ol' Sam and Carl Albert of Oklahoma. Both dependable and respected.

I asked Carl what Rayburn's outstanding traits were.

"Judgment," Albert said instantly. "An especially judicious person. Didn't err many times. Anything required, he could handle. I learned from him, I tell you.

"He was fond of sayings," Albert continued. "One I heard most often was, 'When you're about ready to answer a question someone's asking, wait a minute.'

"Another was, 'It doesn't make any difference how much sense you got if you haven't got judgment to go with it.'

"Another, 'A lot of people with lots of sense don't have common sense. And common sense is about all the sense there really is.' "

I asked Carl how he differentiated between sense and judgment.

"Sense is intelligence and judgment is the ability to come to an appropriate decision under the circumstances," was his sage reply.

When Albert first went to Congress, Republican Joe Martin was Speaker. It was the 80th Congress, which Harry Truman dubbed "Do-nothing." The tag helped Give-'em-hell Harry get elected in '48, along with a majority in the House. So Sam Rayburn became Speaker.

"I saw immediately how much influence Martin and Rayburn had," Carl said, "and in the back of my mind I had a latent desire for the job. Not expectation, just a faint hope.

"There is so much competition for the job and of course I would never have run against Rayburn or Speaker John McCormack. Both were too good to me."

We talked of House Speakers in the past. Carl wanted the record set straight.

"McCormack was the most maligned," Carl instantly declared. "People didn't understand him. He was controversial but thoughtful and judicious. A tremendous debater. Best operator in the House I've seen."

"Going way back," I interjected, "I guess Joe Cannon and Champ Clark were most autocratic."

"Clark wasn't at all," Albert corrected. "Cannon, yes."

Then Carl made another correction, about Speaker Albert. Like McCormack, Albert was misunderstood by many, particularly by the Daily Oklahoman and the Washington press corps.

Media people covering politics, hard-bitten and cynical sensationalists, rarely understand a scholar and true gentleman like Carl Albert.

According to some of the media, Carl Albert was not a strong Speaker. Nor did he possess the power of former Speakers, they said. Not true. Albert was a successful reformer who made the House more manageable.

"I had more legal power than any Speaker since Joe Cannon," Carl explained. "We upgraded the Speaker's post several ways in my time.

"The Rules Committee had always been a thorn in the Speaker's side. Rules had to pass on most bills before they could come to the floor. Sometimes Rules Committee members would simply refuse to let bills out. The Speaker couldn't do anything with them. So we changed the rule."

Before Carl's Speakership, Rules Committee members, once appointed, retained their membership no matter what. They were kings of their hill, beyond control. Albert brought 'em back in line.

He asked and got caucus approval of a new rule granting the Speaker authority to appoint Rules Committee members, not just once, but every two years. The Speaker was also authorized to name the chairman, and without regard to seniority.

"Before this change, the seniority system completely dominated," Albert said. "So we weakened 'he seniority system, strengthening the leadership."

Albert also worked over Ways and Means, a small and still powerful committee which controls tax legislation.

"Since Champ Clark's time, Ways and Means also served as Committee on Committees," explained Albert. "Whenever we got a new Congress, this small committee would sit down and select committee assignments for every new member. Unless someone requested a change, they put all old members back on their same committees."

All new members had to go to Ways and Means for committee assignments, so that committee's members, in particular the chairman, were treated like tin gods. Speaker Albert decided to give the Democratic caucus and Speaker more power in this area.

"We created a new Steering and Policy Committee to handle the committee assignments," said Carl, "taking that power away from Ways and Means. We did it in caucus, as a Democratic Party matter."

This action greatly strengthened the Speaker's power.

"As Speaker, I automatically became chairman and all House leaders were on the committee—Majority Leader, Whip and Deputy Whip," said Carl. "In addition, I was authorized to appoint one woman, one black and one freshman. So about half the committee members were subordinates of the Speaker. What had been the powerful Committee on Committees became pretty much a function of the Speaker."

That's how newly elected Oklahoma congressman Clem McSpadden got on the important Rules Committee, a nod from Speaker Albert. Congressman Jim Jones of Tulsa can also thank Albert for putting him in the limelight, even being mentioned as a likely presidential candidate a few years later.

In politics, you are what you seem to be. And you seem to be what the media says you are, true or false.

"I wanted Carl to take the initiative more with the media," Joe Foote, Carl's press secretary told me, "meet them on their terms. When you've worked in the media like me, you're not in awe of them nor do you hold them in special high regard."

But Foote couldn't convince his boss.

" 'Sam Rayburn didn't give press conferences,' Carl would say," Foote related, " 'and Sam Rayburn was the strongest Speaker ever. He told 'em where to go and didn't worry about it.'

"That was the thing with Carl," Foote added, "upholding tradition of the House. I hated to see Carl hurt by the media but he just wasn't like Tip O'Neill. Tip would put his arm around reporters, walk down the hall with 'em telling jokes. This pleases their egos. They like being seen talking to wheels.

"Carl was gentlemanly but preferred a business atmosphere. He'd rarely invite a reporter into his office for coffee or flatter him."

Once upon a time, dear reader, the media didn't run our government. Even our president is now accorded less courtesy than a skid row bum by certain media meatheads screaming for TV attention at presidential news conferences.

President Franklin Roosevelt, who did away with written questions and started live press conferences for the full media mob, said at the time future presidents might regret his precedent. I assure you they have.

On network TV shows, most government leaders today accept any insulting question with fearful smiles and meek replies. Those who don't aren't invited back. You'd think by their haughty air the arrogant TV interviewers have been elected to the high positions and our nation's leaders are their lackeys.

This is the sad result of the media's power to elect or defeat. Power corrupts and absolute power corrupts absolutely, in the media, too.

I asked Joe Foote about stories implying Speaker Albert was becoming a lush.

I've had a drink with Carl myself but never seen him tipsy, which is more than you can say for me and some of the reporters who wrote those stories.

"Carl really resented such charges," said Joe. "Here's a guy who got up at 6:00 every morning, stayed on the job until 8:00 or 9:00 at night. Not once did he take a drink during working hours.

"Nixon was apparently drinking pretty heavily then and nobody said a word about it. The national press gave us no problem on it either. We had network anchors and top reporters from the *New York Times, Washington Star* and all the rest. No trouble except from the *Oklahoman* mainly.

"And all the things Carl was criticized for resulted from his Oklahoma background more than anything. If he had any fault it was being too much an Oklahoman. All the good things our state has to offer were in Carl Albert — his openness, humble upbringing, honesty. His traits were the best Oklahoma has and the best in him is what brought criticism."

It isn't Carl Albert's style to fake it. Unlike most of today's politicians, he wouldn't butter up someone he doesn't respect. Fairness is Speaker Albert's specialty. Which isn't good enough for media small shots.

After his retirement, I talked with Albert in his McAlester office about greats and near-greats he knew and worked beside.

"Harry Truman wasn't much to lobby Congress," Carl recalled. "I guess partly because he had a Republican Congress for two years. Called me only once to vote for a bill. He talked to Sam Rayburn and John McCormack."

That was traditional. Work through the leadership from the White House, follow the leadership in Congress. The only way to get things done in that day.

"I once did ask President Truman to sign a private bill of mine to get a claim for a boy an army truck hit," said Carl. "Historically the president vetoes such bills but I went to Truman with mine and he signed it."

I told Carl about Truman's telling us in '56, when Gov. Raymond Gary was Averell Harriman's presidential campaign manager, that he had made a mistake pushing Adlai Stevenson for the nomination in '52.

"I see why Truman thought that," Carl replied. "I don't think he thought of Stevenson as an executive. Too much a nice fellow, too persuaded by ideas and maybe not too practical."

I was madly for Adlai in '52 and again in '56 after he beat my man, Harriman. When Eleanor Roosevelt urged the Democratic convention to nominate him again in '60 at Los Angeles, my wife and I shouted ourselves hoarse for Stevenson again. I manned a Stevenson phone on the floor for Sen. Mike Monroney of Oklahoma who was campaign manager for Adlai's last hurrah.

Looking back from where I sit now, however, I think Truman's judgment was better than mine. Stevenson was a superb theorist and wit. He made Illinois one of its finest governors. But as head of the nation, I doubt he would have been tough and decisive enough to handle the bandits abroad in our nation's capital.

"It's my impression LBJ and Bob Kerr were two peas in the same pod," I told Carl.

"Oh, yeah," Carl answered. "Bob would have been Johnson's spokesman in the Senate had he lived. Johnson told me Oklahoma did more for him than Texas and asked less. Said it was all because of Bob Kerr. Bob was an operator and so was Johnson."

We talked about the famous Kerr-Turner U.S. Senate race in '54, when money flowed out of both camps like water down a roaring mountain stream in the spring thaw.

"Some of Kerr's leaders thought Roy Turner would take away his Senate seat," Carl stated. "People liked Roy. Pleasant, easy going. But the price of cattle went down so much during the campaign that the anti-government rancher (Turner) no longer represented the little cattlemen.

"Bob really used that. Lower farm prices nominated Kerr over Turner. No question about it."

Carl Albert's district saved Bob Kerr from defeat in Kerr's first governor and U.S. Senate races. Kerr's majority in Carl's district was larger than his statewide majority.

Most of Kerr's races were tough and costly, partly because of Kerr's personality. Kerr could be abrasive as an outhouse corn cob on a cold winter morning. That was his style, fight at the drop of a hat.

"Kerr would do it the hard way all right," Carl agreed. "He tried steamrolling everything. Ran over everybody he didn't like. He'd sometimes charge in, lambasting away, when a quiet, easy way was needed."

Carl Albert knew presidents Nixon, Ford and Kennedy well. But he knew LBJ best of all. Worked with and for President Johnson to the point of exhaustion.

"Johnson was by far the most ambitious man we had in my time," mused Carl. "He was vain. Liked doing things he thought would give him historical grandeur.

"When first in, he got lots of telegrams congratulating him and he'd always have them on his desk. Then he had phones all over the place, a long string of phones. He'd point to favorable telegrams and polls and say, 'Here, look here. See all these.' He'd just gloat over them.

"Then during the Vietnam war, when he started hurting, you no longer saw the many phones, telegrams and polls on his desk."

Speaker Albert was a loyal follower and sounding board for President Johnson. LBJ knew integrity when he saw it. He used Carl for the toughest jobs, like gaveling the bloody Democratic convention of '68 in Chicago.

Albert made two political speeches in early '68 of great significance. One was in South Carolina, the other in Staten Island, New York. Carl's speeches were historically important because of the unhappy information he brought back to President Johnson after making them.

"I told LBJ one day," Carl recalled, "that I'd made a speech in South Carolina. Told him the governor of South Carolina said, 'The president's in a lot of trouble.' Bobby Kennedy's pictures were all around and the governor said, 'They hate Johnson more than Bobby Kennedy.' He said they'd go Republican in '68 because southern states resented LBJ's civil rights legislation."

Many South Carolinians considered Johnson a traitor to his part of the country.

" 'They hate Bobby Kennedy,' " Carl quoted the southern

governor to LBJ, " 'but they forgive him a little because he grew up in a different atmosphere than President Johnson.' "

The next week-end Albert went to a county convention in Staten Island and talked to county Democratic chairmen.

"One was a strong Johnson man," Carl told LBJ. "All the rest are for Bobby Kennedy. They all said, 'Kennedy's gonna carry New York.' "

"I know it," Johnson replied sadly, rubbing his strong hands together in a slow wringing motion, his habit when distressed. "I'm not even sure I'll get nominated and know I can't get elected."

"Shortly afterward he made his withdrawal speech," recalled Carl. "I felt sorry for him. Nobody ever tried harder to make a good president than Lyndon Johnson and he was my loyal friend."

I vividly recall those spring days of '68. I was working on LBJ's reelection campaign as director of Public Affairs and Research for the Democratic National Committee. My office in Watergate was one of those later bugged by the Nixon campaign committee burglars. I could have told them no information of value would be found. The Democratic National Committee then leaked like a sieve to every columnist in town. Still does, I'm sure.

Watergate was a two-bit deal. Only utter stupidity permitted it to become such a cause celebre it brought down President Nixon and could have put Speaker Carl Albert of Oklahoma into the oval office in Nixon's place.

Mr. Speaker

12

LET THIS CUP PASS ME BY

Die when I may, I want it said by those who know me best that I plucked a thistle and planted a flower where I thought a flower would grow!

Abraham Lincoln

When the day comes for another military draft, I hope to God our leaders are wise enough to draft college students, too. Make 'em equal with others so they won't cry so much. I remember from my army days that once you take the oath and pull KP and latrine duty a few times, they've pretty well knocked the crybaby out of you. You fall in step nice and easy.

So much for personal editorials. Carl Albert knows far more about Vietnam and other national crises than I. We talked of such things.

"Always seemed to me," I began, "that in Vietnam we either should or shouldn't. Once we're in, what choice but go all out?"

"That lost a lot of support for Johnson after a year or two," Albert replied, "because he wouldn't go ahead and finish the war. He was in a no-win situation at home. It would have been easier to win the war in Vietnam than consolidate thinking in this country.

"But I've seen Johnson when he was really good," added Carl. "When the Dominican Republic crisis came up, the revolution down there, LBJ sent in 5,000 troops to protect and bring home Americans. He told me, 'There will not be another Communist country, another Cuba, in the western hemisphere as long as I'm President of the United States.' and there wasn't."

"This Cuban thing worries me," I put in.

"Me too."

"I thought the Monroe Doctrine would always be adhered to by this country."

"We're not doing it," said Carl, shaking his head. "Of course they alibi out of that but Cuba is Communist. Cubans have control but are actually just tools for Russia."

Then Mr. Speaker changed the subject to the Cuban missile crisis and told of the meeting he attended, called by President Kennedy, when we were eyeball to eyeball and missle to missle against Russia. Kennedy sent military planes to pick up Albert and other House and Senate leaders, bringing them to Washington.

"My plane picked up Sam Rayburn first," said Carl, "then me. Stopped in Springfield, Missouri for Dewey Short and at Indianapolis picked up Charley Halleck and Everett Dirkson.

"Kennedy got us in there and told us what the Russians were doing, how we discovered it and that he issued an ultimatum for them to get out. He was ready for any eventuality. Fortunately Russia backed down, removed their missles."

What impressed Albert most about this meeting was advice Senator Dick Russell of Georgia gave President Kennedy, advice not taken.

" 'Mr. President, we will see the time, all of us,' Russell told Kennedy, 'when we'll regret allowing Castro to exist. You're mobilized now. A big chunk of your navy is right off the shores of Cuba. You have soldiers and marines on every ship, more power than you ever had. This is your best chance, with world support, to go in there and knock out Castro forever. We can do it in a week.'

"And Russia couldn't have done a damn thing about it,"

concluded Albert. "We were on top of it at that moment."

The reverse happened when Russia marched into Czeckoslovakia. Russians then held the high cards. President Lyndon Johnson called Albert in to discuss this equally dangerous crisis.

" 'The Russians are in there and mean business. They're ready to fight an atomic war if necessary, just like they were with Hungary,' LBJ told me," Albert said. " 'We can't go in there unless we're ready for atomic war.'

"Russia would have been in this same boat if we'd taken Cuba," Albert continued, "because we are close to Cuba like Russia is to Hungary. They wouldn't have challenged us because we could have immediately started revolutions in every one of those Warsaw countries. With our help, there would have been fighting over there, execution of soldiers and everything else. The Russians knew it. But we didn't do it.

"Dick Russell, probably the smartest man in the Senate then, told Kennedy, 'You'll regret it if you don't move against Castro.' That's probably Kennedy's biggest mistake. He got credit for getting the Russians out but didn't stop the potential for letting more in, as we now know."

Carl and I talked about LBJ the screamer.

"Don't know if I could have worked for him if I had to be with him every day," I began.

"I've had him call me on the phone," Carl laughed, "and you could hear him cussing as if he were right here, 'Who the hell answers these phones? When I want someone on the phone, I want 'em! I want this changed, hear!' Shouting at the top of his voice.

"But Johnson was two-sided. He would tell 'em how sorry they were, cuss 'em out, then turn around and treat them better than they'd ever been treated. He was really tenderhearted underneath, loved his people."

"Any truth to the story LBJ thought he could still stampede the Democratic Convention in '68 and get the nomination after he had already bowed out?" I asked.

"No, Johnson knew the situation," Carl replied. "But the President was on me, calling several times.

" 'Don't let that Bobby Kennedy's bunch disrupt things,' he ordered. 'Ignore them.' But I had to let them sing 'Glory, Glory, Halleujah' for a while.

"I'll do the best I can, Mr. President," was Carl's standard reply when LBJ told him things like, 'I want Hubert Humphrey on TV at 9:00 o'clock tonight. Don't you let anything stop it.' "

A whole lot of Bobby Kennedy and Gene McCarthy people tried to prevent Humphrey from getting on in prime time. *They raised hell every minute and elected Nixon president right there in hot and riot-torn Chicago.*

"I did get Humphrey on at 9:00, in spite of my laryngitis," Carl remembered, "and caught a lot of hell in the process. Some actually threatened murder if I put Humphrey on in prime time."

I handled media matters during that convention, a rugged assignment, with hell breaking out every hour on the hour all over the place, much of it instigated by the media. Carl Albert at the podium was in the media's crossfire at all times.

"What about the media, Carl?" I asked. "Seems to me they're getting a little out of hand. I like my leaders to be elected. To me the Jane Fondas and Jesse Jacksons aren't leaders. They're puppets of the media."

"Well," Carl slowly answered, "it comes out of bias the big

media has for the eastern establishment. The *Boston Globe, New York Times, Washington Post* — they're newsmakers of the country. They literally make news instead of just reporting it. They also create false images of people.

"Biggest criticism I have, the media carries this notion of freedom of the press so far they use it even when it endangers the country. That's the thing I really object to. Still, I recognize freedom of press is indispensible to democracy. But the press should police themselves when the national interest is at stake."

"That'll be the day," I offered. "Printing the Pentagon papers, things like that, would once have been thought treasonable."

"It would. And what about printing how to make a hydrogen bomb? Print how to make it on the front page. Terrible. The Rosenbergs were executed for almost that same kind of activity."

We discussed the Kennedys. Carl was for Jack Kennedy and likes Ted Kennedy but has strong reservations about Bobby, who once tried to unhorse him. We agreed Jack Kennedy would not likely have become a presidential candidate so soon had it not been for his strong early media support.

Carl and Bobby butted heads when Carl was running for Majority Leader. Bobby played hardball, took plenty advantage of his brother's position, and had a lot of people, including LBJ, hating his guts.

"A close friend who worked with Bobby Kennedy in the Justice Department got word to me Bobby was trying to help Dick Bolling defeat me for Majority Leader," Carl said. "What Bobby didn't know is I already had twice as many pledges as I needed.

"When I learned what Bobby was up to, I went to President

Kennedy. 'I'm not surprised,' he told me. The president was nice about it and assured me he was having no part of Bobby's activity. I'm sure he also knew I had the votes. Incidentally, I had no better friend in Congress than Dick Bolling."

Two events stand out in my mind showing the measure of Carl Albert the man. One relates to a rural Oklahoma soldier Albert got relieved of military duty; the other his chance to become President of the United States, which Carl turned down flat.

It is not Carl Albert's usual style to intercede in behalf of someone seeking to escape military duty. His views on exempting special groups are close to mine. We were both drafted and see no reason why anyone of sound body and mind shouldn't enjoy this same privilege in time of national emergency.

"Eliminating the draft was a serious mistake from three standpoints," said Carl. "First, you need intelligent people running the military. Even the job of operating a gun is complicated today.

"In the second place, it's only fair. The only way to get people in the service who get most benefit from our country is to draft them. Many aren't going to volunteer in peacetime. A lot won't volunteer in wartime.

"The third point is it costs so darn much. I went in at $21 a month. I do think you ought to have a draft. Get the people you need, quality types. Those who then don't go are just lucky because they aren't needed or somebody else's number is ahead of theirs."

Carl resented people trying to use political pull to get someone out of service.

"I was always getting those calls, especially during the Korean War. Oklahoma's 45th Division was in it and it was

Let This Cup Pass Me By

rough on them. A lot of good soldiers stayed in the reserves after World War II and were called up, while others didn't have to do anything. Especially those in it and their parents hated the Korean fighting."

Naturally, Congressman Albert got plenty hard luck stories from folks wanting their Johnny or James back home. Most didn't get much house, but one day Albert got a call that was different. It was from the tiny mountain town of LeFlore, south of Red Oak, Oklahoma. Placed by W. G. Stockton, superintendent of schools and longtime Democratic County Chairman. Only phones around there were at the post office, the town's two stores and the school.

"Carl, there's a lady here who's ridden in on a horse wants to talk to you," Stockton said in his measured Oklahoma drawl.

"Well, put her on."

"Mr. Albert, they put my son on a boat in San Francisco and are taking him to Korea," the lady pleaded. "They won't take him off. I've begged them to and now I can't get anyone to talk to me, so I'm coming to you."

"Well, has he made application to get off the ship?"

"No, he won't do that. He's a soldier and wants to fight."

"Don't see how I can get him off then. Are you making it all right?"

"Yeah, I'm making it."

"Do you need him home to help you?"

"Well, he could help around here but I don't *have* to have him. I just *want* him."

"Well, under those circumstances I just have to be frank with you. I see no way for me to get him out. I've been through this too often."

"But, Congressman, let me tell you something. I only had

three boys. Two were killed in World War II. This is my youngest, my last."

She started crying.

"Well, that's a whole different thing," Carl soothed. "I'll see what I can do."

Carl put down the phone, picked it up again and immediately dialed the Secretary of the Army. Bad news.

The sole surviving son regulation, providing the last son in a family couldn't be sent to a war zone, had been repealed.

"I knew I was going to try to do something about it," Carl said, lips tightening. "Guess you've heard of Carl Vinson, former Chairman of the Armed Services Committee. Served longer in the House than nearly anyone. A power. He ran the Army, Navy and Air Force. The works. Mr. Military in the House. I went up to see him.

"Listen to this story, I said, and told him about the mother who wanted to keep her last son alive.

'We've got that sole surviving son regulation,' he answered me.

" 'No, they haven't,' I answered.

" 'Who'd you talk to?'

" 'Secretary of the Army.'

" 'The Secretary told you that?'

" 'Yes, sir, he did. He said there's nothing we can do about it.'

" 'By God,' Vinson thundered, 'they either got it or they will have it, before the sun goes down! You can put that in your pipe and smoke it.'

"I went down to my office," said Carl, smiling, "got a cup of coffee on the way. The phone was ringing when I got there. It was the Army Secretary calling to tell me they had suddenly

198   *Let This Cup Pass Me By*

reinstated the sole surviving son regulation, adding that orders had been issued to take that boy off the ship the minute it hit Japan and send him back to the states on the first plane out.

" 'That sure is great,' I told him. 'It will please a fine old woman.' "

A nice ending but that's not the end.

"When the boy got back home, he sent me the meanest letter I ever got," chuckled Carl.

"You got no business meddling in my business," the soldier complained. "I don't give a damn if you are a Congressman. I joined the army to fight. My brothers fought for their country. They wanted to. I'm proud of them and I'm as good a man as they were."

"It just happens bringing you home is your mother's right," Carl wrote back. "It's not your right but her's. A right she deserves, to keep you, her last son, alive."

Some different kind of American, that boy from the Oklahoma hills, than the kids who high-tailed it to Canada the minute their favored-status college deferments ran out during the Vietnam War.

This Oklahoma soldier who was removed from war's danger zone against his will has something in common with Carl Albert. Both have ideas about honor they won't back off from.

Albert proved his mettle in the fall of 1973. Vice-President Agnew was facing criminal charges and resigning. Important leaders in Congress wanted to impeach President Nixon before a Republican successor to Agnew could be named.

This would have made Speaker Carl Albert President of the United States.

On September 25, 1973, Albert got a call from Vice-

President Agnew, who knew he was in deep trouble and wanted to meet with the Speaker at 4:00 p.m. He had a favor in mind.

At the appointed hour, Albert invited the Vice-President into his office and sent for Majority Leader Tip O'Neill, Congressman Gerald Ford, Majority Whip John McFall, Minority Whip Leslie Arends and Lew Deschler, House Parliamentarian.

What Agnew wanted was for the House to make "full inquiry into the (bribery) charges which have been made against me." He was desperate, pleading for a chance to defend his reputation, saying he was being destroyed by leaks from the prosecution working with a Baltimore grand jury.

"I'm the victim of an ambitious zealot who's trying to make a record for himself (George Beal, Baltimore prosecutor)," declared Agnew. "They're hounding me, taking every individual they can and giving every kind of immunity."

Those meeting in Speaker Albert's office were mostly sympathetic. As politicians, they had often heard and read about false charges made against themselves. They knew grand juries are often used to bear false witness. But Agnew's plea didn't ring true.

Agnew brought with him to this meeting a letter which Speaker Albert read to those in his office. It stated, in part, "I respectfully request that the House of Representatives undertake a full investigation into charges which have apparently been made against me in the course of an investigation by the United States Attorney of Maryland. This request is made in the dual interest of preserving the constitutional stature of my office and accomplishing my personal vindication... No grand or petit jury could fairly consider this matter on its merits. I

Let This Cup Pass Me By

therefore respectfully call upon the House to discharge its constitutional obligations. I shall of course cooperate fully."

Some of the first sympathy for the Vice-President soon started melting away. Agnew's claim, boiled down, was that the constitution protects the President and Vice-President against criminal action. Several members thought the Judiciary Committee should hear the matter. Others said leaving it to Peter Rodino's committee was exactly what Agnew wanted. They worried that Agnew would thus engineer enough delays so the Maryland courts would be elbowed away from jurisdiction.

In the end, Speaker Albert put out a press release saying the Vice-President's request was being turned down. But no action was taken toward impeachment of President Nixon. Carl Albert wouldn't permit it.

Two weeks went by. Vice-President Agnew copped a plea to stay out of jail and abruptly resigned. Congressman Gerald Ford was appointed in his place. At 10:00 a.m. the following August 9, President Nixon, under heavy fire for the Watergate coverup and those tapes he foolishly saved to show history his greatness, tendered his resignation and Gerald Ford was sworn in as president.

Jimmy Breslin in his book, *How The Good Guys Finally Won,* says Congressman Tip O'Neill was first to tell Carl Albert in January 1973 the jig was up, that President Nixon could be impeached.

"They did so many bad things during that campaign," O'Neill told Albert, "there is no way to keep it from coming out. They did too many things and too many people knew about it. There is no way to keep it quiet. The time is going to come when impeachment will hit this Congress and we better be ready for it."

Breslin says Albert was reluctant to impeach Nixon.

"His (O'Neill's) opinion was not received with great warmth," Breslin wrote. "The House of Representatives is not a place of positive action...Albert's caution begins with breakfast. To speak of impeaching Richard Nixon was like asking him to use his shoetip to inspect for landmines."

Breslin's version of how Speaker Albert passed up the presidency flowed a bit too easily and was second hand to boot, so I asked Carl about it.

"I have no recollection at all of Tip O'Neill telling me in January of 1973 that Nixon could be impeached," commented Carl. "I am sure I already knew this. First person to talk to me about it was Larry O'Brien. But honestly, I have no knowledge of anybody telling me the jig was up (for Nixon) before I personally knew it...

"The claims that I had the Presidency on a silver platter and all I had to do was reach out and take it are oversimplifications of a situation far more complicated than that. The trouble is some people are drawing conclusions from 'facts' they must have manufactured."

So what else is new? History, like most things in life, comes down to who's doing the telling.

In July, 1973, Congressman Robert Drinan, a far-left Jesuit law professor from Boston College, introduced a resolution actually calling for Nixon's impeachment. Drinan wanted Nixon impeached on the impossible grounds he failed to inform Congress about allegedly conducting a war in Cambodia. Albert and O'Neill tried to talk Drinan out of his harebrained notion but failed. So a dangerous situation arose.

An impeachment resolution is privileged, must be heard and voted upon. Albert had to make sure some Republican didn't move to bring Drinan's resolution to a vote. Very few Congressmen were yet ready to vote Nixon's impeachment.

Albert knew Nixon, in a vote on Drinan's impeachment resolution, would in effect get a vote of confidence from the House. Drinan's resolution would have gone down four to one or better at that time.

To prevent this, Speaker Albert or one of his leaders was forced to stay on the floor at all times to keep Republicans from calling up Drinan's resolution. Democratic strategy, if that happened, would be an immediate motion to table.

Tip O'Neill was convinced the votes to impeach Nixon would be there at the proper time. Many Congressional leaders also believed Speaker Albert could, if he chose, become President of the United States when Vice-President Agnew was forced to bow out. They were urging Albert to go hard for Nixon's impeachment and the presidency itself.

Albert's press secretary, Joe Foote, remembers those days and confirms there was a strong effort to get Carl actively seeking the presidency.

The trick would be to prevent Gerald Ford being confirmed as Agnew's successor. That done, Albert would be next in line to be president. House leaders, where impeachment proceedings would be brought, were confident Nixon could be ousted if that's how the stage was set.

"Democratic leaders got together and put the heat on Speaker Albert to prevent Ford from becoming vice-president," Foote says. "There was the stormiest meeting of House leaders you've ever seen. They took Carl on head-to-head.

" 'You owe it to the party, Carl,' they insisted. 'You owe it to the nation.' "

Speaker Albert kept shaking his head, no. He thought it improper.

"They became almost violent," Foote told me. " 'You're crazy, Carl. How can you sit and talk like that? Why do you want to protect these guys?'

"I was with Carl when they gave him the news Agnew resigned," Foote continued, "walked back to the House chamber with him. He was really shaken. I think he was stunned by the realization he was at that moment next in line to be president.

"I was with him later that night. He realized the nation was in a crucial state. All dreams of personal fame, riches and the like had to be put aside. I think Carl realized this was the most important thing he'd ever do in his life and he better do it right.

"Carl always uses good justment, restraint; the very qualities he's been criticized for. In that period of our history, Carl was exactly the right person. We sure didn't need a partisan, political guy."

I agree, Joe. So does Carl Albert.

"It wouldn't have been right, Marty, not after Nixon was elected by that wide margin." That's the reason Carl gave me for turning down his chance to become president. "The people elected a Republican," he added, "and were entitled to a Republican president the full four years. That's what I told them and what I still believe."

Carl Albert might have become president. Democrats had the votes in both House and Senate. But such an act would have created turmoil and bitterness throughout America. In politics the general rule is: Do whatever you're big enough to.

Carl Albert did what was right instead.

The world's greatest leader said, "If it be possible, let this cup pass from Me." In His case it wasn't possible.

In Albert's case, letting the cup pass was possible and pro-

Let This Cup Pass Me By

per. But he, too, was crucified by non-believers.

"Scared of being president," some said.

"Too indecisive to grab the brass ring when they practically put it in his hand," several lamented.

"Couldn't take the heat," claimed others.

Wrong. Our boy from Bugtussle is too much a man to rise above principle for political advantage.

Carl Albert let the cup pass him by because it wasn't his cup and he doesn't steal. Having known a few hundred politicians of great importance, by their own admission, I tip my hat to Speaker Albert, rare bird who would rather be right than president.

13

SENATOR REACHOUT

There's always free cheese in a rat trap.

H. R. Gross

It was celebration night before a legislature's closing next day. Certain legislative Romeos and their Angels of Delight were gathering in the plush away-from-home apartment of a now departed State Senator.

Mischief was afoot.

One older Senate member who habitually begins dipping from the merry bowl in midafternoon had his usual head start over merrymakers now arriving as the fiery Oklahoma sun was prettily setting.

This handsome gentleman of bloodshot eye and slightly bloated cheeks, hero of our tale, in his own mind's eye is cock of the walk with women. But legislative ladies refer to him among themselves as "Senator Reachout," a reference to roaming hands.

Somebody's sister, secretary, girl friend, wife or even dearest friend, it makes no difference to Senator Reachout. He honors them, one and all, with offers of his hidden charms.

A sharp slap in the face, loud scream or vicious bite that brings blood he takes to mean, "Not now; maybe later." Anything less he considers passionate desire for his body from whatever female of the moment he is clumsily trying to pin.

Ol' John Barleycorn is his constant afternoon and nighttime companion. Hence, he is more amorous in the head than in bed. Senator Reachout in the hay, alas, is referred to by those who know as "Senator Poopout."

On this final festive night of the session, before these few legislative hearties must return to their normal pedestrian ways of hearth and home, the generous host brought with him, in addition to his regular "monkey girl," a lovely and lonely miss of great beauty and charm. She was to be Senator Reachout's blind date.

Perhaps I should explain "monkey girl." It is a phrase originating in the Oklahoma Senate during the '30's depression days, when almost any job was impossible to get. Secretarial and other legislative jobs for women were strictly patronage, savagely fought after. The competition was fierce, no holds barred. Such jobs went only to young ladies legislators chose. Some could type and others had different talents, but all were close to a legislator or no job.

"I wouldn't take your old monkey job on a bet," one disgruntled female who was bypassed for such a position spit out at the girl selected in her stead. "I'll never take a job, no matter how much it pays, if I have to hang onto it with my tail."

Thus was born the phrase "monkey job." It lives to this day in political circles, a job held onto by one's tail.

A couple "monkey job" holders were in attendance on the occasion of Senator Reachout's historic blind date. Such ladies are pragmatists, like their sponsors, adhering to the respected First Commandment of politricks:

Thou shalt give to get.

On the festive night to which I refer, Senator Reachout's usually lidded red eyes popped open wide when he first saw the lovely lady entering with the host's "monkey girl." He nearly dropped his drink as the gorgeous creature, sweeping in with a smile and laugh, walked straight to Senator Reachout, extending her hand.

"You're Senator Reachout, aren't you?" she gushed, moving beside him warmly in one swift movement. "I'm Gilda. Senator (censored) told me all about you. I thought he was bragging but now I see he definitely was not," she tittered, eyes dropping demurely.

"Honey, I don' know wha' my ol' buddy tole you," Senator Reachout slurred happily, "but I'm damn sure gonna try living up to his billing."

"You devil," the lady trilled, patting the back of her highly piled blonde hair, at the same time brushing Senator Reachout's arm suggestively with an ample bosom. "I've heard plenty about you," she teased.

You could almost see proud peacock feathers rising on Senator Reachout's neck. Gilda was indeed beautiful — deep saucer eyes, double-breasted in spades, perky rear rising and falling like a choppy sea, shiny white teeth and low, sensuous voice.

Senator Reachout was so smitten and flustered he set his drink down, which he rarely did except to answer a call of nature or dire emergency.

All guests in due course arrived as the drinks kept flowing. An hour passed. Gilda and Senator Reachout by now seemed made for each other. They occupied a love seat in one corner of the living room, shielded by semi-darkness, which permitted Reachout to live up to his name without being obvious.

"Not here, honey," in a nervous but not unfriendly whisper were the words emanating at intervals from their little love corner as Gilda sought to keep basic items of clothing in place against Reachout's amorous onslaught. By strength of body more than character, she barely succeeded.

If one fortunate member of the legislative congregation

present could persuade his companion of the evening to become sufficiently enamoured, it was customary at these soirees to award such a lucky fellow use of the apartment's single bedroom. House rules required it never be used secretly, lest someone be inadvertantly spied upon.

Usually the bedroom is only put to use after many drinks and a dare. Senator Reachout had taken the dare before. On this night the bedroom dare was hurled his way again. Would this deliciously long, sinuous blonde lady accept such a public challenge with ol' Senator Reachout her partner?

Not likely, most present thought. Yet, as we say in politics, anything can happen and it did.

There is a fine camaraderie among our legislative princes and kings. They respect fellow members' shortcomings, never think of telling on another. I pried my information from a private eye working for a disgruntled wife, contemplating divorce, who had the place bugged this particular night.

After Gilda's third drink, steam began rising from the shadowy corner where she and Senator Reachout cuddled. Heavy breathing and gurgly sounds were heard. Anyone passing within five feet saw lips and thighs pressed tightly together.

Other couples were nudging each other, pointing toward the passionate pair and giggling. It appeared the Senator, although clearly overmatched, had nonetheless found the secret of this lady's desires.

"Oh, I'm sorry, honey," Senator Reachout was heard saying as he disengaged a hand, seeking a better hold. Something fell and bounced across the floor in sight of everyone. Gilda leaped to retrieve her padded falsy.

"Lose something, Gilda?" someone shouted.

Everyone laughed.

"Mind your own business, jealous bastards," Senator Reachout retorted.

The party by now had the warm glow encouraging reckless behavior. The uncrowned king of the Senate, who brought Gilda to the party for Senator Reachout, felt the time was ripe.

"Anybody here wanna get married?" he asked in a loud, singsong voice.

"Wanna get married?" doesn't really mean, Do you want to get married? Exact translation is, "Wanna get married just for tonight?"

"Who wantsa get married?" all joined in the chant. "Who wantsa get married?" they were soon singing in unison. All but Gilda and Senator Reachout.

This was the dare. If Gilda and Reachout took the dare, the apartment bedroom was theirs for the night.

Hardly anyone expected it to happen but it did. Gorgeous Gilda momentarily stepped out of Reachout's grasp, took her fading roue by the hand and smilingly led him to the bedroom door.

"We wanna get married," she simpered, "don't we, big man?"

"You said it, baby!" replied Senator Reachout proudly, draping a familiar hand across Gilda's high-rise rump. They entered and closed the bedroom door.

All remaining in the living room were surprised, except two.

Their host put a hand to his lips, signaling continued silence and motioning the others forward. Slowly, stealthily everyone gathered next to the bedroom door to listen.

One Senator peeked through the keyhole but backed away, shaking his head. Nothing could be seen but everyone had an ear tuned, listening to cooing and giggling inside.

"Oh, no, not now," Gilda was saying. "Let me, you big, beautiful beast. Let me, please."

"OK, honey, have it your way," Senator Reachout sighed contentedly. You could almost see him gratefully lying back.

Several minutes went by with no sound except soft rustlings. Two or three couples left the bedroom door huddle, refilled their drinks and went back to sofa and deep chairs to stoke their own fires, titillated now by the bedroom sounds they'd been hearing.

The host and his lady, however, kept close vigil at the bedroom door. They knew Senator Reachout would soon make a startling discovery.

When it happened, Senator Reachout's wounded roar was thunder, lightening, cannon fire and wild animal scream rolled into one.

"Sonsabitches, sonsabitches, dirty rotten sonsabitches!" he was shouting at Gilda. "Get outa here, you damn fag, or I'll kill you!"

The Senator who brought Gilda for Senator Reachout's blind date leaped away from the door, bursting into uproarious laughter. Sounds of scuffling, panting and hurried footsteps came from inside the bedroom.

"Don't hurt me, please," pleaded Gilda. "Oh, honey, just let me go on home."

The door burst open. Gilda was literally thrown out, her clothes in disarray and minus her falsies. Her figure was utterly flat without them. Shoes in hand, it was also clear she had frightfully large feet for a girl.

Senator Reachout, buckling his belt, pushed Gilda roughly aside.

"Did you hear me?" he shouted, "beat it before I kill you."

"Just you let me alone," lisped Gilda tearfully. "You're not much anyway," she taunted.

Others in the room were rolling on the floor in glee, laughing their heads off. Senator Reachout had overreached himself.

"Some pals," Senator Reachout whined, deep pain in his voice, "fixin' me up with a female impersonator. I oughta shoot every one of you bastards."

"Don't worry," soothed the host mastermind, "we all love you. If we didn't," he added with a snicker, "who the hell would?"

The laughter rose higher.

Gov. David Hall won the prize he so coveted, then found it not worth the price. He lost it all and much more through carelessness, overconfidence and failure to realize how powerful were his political enemies.

14

TANGLED WEB

Oh, what a tangled web we weave
When first we practice to deceive.

Sir Walter Scott

David Hall isn't alone.

Two Oklahoma governors were impeached. One, the tall, kindly and generous Henry S. Johnston, got a bum rap. Done in by a demanding legislative clique to whose will that honorable governor wouldn't bend.

"Iron Jack" Walton, who threw the famous week-long barbeque and booze party, was also drummed out of office by the legislature. He got what he asked for.

Four other Oklahoma governors faced criminal charges. C. N. Haskell, Oklahoma's first governor, and J. A. B. Robertson, its fourth, were indicted while in office, charges later dropped. Leon C. "Red" Phillips of the fiery hair and temper to match went to trial twice. He escaped with a hung jury the first time, acquittal in his second trial.

Political battler George Miskovsky, famous for his million-dollar libel suit against Oklahoma Publishing Company, was then county attorney of Oklahoma County. Miskovsky and Gov. Phillips had mutual hatred for each other's guts. On July 2, 1943, Miskovsky filed bribery and conspiracy charges against Phillips but couldn't make them stick.

Which brings us to Gov. David Hall, only Oklahoma governor in history sent to prison.

Here my typewriter sticks. How to be fair to both Hall and the man most responsible for his downfall, former Secretary of

State John Rogers, Jr.?

To those who claim Gov. Hall was a "cynical crook," I can name you 100 people I trust less. Hall couldn't climb the staggering twin mountain peaks of hostile press and bitter political enemies in both parties.

Which is not to say he was blameless. Far from it.

John Rogers, Jr. came close to being impeached for blowing the whistle on Hall. He traded his office for the hated title "snitch." John-John, as the junior Rogers was called, to distinguish him from his State Examiner and Inspector father, was caught in the old Wewoka switch.

He and his father faced grand jury charges, caused by a $37,000 donation to Hall's successful gubernatorial campaign. Both father and son claimed Fifth Amendment protection to avoid testifying about collecting this giant campaign contribution for Hall from the senior Rogers' state employees.

When John Rogers, Jr. took his tale of a bribery attempt by Gov. Hall to then Attorney General Larry Derryberry, he didn't realize he would soon be talking to the FBI.

"I gave it to him (Derryberry) because it was his responsibility," Rogers told me. "If he had handled it, he would have been the guy to have taken the heat rather than me."

Once Rogers informed Derryberry about a possible law violation involving Gov. Hall, a black cat jumped out of the bag and scooted across Rogers' jinxed trail.

Once the accusation was made, the FBI demanded Rogers truss himself up in electronic gear and become one of their operatives. Too late then for Rogers to say, "Aw, I was only kidding, boys."

The dice were tossed, coming up snake eyes for both Rogers and Hall.

I just finished the last sad tape transcripts involving this pair. If there's an ounce of forgiveness in your soul, you'll sympathize with both. They endured the tortures of hell.

You place blame where you like. I say Rogers had plenty reason for acting the "good citizen" and revealing Hall's alleged bribe offer. I also say David Hall — lawyer, former prosecutor and governor — could easily rationalize in his lawyer mind a "finder's fee" for getting a financier $10-million worth of legitimate business.

Gov. Hall had no plans to collect the $50,000 "finder's fee" involved until after he left office. Furthermore, taped conversations between Hall and Rogers indicate Gov. Hall and financier W. W. "Doc" Taylor, convicted along with Hall, may have been considering doing business together in California after Hall's term ended.

If Hall thought he was doing a lawyer chore, he's not the first, nor last, to practice law while in public office. It's going on right now.

Doc Taylor, convicted along with Hall, was a legitimate businessman with a legal deal for the State of Oklahoma. Those in Taylor's business are used to paying finder's fees. Some pay them, usually indirectly, to public officials.

Taylor had his go-between, attorney R. Kevin Mooney, a friend of Hall's. Mooney was arrested and cuffed by FBI agents in Rogers' office when he came to finalize the alleged bribe.

Financier Taylor couldn't believe it when he was convicted along with Hall. He didn't understand that when you deal with public officials, it's a different ballgame. One businessman using influence in behalf of another for a price is not illegal.

It's a close question whether it was illegal for Taylor to pay Mooney for help in getting business for his company from the State of Oklahoma. Taylor could have copped a plea or agreed to testify against Hall, as Mooney did, and surely gone free. I think he went to jail for a principle, convinced he did nothing illegal.

Which is not to say Doc Taylor is ready for sainthood either.

What I hope you will understand is that all four principals in this first felony conviction ever for an Oklahoma governor were mortals not much different than you and me.

Rogers was between the crack and hard place. He's the one who encouraged raising $37,000 for Gov. Hall's campaign from his father's employees. He had been before one grand jury over it. Got big, unflattering headlines when taking Fifth Amendment protection on his attorney's advice. There was likelihood both he and his aged father could be indicted, all because they helped Hall.

The smell of cold iron was in the Rogers' nostrils.

"I'm the culprit who got my father to support Hall," Rogers told me. "I was supporting him and I wanted dad to support him. I look back on it as one of the biggest mistakes of my life.

"I learned to recognize different personalities in Hall," said Rogers. "A split personality. He thought he could just get over anything. It's practically impossible to convict a governor. He knew it."

While being investigated, Hall set up devices around his office to detect transmitters. They went off frequently, so he knew he was being monitored. Yet he remained confident, although cautious.

"I know he suspected me at first," Rogers told me, "or he wouldn't have written notes back and forth. We conferred by notes several times. When I would go in his office, Hall's sensors would pick up my transmitter.

"During our first meeting, I wasn't aware Hall's sensors went off. That was his only chance of knowing it was me. After that the FBI took care of it by turning on other transmitters before and after I went in. There were probably ten guys involved."

I asked Rogers how Hall reacted when his sensors alerted him he was being taped.

"Well, it really didn't scare hell out of him," replied Rogers. "He was overconfident. He would let me know we were being bugged and he'd tell me not to talk to him. Start writing notes."

Rogers explained what he called Hall's split personality.

"There's a part of Hall," he answered, "that's honest, straightforward. Then there's a part of Hall that is kinda little boyish, not dealing with reality. There's a part of Hall that's really mean, too . . . I mean he would do anything to gain for himself."

I asked what Rogers considers Hall's greatest failing.

"Underestimation of others," he replied. "Thought he could handle anything. But we have a moral standard that seems to be different for politicians than working people. And seems to be different for business than working people . . . You know, you can justify anything, really."

I asked Rogers why he resigned his office.

"I resigned after I polled the State Senate," he answered. "They had the power to impeach. When I decided to resign it was because I knew I was going to be convicted. Of course, I

Tangled Web   219

didn't know what I was going to be convicted *of* because *they* didn't know.

"My dad got involved in problems I wouldn't have him involved in at all, for any price. Money was collected in his State Examiner and Inspector office and I helped raise money for Hall."

Rogers and his dad were on the hot seat, while Hall seemed home free. Causing resentment. It didn't seem to Rogers that Hall was much concerned over the Rogers' troubles.

So Rogers was secretly resenting Hall.

Hall was unaware of these feelings. He considered Rogers maybe his most trustworthy political friend. He knew his conversations were bugged but for a long time it never crossed his mind ol' buddy John Rogers, Jr. was the one wired for sound.

Hall was in dire financial straits, had just been defeated for reelection. Not wealthy, he would need money when his term ended.

It's a short step from there, I believe, to rationalizing a "legitimate" finder's fee or getting paid for "legal help," especially since payment wasn't to be made until months after Hall left office.

That's how I think David Hall worked it out in his troubled mind. Not much different, I'm sure he thought, than being a lawyer legislator. Lawyer legislators are in greater demand today than ever. Nor will they be less useful to special interests tomorrow.

Now a few rare kind words for former Secretary of State John M. Rogers. He's more complex than even David Hall. When Rogers blew the whistle on Gov. Hall, he also blew it on himself. Cut his own throat along with Hall's trying to save his father.

"Nobody likes a snitch," John told me. "I knew it would be tough on me. But I felt it was right, although I didn't realize it would get so big and involved."

Rogers doesn't live with fear. He can be impulsive. His mind is quick and clever. Like many men who are not tall, he walks with head high as if trying to stretch himself. His speech is rapid, clipped.

He didn't leave town when his bad days came. Opened a restaurant in Penn Square, Oklahoma City.

Most legislators and others at the capitol who knew Rogers figure he helped the FBI nail Gov. Hall in order to make himself a big man. Rogers says no. If this were his motive, it was a miserable failure.

I personally think the whole thing snowballed on Rogers. He was trying to get Hall's attention but got the FBI's instead. And those boys don't fool around.

I'm convinced Rogers bears no ill will today against any of those involved with him.

"I wasn't mad at Doc Taylor," Rogers told me. "I figured he was just trying to pay some crooked politicians. I told him face to face, right in the courtroom, 'Doc, if you will just plead guilty, you won't get anything.' Doc was mad. Called me a piss-ant."

One thing that put Taylor away was a check stub.

"When we agreed to get it done, Taylor got a check. It was about $32,000, made out to me," explained Rogers. "I told him I didn't want it. So he destroyed that check but after the whole thing was over, the FBI seized his records and that check stub was still there."

It could not be explained away, Doc Taylor learned to his sorrow.

Like Hall, Taylor was overly sure of himself. It's a close question whether Taylor actually did anything illegal. But he should have known, dealing with politicians, presumption of guilt will be heavy with any jury.

As for Hall, Rogers is convinced overconfidence was his greatest enemy. Hall is smart and knows it. He is clever and knows that, too. But so is the FBI.

There is one other important character in this drama, Jan Eric Cartwright. Young Cartwright, friend and supporter of Gov. Boren, who defeated Hall, filed a lawsuit against John Rogers, Sr. shortly after Boren's election. The suit alleged the senior Rogers set quotas on the amount of money each category of employee in his State Examiner's office was required to cough up for Hall's campaign.

I'm sure the spectre of prison bars was appearing in nighttime visions of both Jr. and Sr. Rogers. They knew well the dangers any elected official faces before a politically inspired grand jury.

Had there been no Cartwright lawsuit, I doubt Rogers would have complained to Derryberry about a bribe offer from Gov. Hall. Above all, young Rogers sought to protect his devoted, aging father. Hall was powerless to stop Cartwright's lawsuit or the grand jury, yet young Rogers felt, understandably, "Hall might have done something."

Hall's seeming ingratitude was deep in Rogers' craw when the governor allegedly offered, in the final days of his administration, to cut a deal with Rogers. The proposal was for Rogers to get the State Employees Retirement Fund to invest $10-million with Doc Taylor's financial firm in Dallas.

As this scheme was planted, watered and finally flowered, Rogers was the one out front. This, too, caused resentment in Rogers, a feeling of again being used.

Taped conversations between Rogers and Hall make clear Hall was twisting many arms to get the state investment approved. But the governor's tracks were hard to find. His lawyer and prosecutor training show strongly throughout the bugged conversations.

Rogers was to be Hall's front man. Hall would be in position to say, "Who, me?"

Without Rogers' tapes, Gov. Hall would have gone free as a bird. Without those tapes, Rogers could himself have become the fall guy. Rogers was smart enough to know it.

Hall carefully kept himself clean, refusing to say one word about payment of money from or to anyone. When he finally did become suspicious of Rogers it was too late. The cheese was tasted, the trap snapped and Gov. Hall was caught.

Hall made the common mistake of judging others by himself. He thought he had every reason to trust Rogers. Hadn't Rogers given him $37,000 for his campaign? No other friends were so generous. Didn't that make him and Rogers buddies? Of course, in Hall's mind. But not in Rogers'. Rogers and his dad were in bad trouble and angry about getting no help from this governor they had risked so much to help.

So once more the human ego toppled a kingdom. King David took his "Jolly Rogers" too much for granted. For which he paid dearly.

It was a sorrowful 1974 Christmas season for Gov. Hall and Secretary of State John Rogers. Goodwill toward men was not foremost in either's mind.

Rogers' jaunty walk, head high and chest out, was slowed by a tangle of wires and radio equipment padding his ample stomach. He had trouble staying at arms length from Hall, trying to prevent detection of the bugging apparatus he wore. It was a chore doing so because no one is more arm-around-waist buddy-buddy than David Hall.

Rogers worried about Hall finding him out. He sweated hard to follow difficult, dangerous instructions from FBI agents. He worried about his elderly father's health, the fact both Rogers' political careers might go down the drain. His brow furrowed deeper over how he would be accepted by the public, friends and acquaintances once his secret activities were revealed.

Hall had even greater cause for concern. He was being investigated by the IRS. Much of the media, *Daily Oklahoman* in particular, searched diligently daily for any past action to criticize.

It was tough on Hall's lovely wife and his bright, beautiful children. Yet they bore up bravely. Hall was leaving office deeply indebted to lawyers, with no big bucks in view.

He was also suffering the downer of a lost election. Many he felt should have supported him, because of his exceptional record as governor, didn't.

Par for the political course but nonetheless gagging. When reality sets in for all defeated high public officials I have known, the political contractors and yes-men flap their vulture wings and move in with the newest public hero. They forget immediately they ever knew you.

So was it with David Hall.

The Hall indictment claimed a conspiracy starting in September, 1974 between Hall and Doc Taylor, president of

Guaranteed Investors Corporation; R. Kevin Mooney, alleged bagman and contact for Taylor; and John Rogers, Jr., Secretary of State. The payoff was to be $50,000 for getting Rogers and Hall to swing $10-million worth of state business to Taylor's company.

Initially, half the $50,000 was supposedly ticketed for Hall, the other half for Rogers. But as negotiations went on and tapes around Rogers' body kept turning, the ante went up.

Rogers played his part so well, he's now in the FBI's acting hall of fame. He sold Taylor and Mooney completely on his character of a greedy politician out for every dime he could steal.

Time was running out on Hall December 22, 1974. He would be out of office in three weeks. If the deed was to be done, it must be quick. Yet most members of the Oklahoma Public Employees Board, required to put their stamp of approval on the transaction, disliked its smell.

Members of the Retirement Board, besides Rogers as chairman, were Jim Cook, Commissioner of Charities and Corrections; Leo Winters, State Treasurer; L. P. Williams, Commissioner of Labor; J. O. Spiller, Director of State Finance; Richard A. Ward, State Highway Director; and J. L. Merrill, member of the State Tax Commission.

It should be noted Hall appointed three of these men — L. P. Williams, J. O. Spiller and J. L. Merrill. Hall was also responsible for appointment of State Highway Director Richard A. Ward.

Four out of seven beholden to Hall. But that didn't mean automatic approval; Hall was out and these people weren't about to take serious risks for a dying lame duck.

They were understandably fearful of unknown quantities. Taylor's company was not well known at the state capitol.

"When I was chairman," Rogers told me, "we were leery and kinda hostile about accepting securities from people not big and reputable in the state, whose backgrounds we didn't know. We liked securities to come from one of the big brokerage houses or at least a bank in Oklahoma. So we would have some place to go back to ... do business with the public's money with people who couldn't run away."

Competition was hot and heavy for these state retirement funds. Banks, insurance companies and brokers all fought for an "in." On occasion a legislator or two would put in a word for someone. The "best bid" the board was after is always subject to interpretation and politics.

Max Strange, strong, unflappable man of serious mein ran the retirement fund as secretary. Taylor's $10-million proposal was first presented to Strange, who routinely explained it to the board.

At this point no pressure was being applied.

"Hall did tell me in a nonchalant way he was aware of it," said Rogers, "but it was perfectly all right (with him) whatever we wanted to do with it. I got the idea he didn't care, one way or the other.

"Mooney was a friend of his, a former classmate or something, and he (Hall) would appreciate it if we would just look at his proposal and do whatever we thought right.

"That was his first pitch. Nobody on the board was favorable so I tossed it in the trash."

Hall got more seriously involved after a Texas visit with his friend Mooney a month later.

"The second pitch," Rogers laughed, "was a little different. He said, 'John, this is not an ordinary deal.' That's when he told me (about the $50,000). We had several conversations about it."

Rogers says he told Hall everyone on the board was cool.

"We felt secure, see, in not having strangers involved in the money," Rogers explained the board's attitude. "It wasn't we felt they were crooks or anything. Just that we weren't interested in having anyone who could possibly be a crook."

Rogers admits there was no direct offer of a payoff even when Hall suggested the board consider Taylor's proposition a second time.

"I believe I talked to the board," he stated, "and said the governor told me ... maybe we shouldn't have thrown it (Taylor's proposal) away. But no payoff or anything like that ... until it became evident we weren't going to do anything about it."

That's when Rogers says the arm-twisting by Hall started. He adds that the price also went up, far higher than the original $50,000 to be split two ways.

"But the first offer was $25,000," declared Rogers. "He (Hall) said, 'We can make 50 ... 25 for you and 25 for me.' He just told me to get it through. Twenty-five thousand in cash apiece."

BUDDIES...

Carefully keeping his distance, John Rogers offers his hand to Gov. David Hall, who grasps it with the true love of fear and bestows upon Rogers his warmest insincere political smile. At the time, Rogers' stomach was carrying the added weight of a cumbersome recording device and Hall's mind was weighted down with knowledge someone, he knew not who, was taping his conversations. (Jim Weems photo)

228

15

THE NOOSE TIGHTENS

A wise man feareth.

Proverbs 14:16

When Rogers made his final presentation to the board, recommending approval of the $10-million deal, he was wired for sound.

I again asked Rogers why he took his complaint of being bribed to Attorney General Larry Derryberry.

"I knew Derryberry was not in the same camp Hall was," replied Rogers, "otherwise I wouldn't have gone to him. I felt reasonably safe with Derryberry. Something that big, you have to weigh things and take a risk.

"He (Derryberry) felt it should be a federal thing as opposed to him handling it. I think he wanted out. He would like to be in for the glory but he didn't want in for the bad."

Who does? Derryberry, remember, got burned once when he recommended impeachment proceedings against Hall. The legislature turned him down. His face was still red.

"So the next thing," Rogers says, "I'm in the FBI office with the agent in charge for Oklahoma City. Derryberry set the meeting up for me to meet him . . . From then on, Derryberry was informed as an officer of the state. Anytime I met with the FBI, Derryberry was there."

Rogers says they met nearly every day for a period of two months. Rogers was fitted with recorder and transmitter. His conversations with Hall were picked up in cars near the capitol, driven by FBI agents.

"Reason for this," Rogers explained, "is the complication

of presentations in federal court. There must be witnesses on the scene at the time. They (agents) have to put the equipment on you and take it off. They have to write or sign (proof of) whatever action taken, identify the tape you take each time."

Thus the tedious, complicated and expensive gathering of evidence was carried on. Meantime Rogers, who up to his meeting with the FBI had been noncommittal to Hall, agreed to help sell the $10-million investment by the state in Taylor's proposition.

"My instructions were to go along with the deal," said Rogers, frowning and shaking his head. "But there were problems with that, too, legal problems."

Other board members had no idea what was going on. Hall was twisting their arms and Rogers was pushing for approval. They met strong opposition but in the end were almost too successful.

"At one point," Rogers revealed, "it looked like the board was going to issue the damn check for $10-million. That would have raised the legal technicality of how the money was to be later recovered. But we did manage to delay issuance of the check until the bust was made."

It took four or five meetings, and countless conversations with Hall, before the deal was signed, sealed but not quite delivered.

The noose really tightened around Hall's neck December 22, 1974 when the most damaging phone conversations between Hall and Rogers were taped. As you will see, it was a time of terrible torment for Hall, yet he maintained his confident air to the end.

Key parts of conversations between Hall and Rogers follow:

8:00 a.m., December 22 — The morning after Hall promised Rogers he would get in touch with doubtful board members and "twist arms."

"Still got to touch base with two or more this morning," Hall tells Rogers. "Cook'll be here but Merrill and L. P. (Williams) I haven't talked to yet . . . I think I'm just going to call Merrill over and have it face to face with him."

Rogers asks if he should call a meeting of the board for 3:00 p.m.

"I'd rather wait until I've got 'em," replies Hall.

"Yeah," Rogers laughingly replies, "I don't wanna go through that again . . . I'd rather not have to face J. O. (Spiller) again until it's all over and they've made an interest payment."

"Now you're talking," says Hall.

There was trouble with Spiller. He understood finance and wanted no part of anything questionable.

Rogers and Hall discuss Doc Taylor and Kevin Mooney coming up from Dallas that day for a possible meeting of the board in the afternoon. Hall displays his usual caution against involving himself.

"You wouldn't want to pick 'em up at the airport, would you?" asks Rogers.

"Oh, no, no I wouldn't . . . I gotta be careful."

4:37 p.m., December 22 — This phone conversation reveals board members were a hard sell. Nothing on the surface indicated something wrong but the board had good radar, especially J. O. Spiller.

"Just talked to Kevin (Mooney)," says Hall. "He tells me Cook didn't show up at the meeting and he didn't have enough votes."

The Noose Tightens   231

"Cook didn't show and Ward wouldn't go for it without Cook," Rogers replied.

"Ward would go for it if Cook had been there," Hall countered. "That's what the deal was. What I can't understand is why Ward didn't go ahead and vote with you."

"There was no way," Rogers replied, "with J. O. (Spiller) spouting off. J. O. was really the bad guy. He doesn't think it's a bad deal but his remark was, 'In the waning days of an administration, we're not going to invest in all this stuff.' "

At this point Rogers reminds Hall of a meeting scheduled for the following day — Hall, Rogers, Doc Taylor and Taylor's man, Kevin Mooney. Here Hall shows his first sharp suspicion of danger. He begins separating himself even more from other participants.

"I don't really think it's necessary for us to have the meeting," Hall interjects. "I don't want Mooney showing up in my office the same day they're going to vote on it ... I'd much rather you-all just go ahead and handle it all."

Although suspicious of others, Hall's trust in Rogers appears stout as ever. So the more he talks to Rogers, the more he incriminates himself.

During these conversations Rogers is sometimes prompted by FBI agents. Now he asks Hall to meet with Mooney and Rogers in the governor's office before the next day's board meeting. The FBI wants this, of course, to prove a conspiracy.

"I just don't think it'd be a good idea," Hall protests. "If somebody saw you and Kevin coming into my office at 11:30, before the meeting at 3:00, why, that's not a good idea."

"OK, then," Rogers shoots back, "are you and I going to get together prior to the meeting?"

"I don't, uh," Hall hedges, "uh, other than just check

signals on the phone. But, John, I'm going to call Kevin now and explain this to him and he may want to turn around and call you right back."

Hall calls financier Taylor's intermediary, Kevin Mooney, and Mooney, in turn, makes a call to Rogers.

"How hard did you bend his (Gov. Hall's) arm?" asks Rogers.

"Real hard. He guaranteed Merrill, Cook, Williams," says Mooney.

"Ward?" asks Rogers.

"Well, he said we'd still have it."

Here Rogers' resentment of Hall surfaces.

"I'm gonna stay away from the governor's office unless he calls and wants me," Rogers declares.

"I'm staying away, too," Mooney responds. "I don't want to go around there much."

"OK," adds Rogers, "and just like we said before, *he* (Hall) *just kinda lets other people do it if you're not real careful.*"

A definite warning had Mooney sensed it.

8:37 p.m. the next night, December 23, 1974 — phone conversation between Hall and Rogers following a 3:00 p.m. meeting of the Retirement Board:

"Hello, Big John," Hall greets Rogers warmly. "Tell me some good news."

"Well, I've got some good news and some bad news," replies Rogers. "I went the way you suggested on the second vote . . . and we got unanimous approval."

"Excellent," enthuses Hall.

"So all we need do is have the bank write an approving letter. They're going to start writing it tomorrow."

First National Bank of Oklahoma City was advising the Retirement Board. According to Rogers' various conversations, they didn't like the idea of a company from Texas getting such a big deal. They are in the investments business, too, and First National is used to having its way in Oklahoma City.

Rogers tells Hall the First's Trust Department thought it might somehow be able to get the deal disapproved.

"Said they were gonna disapprove the damn thing," is how Rogers put it.

"Oh, I may approach them entirely differently," replies Hall. "I may go to Leo (Winters) and ask him to get them to do it."

"You want me to work on it at the same time?"

"Oh, gosh, yes . . . It's going to take both of us."

"It's been voted upon their (First National's) approval and they don't have any legitimate grounds for not approving it," declares Rogers.

"I just feel this way," Hall says, "I'm going to give Leo an indication the board might just want to drop that account (with First National Bank) if they don't go along with it."

"You better get him in it," Rogers agrees. "They might think I don't have the stuff, you know."

"Leo's in a terrific position. He's not involved in the vote on it," Hall notes.

Although a member of the board, Winters rarely attended meetings. He was then a close friend of Attorney General Derryberry. Rogers told me he figured Derryberry, who knew everything going on, may have warned Winters away.

"When can you reach Leo?" Rogers asks.

"First thing in the morning," Hall assures him. "I don't

The Noose Tightens

want to take a chance on them getting a letter out tomorrow saying they won't do it . . . What was the vote today, five to nothing?"

"Yeah, five to none."

"That means everybody but Leo and J. O. Spiller were there and all voted yes."

"That's right, all voted yes, (but) upon approval of the bank."

"As far as the bank is concerned, they'd like to do anything to keep it in their possession longer," says Hall.

"Doc Taylor even (offered to) pay them something for being a trustee. He indicated to them he would."

"That didn't cut any ice with them, did it?" asks Hall.

"Hell, no. The guys there, Patterson and some other guy, they're going to write a no deal," warns Rogers.

"Well, we'll get on that stick right quick," promises Hall.

8:55 p.m. the same night, another Hall-Rogers phone conversation. Hall has more thoughts about Leo Winters using his influence as State Treasurer, seeking to get First National Bank to endorse the idea of the Retirement Board investing $10-million with Doc Taylor's company.

"He (Winters) is going to call me back after 9:30 tonight," Hall tells Rogers. "If it's on a good phone (not one likely tapped), I'll just go ahead and tell him what we need to do."

"He's going to need to talk pronto," Rogers urges, "before they get down there and put the quietus on us."

"If we could get them to approve it," Hall declares, "then there's no way anybody can come back on you."

"That's right, not ever," Rogers agrees.

"Now," Hall adds, "I'll tell you what we'll do if they don't approve it . . . We'll just get five votes and we'll change that (account) back to Liberty Bank. I can do that."

This conversation brings back banking memories of my own. Liberty and First National are strong banking rivals. I remember handling a city council election in Oklahoma City in the early 60's at request of Liberty Bank and other top dogs of Oklahoma City.

They were interested, they told me, in better city government. I found out later they were being cut out of the Atoka pipeline deal and were sore. Furthermore, First National Bank had the city's main account. Liberty Bank coveted that money-maker account.

"Think we can elect a couple new councilmen, Marty?" I was asked.

"Don't see why not, providing you guys pay for the election," I answered.

They were willing to pay but wanted their part kept quiet. *The Daily Oklahoman* was against us and most of the Oklahoma City big shots I was dealing with had more gall and greed than guts. Rarely does an Oklahoma City bank openly embark on a political project not sanctioned by the *Daily Oklahoman*.

But stakes were high in this rare case. We elected two honest, capable councilmen who caught hell from the *Oklahoman* every day they served — Bill Kessler, now Judge William Kessler, and Harold Johnson. I may fry in hell for helping put them on the city council, where no man whose soul is his own has yet pleased the *Daily Oklahoman*.

"We need to get the city account moved to Liberty National Bank," was the first request my clients made after our successful election. The deed was done. Liberty got this cream pie away from First National. Thus the struggle for "good government" goes on constantly in Oklahoma City's top business and banking circles.

Gov. Hall understood this "good government" principle well. Lord knows he was beaten over the head day after dreary day by Oklahoma City's power brokers. He knew Liberty National Bank would jump at a chance to replace First National in any big money deal.

"It'd be much better to take it back to Liberty," Hall continued his conversation with Rogers. "Then Liberty can tell us it's a good investment."

Next day was Christmas Eve, a happy time for Gov. Hall. He and family were in Utah on a ski outing. I suspect he did some heavy thinking cruising down those unblinking white mountain slopes.

Hall's caution intensifies in the next conversation, December 26. He's now definitely become suspicious of Rogers. Not everything is going according to plan.

"Did you have any luck with Leo?" Rogers wants to know.

"Leo doesn't want to approach them . . . I don't think he'll do much more," is Hall's unenthusiastic reply.

Leo Winters' mama didn't birth a dummy. Prosecutor Bill Burkett was hot and heavy after Winters, too, but Leo outsmarted him. Cost Winters a bundle, destroyed his peace of mind and harmed his health. But he beat Burkett at his own game on his own field, the federal courts.

Had Burkett not overmatched himself with Winters, I doubt the effort to nail Hall's hide would have been so determined. With Rogers now forced to follow his commands, Burkett had his second chance to become a prosecutor hero.

"How are we going to do it?" is Rogers' next question,

seeking an incriminating reply.

"I wouldn't worry about that," cautions Hall.

"You sonofabitch," laughs Rogers, "I don't know about you but *I* worry about it."

Hall ignores the bait.

"I wouldn't worry about that," Hall says again. "Uh, don't worry. *You know, people that don't play fair and keep their word get in trouble.*"

Oh, oh, there it is. A subtle threat to Rogers and clear indication Hall mistrusts his ol' buddy. Something has happened.

As the sun sets on this historic Oklahoma day, the governor, for the first time, is clearly mistrustful of his Secretary of State.

16

"OH, GOD, YEAH, JUDAS!"

Wisdom comes through suffering.

Agamemnon

The new year started off bad for Hall, got worse, then terrifying.

On January 4, Rogers talks by phone with Doc Taylor in Dallas. Fierce pressure is on by the FBI to tie Hall firmly to the conspiracy.

"I was wanting to get together with David," Rogers advises Taylor. "Have you guys talked to him?"

"No, John," Taylor sounds irked, "I've been busy running all over the damn country getting the trustee set up . . . You know, this isn't a bag of groceries."

"I just can't believe the governor's not more attentive to this big a situation," Rogers sympathizes.

"I think," replies Taylor, "the governor feels his role in it · was just to recommend it as being a good deal and for *us* to do it."

"That wasn't his instructions to me," shoots back Rogers. "He called me in the Blue Room . . . instructed me as to the way everything would go, including a split."

"OK," is all a cautious Taylor answers.

So Rogers again threatens the deal may fall through if Taylor isn't careful.

"I want to remind you now, on the 13th David Hall's out," warns Rogers. "It's not unusual for the new governor to call a special meeting of various boards . . . and get control of them."

"I understand."

"Uh, we got to get this thing where the new board can't reverse an action."

"All I need there is the commitment," Taylor puts it back on Rogers. Then he adds, "I know that Mooney did talk to your attorney (Dick Hampton) . . . on your building deal."

Rogers was at this time on a note for a 100,000 foot building in south Oklahoma City, formerly a discount house but then without a tenant. Taylor questions Rogers at length about this building and his heavy obligations for payment on it.

"We're in the business of purchasing property like that. . . ." says Taylor slyly, "and leasing it to people like K-Mart. . . . You're on the paper?"

"Yeah," admits Rogers, "I'm on the paper."

Taylor then goes into a long discourse about how he has sold and leased such buildings to hardware stores and grocery chains. All legitimate, legal.

"Maybe we could get lucky and rent half of it to Handyman and half to Skaggs Albertson. Everybody'd be home free," Taylor dangles his carrot. "One other thing, we might be very interested in taking your partners' place, coming in with you."

"I see."

"And picking up any back payments on the loan."

"Oh, shit," exclaims Rogers, "that would be a deal!"

The master actor at work again. Rogers knows Hall, Taylor and Mooney are suspicious. Yet by pretending great interest in getting something for himself, Rogers lays to rest many of their suspicions.

"I will just make a pledge to you," coaxes Taylor. "We'll do everything humanly possible to get it done. . . . That's our business, see? So this isn't something we are doing as a favor to

"Oh, God, Yeah, Judas!"

you."

Shrewd man, Taylor. He next goes into detail about how much he's going to do for Gov. Hall after he leaves office. The implication is if he's doing all this for Hall, might he not do even more for Rogers, who'll still be in office and have influence.

I'm persuaded Taylor is a man of his word. He is stolid, a bit heavy-set, with kind eyes and more a listener than talker. Key word in his conversations with Rogers is always "maybe." He never promises for certain that things will be done. He's probably had a bellyfull of Rogers by now. But he doesn't lie, although desperate to get Rogers to take the final action necessary.

"If you help us and we help you, hell, that's just the way the world goes," Taylor soothes.

"OK, so I guess it's up to me to get the big teddy bear (Hall) to talk."

The following day, January 5, Rogers initiates a call to Gov. Hall, still reluctant to talk.

"You know I've got this thing just done, David," says Rogers.

"Well, I don't want to talk about anything on the phone," Hall brusquely cuts Rogers off. "Let's wait and get together Monday or Tuesday."

"And you want to see me in the capitol?"

"You betcha."

"Don't be too busy for me this week, goddammit," Rogers threatens.

"I've been gone," Hall apologizes, "and had more to do than I could say grace over...."

"I know ... *but I think you'd be proud of me* ... I just don't

"Oh, God, Yeah, Judas!"

want to go there for nothing."

"Whatever it is," laughs cautious David Hall, "I hope it's good for you."

"*OK, you wise bastard.* I'll see you later," Rogers ends the conversation.

Calling Hall "You wise bastard" speaks volumes. I'm convinced Rogers is subconsciously seeking revenge for spurned friendship. He is so full of this feeling, as you will soon see, angry words spill out in spite of himself.

Rogers' FBI coaches get him to make another try the next day, January 6, with extremely apprehensive Gov. Hall. To cover Rogers, they set off sensors in the governor's office when Rogers is nowhere around. Not too smart, really. It makes Hall jumpy about everything and everyone, including Rogers.

The ham in Rogers surfaces as he prepares to meander down the hall toward the governor's office.

"Let me get my pipe," he tells those saddling him with his tape recorder, "so I'll have something to fiddle with. Do I look OK?"

Rogers looks OK, except fatter due to the heavy recording device taped to his body.

"I'm on my way," he tells those tuned in. "There's the main door to the governor's office. Approaching the Blue Room . . . I'm going to go in the main entrance here, down the hall toward the boudoir."

"Why don't we walk over in the Blue Room?" Rogers suggests to the governor when they meet. "You want to?"

"That won't do any good," Hall replies. "I'm just very apprehensive about everywhere . . . I'm not interested, John, in anything except what's good for the state . . . that's what you and I have discussed from the first and that's just the way we

242   *"Oh, God, Yeah, Judas!"*

want to keep it because our job is to represent the people."

David Hall for the defense. He knows every word is being recorded.

Four days before Hall leaves office, January 9, 1975, Rogers is instructed to make a final effort to coerce Gov. Hall into talking about bribe money. Again you'll see what an accomplished FBI accomplice Rogers is. Don't forget he, too, is operating with fear and trepidation. People doing what Rogers did have wound up in cement coffins.

Rogers is getting instructions from someone called Jack. The prosecutor's associates aren't identified other than by first names.

"Go right up there and keep your coat on," Jack advises. "If you have trouble, just back off . . . If he frisks you and finds it, it's for your protection."

"What about it, Jack?" asks Rogers.

"You look good," replies Jack.

Rogers is greeted by a highly distraught Gov. Hall.

"Let's go in your hall," suggests Rogers.

"Oh, no, no, no, let's don't do that."

"Well, let's get out of here."

"Oh, no, no, no. . . ."

"Please," pleads Rogers, "let's just walk up the street."

"No, no we can't do it."

"Go in this conference hall across the. . . ."

"No," says Hall firmly. "I tell you I don't wanna do that . . . You're doing an outstanding job," Hall brags on Rogers too late.

"OK, OK," Rogers backs off.

"What about this grand jury coming up?" Rogers then asks. "I know . . . we're all going to get called. I just wish that . . .

you'd go with me someplace . . . in a helicopter, anywhere, and just do some real talking."

"It's best not to do any of that 'till this is all over."

"But governor, you're going to be gone. Let's do it."

"I don't know, John," Hall draws a bead, "but what they've got something stuck on me. That's what I'm worried about."

"Oooooh."

"I don't know whether they've got something on me, something stuck on you."

Although the tape machine strapped to his body is running full speed ahead, Rogers doesn't hesitate.

"Let's go get a steam bath," Rogers challenges Hall.

"Let's wait until I get out (of office) . . . They won't have near the opportunity they do here."

"I'm going to tell you this much . . . The die is cast, everything is OK," Rogers soothes. "You understand what I mean?"

"Well, I don't think they're going to stop until after Burkett leaves office," says Hall prophetically. "I'll tell you what they don't have," adds Hall, whistling past the graveyard. "They don't have evidence of anything wrong. That's where they're screwed. They got all kinds of rumors. They got all kinds of political enemies that want to say things but I'm talking about actually doing things wrong. Being stupid maybe. Being dumb. Choosing bad people. . . ."

"That's not dumb," is Rogers' strange answer from the subconscious, "because Jesus Christ chose twelve."

"Oh, God, yeah, Judas."

"Yeah," echoes Rogers.

"That's right, one in twelve . . . I could have chosen better than that," declares Hall.

"Every one of 'em denied Him, baby," Rogers concludes his Biblical admonition.

It doesn't take a psychiatrist to see hidden meanings in this conversation.

On January 12, day before Hall leaves office, Mooney calls Rogers after talking with Gov. Hall. Hall, Mooney and Taylor are now *all* in that old Wewoka switch. They keep talking about a thing called "trust," which has long since flown the coop.

"Got a call from the fat man," Mooney begins. "Said he talked to you and said it's best I stay in contact with you . . . Said there was some concern whether I could be trusted and said he reassured everyone I could be."

"Yeah, sure, I trust everybody," Rogers airily replies. "I just want the money, that's all . . . You know, he won't talk to me except in riddles."

"He's scared to death," says Mooney. "I want to tell you, John, the man is scared to death. He's so cautious, John, I haven't been even able to talk to him. But he's still committed, as is Taylor committed, and that's all there is to it."

"In other words," Rogers gets down to it, "David was worried about me?"

"I'm going to tell you the truth, John . . . The answer is yes."

"He's afraid of *me*? Goddamn," Rogers snorts, "I took the Fifth Amendment to keep that sonofabitch out of the penitentiary . . . And so did my dad (who) just about lost his race. . . .

"I'm going in and see David tomorrow," adds Rogers testily. ". . . We been writing notes. Well, I'm just going to write him a note: 'No money, no deal.' Hell, I'm the guy that's still responsible for everything."

This is the real John Rogers talking. His gripe: Dad and I aren't appreciated by you, Mr. Governor. Never have been. Now it's your turn to be unappreciated.

"OK," says Mooney, "just don't press for a payment. Don't press him right now. This is a different kind of business deal. It'll all happen. Goddamn, it'll all happen so good you can't believe it!

"Pressing kills 'em all," warns Mooney. "It's the way you play that piano."

"I pound it, huh?"

"You pound it hard. You scare people ... It's that loud music that scares people."

"Well, you know," says Rogers casually, "a barking dog never bites."

This one does.

Had he known of events to follow, I believe Rogers would have laughed Gov. Hall out of any offers he thought improper. But when the FBI came in, Rogers was stuck with being a spy. I grade him A-plus in the role.

"I just didn't want you to be pissed," Rogers apologetically finishes his last talk with Hall, "because I've got good reason ... We can't, you know," he floundered, "later on we'll explain it and say, 'Well, we're sorry.' But that's the way it is."

Yes, that's the way it is and was. You can't stop the wind from blowing, John. Not in Oklahoma. It comes sweeping down the plain as we play hardball politics, throwing knock-down pitches, spitters and curves.

The curves strike you out. Even a governor.

17

ON TRIAL

Every man has a scheme that won't work.

Howe's Law

Jan Love, gracious young lady on Secretary of State John Rogers' staff, unwittingly helped put the final nail in Gov. Hall's coffin when she was chosen to greet Kevin Mooney at Oklahoma City airport the day Mooney arrived to be arrested by the FBI. Mooney's plane was late and Jan was nervous.

She had been told by FBI agents they would follow closely behind as she drove Mooney to the state capitol for a meeting with John Rogers, Jr. It was high noon when Mooney's plane dipped down.

While Jan transported Mooney to Rogers' office, the FBI was harnessing up Rogers for the final act in this drama. Agent Ted Rosack was in charge.

He and other agents outfitted Rogers with a special corset-type elastic belt. It held a tape recorder fast to the small of Rogers' back. A transmitter was slipped into the pocket on a belt fit just above Rogers' left hip. Two gold-colored cotton and felt urethane foam chairs were placed at the corners of Rogers' desk.

Rosack and other FBI agents positioned themselves in Rogers' next door conference room, hearing every word spoken. Derryberry and Marvin C. Emerson, his first assistant, waited with FBI agents. They kept their presence secret, as they had throughout the investigation.

The letter authorizing the $10-million deal was placed in a

visible spot atop Rogers' desk as Jan Love's car carrying happy, unsuspecting Mooney entered the capitol compound.

Handsome, gracious Mooney was acquainted in Rogers' office, known as "a good guy." He hadn't been to lunch. So when Jan Love went to advise Rogers of Mooney's arrival, Mooney sat down beside pretty Judy Bishop's reception desk. In a pleasant mood, he invited Jan and employee Linda Norfleet to lunch. He asked Jan to see if Rogers wanted to come along.

"No time for lunch," Rogers told Jan. "Send Mooney back to my office."

Then Rogers whispered into his transmitter, "Mooney's coming in."

Reporters later asked Rogers if he was nervous at this moment.

"Goddamn, who could be nervous?" he replied. "I had the FBI all over the place."

Rogers picked up the vital $10-million letter, handed it to Mooney and then, on a prearranged signal, Rosack and other FBI agents swarmed Rogers' office, grabbed Mooney and slapped the handcuffs on.

When burly 6'5" Rosack flashed his badge and agents started frisking Mooney, the affable Dallas lawyer turned white. He knew this dance was over.

"I hated bringing him into such a trap," said Jan Love sadly. "I like him."

Linda Norfleet, the other young lady invited to lunch by Mooney, burst into tears.

Without a program, it's hard to tell villains from heroes in these real life dramas.

Mooney decided to cooperate with federal officials, who didn't want him. They wanted Gov. David Hall. They got him the hard way, through Mooney and Rogers.

Gov. Hall was indicted at 2:14 p.m. Thursday, January 17, 1975. Big splash for the 6:00 o'clock news and morning papers.

He was charged with extortion, illegal use of interstate facilities and conspiring with Kevin Mooney and Doc Taylor to bribe Secretary of State John Rogers Jr. to influence him in investing $10-million of state employees' retirement funds.

There were other Hall troubles. The grand jury was also investigating alleged kickbacks and laundering of Hall campaign funds. Hall was under further investigation by the IRS. To say nothing of the never-ending investigation and daily tirade against him by the *Daily Oklahoman.*

Twenty FBI agents had been on the case and Lord knows how many IRS people.

"But the real credit must go to John Rogers who immediately reported to Mr. Derryberry the first approach to him," said Ted Rosack, FBI agent in charge. "He (Rogers) thereafter carried on the scheme, with close assistance of a team of law enforcement officers, with great skill and ingenuity. Without him, we wouldn't be here today."

Gov. Hall was bitter.

"For the past four and one-half years," he spit the words through tight lips, "myself and my family have been subjected to harassment and abuse. That harassment has included wiretapping, burglary, mail tampering, malicious accusations and taping of conversations.

"I'm glad today we take this out of the newspapers and put it in the courtroom where it belongs. I feel when the evidence is presented, I will be fully vindicated and those who have conspired against me will be exposed."

Hall's handsome face was set in hard, cold lines. His clothes matched—black suit, black and white striped tie, black socks and black boots. His time of mourning. Yet Hall stood firmly erect, a soldier at attention.

When Gov. Hall's trial started, jurors were fitted with headsets. Thirty banks of headsets were ordered to permit jurors and officials involved to hear the volumnious Hall-Rogers conversations.

A small thing hurt Hall badly, looming large to the jury. The log on the governor's state plane showed that W. W. Doc Taylor and R. Kevin Mooney were picked up in Dallas Nov. 3 and brought to Oklahoma City, then flown back the following day.

Not everyone in Dallas gets this special service from Oklahoma governors.

Prosecutor Burkett was never able to put a "smoking gun" in Gov. Hall's hand during the trial. But a lot of these "little" things, plus the taped conversations, added up in the jury's minds to a criminal conspiracy between Hall, Rogers, Mooney and Taylor. Still, it was a close call that could have come up not guilty, or at least a hung jury.

Mooney escaped trial by entering a guilty plea. Rogers, of course, was granted immunity. He testified at Hall's trial that his immunity, granted by federal prosecutor Burkett, also covered all acts committed by himself and his father, John M. Rogers, Sr., between January 1, 1970 and December 23, 1974. That took care of Rogers on the $37,000 he and his father raised from the Sr. Rogers' employees for Gov. Hall's campaign. Most important part of the tradeout.

Rogers also admitted he had been under IRS audits. But he declared these matters had no bearing on his decision to cooperate with the FBI in seeking evidence against Gov. Hall.

Initially, Burkett said Rogers hadn't been the subject of an investigation but later admitted he was wrong in saying so. Rogers said when he offered Burkett his help he no longer wanted to "take the Fifth" before the grand jury. Burkett immediately offered not to prosecute him or his father.

Thus are cases "made." Rogers had no other choice.

It was tough preparing a defense for Hall and Doc Taylor. Taylor's lawyer, James P. Linn, tried to make young John Rogers the culprit. He mentioned "sickening conduct" on the part of Rogers toward Taylor and Mooney. Linn pointed out Rogers continually demanded "money, money, money."

Linn claimed Rogers first solicited a bribe. Said it happened almost a month before Rogers disclosed Hall's alleged bribe attempt to Attorney General Derryberry.

After the trial's first day, Hall left court with that usual spring in his step.

"Grimm's Fairy Tales," he laughingly remarked about Prosecutor Burkett's opening statement. "I wish I could say something, but that's up to the attorneys. But it was about as wild a story as I've ever heard," Hall told the press.

The prosecution claimed Hall, Mooney and Taylor held a conference, at which Hall allegedly offered to arrange a meeting with Max Strange, executive director of the retirement fund. At this meeting Hall, the prosecution declared, told Mooney he would get a one per cent "finder's fee" if the proposal went through and Hall wanted $50,000 "as future legal fees."

When Mooney told Taylor of the proposal, Taylor calmly stated he was "used to paying points and was agreeable," said the prosecution.

Defense attorney Linn concentrated on Rogers' own problems with federal authorities. He claimed Rogers went to the FBI because of his involvement in raising $37,000 from his dad's state employees for Gov. Hall's campaign. He pointed out Rogers had taken the Fifth before the grand jury himself and was merely spying on the investment proposal as a way "to clear himself" and get Hall.

It's toughest on the wives. Both Hall's and Rogers' wives were in court with their handkerchiefs. Jo Hall looked at Rogers coldly, with obvious distaste, throughout his testimony.

Pretty Jeanne Rogers, then an outstanding Oklahoma golfer, was also on the front row, offering an occasional nervous smile of encouragement to her husband.

"I feel very uncomfortable," she said, sitting in the same pew with Mrs. Hall.

Rogers made his pitch exclusively to the jury, rarely looking at Hall. The governor kept his eyes fastened on Rogers with hard, menacing looks. Even when standing to pour himself a glass of water, Hall held his stare firmly on Rogers.

Kevin Mooney, the other key government witness, readily admitted he agreed to split a $100,000 finder's fee with Hall. The tall, ruggedly handsome black-haired witness added that Hall told him he intended to give Rogers $25,000 of his share so Rogers would get their investment proposal approved. He declared Hall suggested the scheme to him at a meeting they held in Fort Worth.

Mooney graduated with Hall in 1959 from Tulsa University's law school. He said he and Taylor considered the finder's fee a standard practice but failed to realize any split with Rogers was illegal.

"I don't think Taylor ever thought he was paying a bribe," said Mooney.

During the trial it came out Gov. Hall definitely got scared of Rogers December 31, 1974, after his skiing vacation and long conversations with Rogers. On that date Hall phoned Mooney, telling him he had been tipped off by a friend that he was being "set up" by Rogers.

The trial was not without its touch of humor.

"I shall walk through the valley of death and fear no evil because I'm the meanest sonofabitch in the valley," Rogers said on tape at one point.

Rogers on the stand had a moustache which he occasionally wears. He arrived daily in a half size winter coat with black fur collar. He was a lonely figure but unafraid and determined.

I asked Rogers if Hall ever accused him of a double-cross.

"Only in the courtroom," said Rogers. "When I was on the stand he told me he was going to get me. Mouthed it. The jury saw it; I saw it. He was in a rage . . . could hardly control himself at what I was saying on the stand."

Rogers insists he was never really angry with Hall. Nor was he trying to become a hero. You may find part of his motive in what follows:

"I never had an emotion of being mad at Hall," Rogers told me. ". . . I never had sent anybody to the pen either. But I was well aware of what I was doing.

"It turned out just like I knew it would turn out and I'm not any hero; it was just one of those things.

"My father's predicament influenced me . . . Gave me the resolution to go through with what I was doing. It wasn't only the fact he was trying to steal the money because I could have stopped that without putting him in the penitentiary.

"He (Hall) took our money . . . and then did absolutely nothing to help us over our hard part . . . If that hadn't been in it, I would have probably tried to help him from getting into more trouble. Said, 'Leave it alone' or something.

"My attitude when he approached me was definitely against him. Hostile. Because here he was going to use me again. It made me mad that he honestly thought I was stupid or something."

"It took a bit of guts to go ahead and do it," I suggested.

"Really it didn't, Marty," answered Rogers. "There's nothing gutty about it. I was put into a position of being able to do it . . . Just something you wish hadn't happened to you but . . . there it is.

"I would not want to do it again," Rogers added softly.

Rogers told at the trial about what was on the notes Hall wrote warning Rogers they were being bugged. He said Gov. Hall, after showing him the notes, lighted them with a cigarette lighter and flushed them down the toilet.

"When I walked in, he put his forefinger over his lips and told me to sit down in a chair," Rogers testified. "He took out a piece of cardboard and wrote a note and held it up.

"We are bugged. Office bugged for 10 days. Wait eight months. Trust me."

Reporter Mike Hammer of the *Oklahoman* wrote in his story, "The apparent hand-writing of notes is audible on the tapes, as is the flushing of the toilet described by Rogers in his testimony."

On March 6, 1975, Gov. Hall took the stand in his own defense.

"There was no bribe," he said firmly, standing tall and straight. "There was never any discussion with Mr. Mooney or Mr. Taylor with regard to their paying me any money with regard to that plan."

Asked by his attorney if he was available for a price, Hall replied, "Money has not been my concern. That's probably the reason I'm in debt ... My prime objective has been to accomplish my goals of leaving my mark in history by doing something for the good of the people. I consider life something more than a big car, a nice house and a bank account. Money has never been an object of mine."

I knew Hall well enough to say he didn't appear overly concerned about money for himself. He was broke and deep in debt. I must add that when they call the roll on Oklahoma governors whose administrations did most for we, the people, Gov. Hall will rank near the top.

His tax program, making the fat cats pay a fairer share, caught him hell in the country clubs of Oklahoma City and Tulsa. The privileged were after him hard. They finally got him. But a lot of school teachers, state employees, handicapped citizens, and others beholden to state government would be worse off today had not David Hall sat in the governor's chair.

Hall's press secretary, Ed Hardy, cast doubt on Rogers' testimony about the note writing. He was in and out while Hall and Rogers met but said he saw no notes written or changing hands. Hardy added he didn't understand a need to burn anything because Hall had a paper shredder beside his desk that was used regularly to destroy papers.

Attorney General Derryberry admitted putting Rogers in touch with the FBI.

"He's extremely brash, to the point of arrogance, but he had the guts to see it through," Derryberry said of Rogers.

The defense came to bat March 6, 1975 without any heavy hitters.

"The evidence for David Hall will show he didn't do it," was attorney D. C. Thomas' opening statement.

Hall witness Robert R. Sanders, a former political pollster for Rogers, revealed he was the one who, in late December, tipped Hall off that Rogers was helping investigate the governor.

"David was very shocked about it," said Sanders, adding that he felt Rogers was assisting federal authorities to help his "own image and political improvement." He also claimed Rogers told him, "Burkett has promised to help me with the press."

Both Hall and Doc Taylor counted heavily on testimony from Dallas financier Richard R. Finley. He and Taylor declared Rogers demanded money from them a month before he started working with the FBI.

Doc Taylor claimed Rogers told him and Finley that he put all his money in trust when he took office "and it costs me twice as much to live as I make."

Finley testified he heard Rogers say, "You realize, gentlemen, that the earnings I make as a public official do not begin to meet the expenses of my living."

Two business associates of Taylor, Rex Scott and William Boone, tried to bolster the claim that Rogers himself was seeking a bribe. They stated Taylor had told them his investment proposal in Oklahoma was going well except for one official who "had his hand out," meaning Rogers.

The jury didn't buy this testimony. Not after all those tapes. Another reason, Taylor and Mooney couldn't keep their stories on the same track.

Mooney told of Hall proposing the finder's fee. Taylor, who wasn't blessed with the immunity granted Mooney, had to deny Mooney's statement.

Hall at one point accused prosecutor Burkett of being "duped by Rogers," who he claimed conspired with Attorney General Derryberry to frame him. Hall added he thought Rogers was trying to set him up and that the FBI became part of the alleged conspiracy because Republican prosecutor Burkett was willing to believe anything to nail Hall, whom he had been investigating more than a year.

On cross-examination, Burkett wisely kept playing the damaging tape recordings between Rogers and the others. Best Taylor could come up with was that these conversations were "half straight and half double-talk . . . I was just trying to avoid his demands," Taylor added. "I made Rogers tell me the whole story so I could report it to the highest authority in Oklahoma, Gov. Hall."

Taylor's story didn't ring true to the jury. Not after those volumnious tapes. Mooney, although obviously trying to be helpful where possible, couldn't avoid disputing Taylor's claims. Rogers wasn't bashful about backing up Mooney.

Had he not been involved with politicians, I doubt Taylor would have been convicted. I'm convinced he was only trying to get himself a reasonable, legal business deal. Taylor said after the trial he still felt his proposition was legitimate.

"I have a deal with them (retirement board)," he stated. "I don't know about legally but I think they are morally obligated. They all voted for it . . . I felt like an innocent party trapped in the middle."

After his release from prison, Taylor again reminded the retirement board of what he claimed was their unfulfilled obligation. He demanded they now perform as agreed. Everybody laughed. The world is cruel when you're down.

It was unkind when Taylor was arrested in Jackson,

Mississippi and forced to post $25,000 bond. The partly bald, bespectacled Taylor, 48 and a touch heavy, was tearful on the stand as he told of his humiliation.

He said he was hounded by reporters, tipped off by the media in Oklahoma City. His attorney told him Jackson reporters admitted prosecutor Burkett had tipped off the Oklahoma City press, claiming Burkett did so to get a lot of publicity.

Taylor lost his composure altogether at this point. He sobbed while relating his sad tale of being led down the streets of downtown Jackson to the city jail, wearing a belly chain. On leaving Jackson, Taylor said he stopped at a gift shop to buy his wife a present and saw his picture in chains on the front page of the Jackson paper. It was his wife's birthday.

All I can say is anyone who figured mild-mannered Doc Taylor, dealer in stocks and bonds, needed a belly chain to restrain him shouldn't be in law enforcement. Too big a coward. But when the media wants a show and prosecutors are looking for public praise, many a person of unproven guilt is put in the stocks to be spit upon. Always done in the holy name of "upholding the law" and "protecting the public's right to know."

If you figure I feel sorry for Doc Taylor, you got it right. As Rogers says, Taylor could have pleaded guilty to something minor and probably gone free. I like a guy who'll fight when he thinks he's mainly right and won't turn on an associate to save his own hide. I'll trust Doc Taylor on a handshake anytime.

There's no sissy in David Hall either. He lost his composure once. That's when he was talking about how hard the many investigations and newspaper accusations were on his lovely wife, Jo. Hall swalled hard a couple times, blinked his eyes rapidly, then in a low voice asked for a cup of water.

After clearing his throat several times, his brilliant blue eyes hardened. Ready again for more questioning. But good answers were hard to come by.

Burkett relentlessly repeated comments from the Hall-Rogers tapes, all sounding bad for Hall. There were so many things Hall couldn't explain.

"I just don't know why I said that," he would parry.

Hall's main defense was his claim that Burkett, Derryberry, Rogers and the FBI were all conspiring to destroy him. He added he felt Mooney also became part of the conspiracy "after he entered a (guilty) plea and you (Burkett) talked to him."

Hall and Taylor ran up expensive lawyer bills. They might have done as well with less costly talent. Hall was convicted on four counts, Taylor on three. Hall was found guilty of extorting $50,000 from Taylor and Mooney, attempting to bribe Secretary of State John Rogers and two violations involving interstate operations. Taylor was convicted on the interstate operations, plus conspiracy to attempt to bribe.

It was a close call. The jury of seven men and five women took 16 hours to agree. Courthouse regulars were predicting a hung jury.

"I was very much surprised," Hall told the press. "I expected a verdict of not guilty or a hung jury."

"I just can't believe this happened to me in this country," declared bewildered Doc Taylor.

"That jury had a lot of courage," was Rogers' comment. "I'm sorry for the fact he (Hall) is the kind of guy who offered me a bribe."

The press reported Derryberry, who had unsuccessfully tried to get impeachment proceedings against Hall, "was quite happy over the verdicts" and went to prosecutor Burkett's office.

"I'm proud of you," Derryberry told Burkett.

Burkett was happily taking calls of congratulations from Justice Department friends throughout the country.

"I think the verdict speaks for itself," Burkett said, "but it isn't something you rejoice over."

As in any poker game like this trial, the winners laughed, losers cried. But nobody hollered, "Deal the cards." The deck was used up. No more shuffles allowed. Burkett and Rogers sacked up the game.

Even Congressman Tom Steed, who had been highly critical of Burkett, pulled in his horns. Some of Steed's friends and constituents were also in deep trouble over serious revelations before the grand jury.

"It went on for two years," declared Steed. "You heard charges and saw headlines and people were dangled along. It had come high time that he (Burkett) ought to do something or quit pulling those tactics. It seemed like an awfully long time to get to the bottom of it."

But then Steed added, "I think Burkett has proved his case, so that's that. I'm satisfied. I hope this wraps the deal up."

Which it did, except for Hall and Taylor. U.S. District Judge Fred Daugherty sentenced Gov. Hall to three years, Taylor to 18 months in prison.

A huge crowd of shouting media people surrounded Hall as he emerged from the courthouse, heading toward his 3-year sentence.

"What's your comment, Governor?"

"A bum rap?"

"Gonna appeal?"

"How you feel?"

"What's next?"

All the media rushed to get close, including Pam Henry, then a political reporter for Channel 4 in Oklahoma City. Pam, badly crippled from polio, was in the worst crush, struggling to get herself and mike close for cameraman Darrell Barton.

Pam carries with her everywhere a smile that lights up the world. But at this important moment it faded. Someone shoving alongside knocked a crutch out from under her.

Pam held her ground, teetering on one crutch while holding her mike in Hall's face until he completed his statement.

"Then Gov. Hall did a beautiful thing, Marty," she told me. "He reached over, picked up my lost crutch and set it up against a fire hydrant beside me where I could reach it unobtrusively. He nodded toward the crutch and smiled sweetly. I was so touched 'cause I loved his wife, Jo. I held it in until we got our story finished, then went home and just bawled like a baby."

Again, how do you pick the good guys?

"It could happen to any of you like it happened to me," was Hall's statement to Oklahomans after sentencing.

He's not too far wrong. Gov. Hall was battered from pillar to post by the *Daily Oklahoman*, IRS, FBI, politicians anxious to see him defeated and by contractors and others out to save their own skins.

Gov. Hall was the big fish they wanted to catch, show off and enter for a prize. Once he was netted, weighed and held aloft for pictures, the prosecutors' interest in fishing for political chicanery waned.

John Rogers didn't fare much better than Hall and Taylor. He was forced to resign his office to avoid impeachment. Yet he had good reason for doing what he did and grounds for impeachment against him would have had to be trumped up charges. Yet I'm certain he would have been impeached had he not resigned.

Doc Taylor spent more than $100,000 in lawyer fees, which he learned are more expensive than finder's fees. Doc's business was also immediately placed in deep jeopardy.

"All doors just slam in your face," complained a tearful Mrs. Taylor.

Prosecutors got their glory; lawyers their big money. Gov. Hall and Secretary of State Rogers got it where the chicken does, in the neck.

As always, one man's pleasure is another's pain.

18

MABELLE

Light of step and heart was she.

Walter De Le Mare

Her name describes her exactly.

Mabelle Kennedy was bright as a shiny May morning, lively as a ringing bell. She was also thin steel hidden in a velvet glove, a laughing black-eyed beauty who held her own in the cowshed world of Oklahoma ranching and at the nation's highest level of politics and government.

Mabelle, Sue Ruble and Donna Nigh are my favorite women of all time in Oklahoma politics and my wife, Helen, puts Mabelle ahead of most men who won high political office in Oklahoma. I kinda agree. Mabelle was class and true grit.

Harry Truman in 1951 appointed Mabelle Assistant Secretary of the U.S. Treasury, highest government position ever held by an Oklahoma woman. But this was only the icing on Mabelle's huge achievement cake.

The little girl who emigrated to Indian Territory from Missouri at dawn of the 20th century became rancher, banker, city councilwoman, mayor, Democratic national committeewoman and more. These honors were mere sidelines to her main job of wife, mother and grandmother to a houseful of children until her death at age 93 in 1981, leaving behind 22 grandchildren and great-grandchildren.

"Brains have no sex," she chuckled at 92, explaining why she was always equally comfortable astride an Indian pony on her grassland range or chatting with the President of the United States, which she did frequently with President Truman.

Her accomplishments were many but Mabelle was no strident half-male women's libber. She was an orchid and silver slipper lady all the way.

"I was born a woman and like it," she said. "I want all niceties of being a woman. But if women want to make it in business or politics, their brainpower will put them there if they go after what they want.

"Many women feel dependent. Not me. I've always been a free spirit, going and coming as I like. Some women are their own worst enemies."

Oklahoma was wild when Mabelle came to the Osage country of northern Oklahoma at age ten. This lively little girl enjoyed her family's treck to Indian Territory by covered wagon.

"It was delightful," she laughed. "We bought vegetables from farmers along the way. My father sold his farm in Missouri and outfitted two wagons and teams. We didn't drive hard, took six weeks for the trip.

"Father made me a rope swing to use when we camped. It was a happy picnic for me all the way. I loved the adventure."

Mabelle didn't get her distinctive name until the family settled in the Osage Nation, after first landing in the Enid area.

"My mother hated the wind and sand there," she said. "We were told that across the river in the Osage (near Ponca City) there was more greenery and rivers, like our old home in Missouri. So we rented a farm near Fairfax, where I celebrated my tenth birthday."

Shortly thereafter Mabelle started school and was embarrassed because she couldn't properly pronounce her name.

"My mother named me after two aunts, May and Belle," she explained. "When the teacher asked my name, I tried to say both names but couldn't get the 'y' out. Sounded like I was saying Ma Bell and the teacher couldn't make out exactly what I meant.

"My mother sympathized, saying, 'You have a right to a name you can say and like, so from now on you're Mabelle.' Suited me, so Mabelle I've been ever since."

Roman Catholic Mabelle had a strict upbringing and was always a proper lady. Well, almost always. There was a mischievous elf in her too, part of her charm.

I remember Mabelle grandly entering the old Biltmore Hotel with a couple lady friends and a clutch of rugged, red-faced cattlemen from the Osage in case there was trouble, which there often was the night before a Democratic Party convention.

She and my wife, Helen, were both lookers and "good sports" who could stand a little coarse talk if the festivities were otherwise friendly. I can see them now, heads back and smiling, each with arms around two Oklahoma Supreme Court Justices, making the then famous high court quartet into a sextet, as they joined in booming out *Carolina Moon, Down By The Old Mill Stream, Old Black Joe* and all the rest.

Years later, my wife and I attended Mabelle's 90th birthday party in Pawhuska. A couple days later we got a thank-you note for flowers sent.

"My house was so filled with flowers," she wrote, "I got up next morning and asked, 'Where's the body?' "

For 40 years Mabelle reigned as Oklahoma's first Lady of Oklahoma politics. Much of her heritage was deep south, so she was a natural born Democrat to her toes, although I suspect she crossed over a time or two to spare the Republic some Democratic highbinder she knew too well.

"I had a southern grandmother who nearly expired when told we were moving to Indian Territory," said Mabelle. "She worried we'd be killed by Indians or outlaws and that her granddaughter would be tainted by frontier coarseness. So as a young lady I returned to Missouri each fall to attend Oaklawn College, a private school, and became as civilized as elocution lessons and studying three foreign languages could make me."

Mabelle was reared a proper southern lady who always dressed for dinner but she learned some better things in the Osage that never left her. Blanket Indians were then more common than businessmen and ranchers but all lived together in mutual respect and acceptance. Mabelle acquired the common touch riding her Indian pony to school and playing with all types of children. This background served her well in politics, especially with one common fella whose stature grows daily, Harry Truman.

Those regular college trips back to Missouri netted Mabelle a handsome husband with outstanding prospects, Edmund Kennedy. He was an ambitious young Kansas City banker who visited the Territory and liked it because of a trim beauty living there he sought to marry. His chosen lady, Mabelle, was not hesitant to point out the area's potential as a place for a young man to put down roots and acquire cheap land.

"I also wanted to be close to mama," Mabelle confessed, and she got her chance.

The Missouri bank Ed Kennedy worked for was moving into new locations. Young Kennedy was given his choice of three new banks to head. One was the National Bank of Commerce in Pawhuska, which he chose after a little prodding from Mabelle and her mama.

The young bride urged her husband to buy land, and Ed Kennedy bought his first 5,000 acres at Mabelle's specific request.

"I told Ed I wanted land," Mabelle recalled, "that we'd find plenty things to use it for in this new country. In those days people overlooked the future prospects of all that plentiful cheap land. It was a big journey from Pawhuska to Bartlesville, 35 miles over horribly rocky trails, even fording a river. The land seemed worthless but it sure wasn't."

Ed and Mabelle bought up big chunks of the territory. When President Truman appointed Mabelle Assistant U.S. Treasurer, she owned the Soldani Ranch, 12,000 acres; the Allred Ranch, 6,000 acres; the Gray Horse and Comer-Craddock ranches, 5,000 acres each and, "Oh, yes, a small place, about 2,000 acres, near Pawhuska," said Mabelle.

"I'm sure glad you loved your mama, honey," husband Ed remarked more than once to Mabelle after these fruitful acquisitions.

Land and her bank provided Mabelle income to play big time politics. Her son, Edmund Kennedy Jr., still heads the family bank in Pawhuska. Her other four children were Mrs. Matthew J. (Marge) Kane, Mrs. Harry G. (Julia) Lane, Mrs. Horace (Pat) Schmidlapp and Anne Blake Dell.

Oklahoma almost had two lady ambassadors under President Truman, Mabelle and another rich and famous Oklahoman, the hostess with the mostes', Pearl Mesta.

In 1949, *Newsweek* predicted Mabelle would be named ambassador "to the first Central America vacancy." *Newsweek* also predicted, correctly it turned out, that Mrs. Mesta was in line to become ambassador to the tiny European duchy of Luxembourg.

Mabelle in politics lived by a personal rule which caused her appointment to the Treasury post rather than an ambassadorship. She wouldn't take a job for which she didn't feel qualified. She was asked by the State Department if she would like to go to Norway, home of all my ancestors and most of my relatives.

"It was flattering," said Mabelle, "but I replied, 'No thanks.' I know nothing of Norway's people, industries or problems. On the other hand, I do know the Indian temperament, being around it all my life.

"I knew I could be useful in a Latin country. I have some definite ideas about helping these people — in Guatamala for instance — which would do a lot more good than in the past."

But it was not to be. Mabelle had connections all the way up to President Truman but Guatamala Ambassador Richard Patterson decided to keep his job to the end of Truman's term. Mabelle's interest in other ambassador posts was nil so she gave up that idea.

"I don't hold with the way these ambassador things usually pan out," she explained. "Some party worker and contributor is too often given one of those jobs without regard to qualifications.

"Which is a stinking shame," she snapped. "For the State Department's foreign service, it's the worst thing that can happen."

Mabelle pulled her weight or didn't join up. This was basic with her and the reason she went to the U.S. Treasury. I personally think she enjoyed it more than she could Guatamala.

President Truman was high on Mabelle. She and Gov. Roy Turner raised a bundle of money in Oklahoma and elsewhere to keep Harry's whistle stop campaign train rolling in '48, when many big shots in the Democratic Party turned their backs on the guy all polls said was a sure loser.

Mabelle had other political credentials. She was a buddy of

India Edwards, head lady at the Democratic National Committee, a real pusher who wouldn't rest until Mabelle got a top appointment. She was also strongly supported by her cohort, Oklahoma Democratic National Committeeman Bill Doenges, than whom there is no more effective lobbyist anywhere to this very day in 1983.

I worked with India in '56, when she, I, Gov. Raymond Gary and Harry Truman were all hot for Averall Harriman of New York for the presidential nomination. We came in second in what turned out to be a two-man race at the convention in Chicago, where we had to politely ask Mayor Dick Daley's permission to get into the hall. Daley and most other delegates were for Adlai Stevenson.

India didn't stand on ceremony. She kept badgering the White House daily and Gov. Turner, who turned down a proffered cabinet appointment, also went to bat for Mabelle. Sands at the top level shift slowly but ultimately there was a vacancy and Mabelle got her appointment. She was sworn in January 7, 1952, gussied up in a navy blue faille suit trimmed in velvet and rhinestones, a perky white and violet hat and sporting her special-occasion trademark, two huge orchids.

She took the job knowing she could do it.

"This is the most right woman possible for the job," boasted India Edwards of her friend. "Mrs. Kennedy's long banking experience makes her eminently qualified."

Mabelle wasn't in Washington long enough to set the town on its ear but she let 'em know she was around. Teamed with Gov. Roy Turner, she brightened up the liveliest party of one season, hosted by Turner at the Mayflower Hotel in downtown Washington.

Starring at this bash were Mabelle and a simulated Oklahoma bronco, named "Hollywood Hobby," imported from California. Hobby was a party horse made of nuts, bolts, wires and springs — forerunner of the mechanical bulls, a later fad in nightclubs.

Mabelle was the come-on to entice a stiff-necked eastern crowd into the saddle after the party got oiled up and nicely underway. She pulled herself astride the mechanical bronco and easily rode it around the room, laughingly holding one hand high.

What some of the elegant guests didn't know was that Mabelle was at home on any horse. She and Gov. Turner had also benefited from a few practice rides on their new steel bronc.

"Mabelle made it look like a snap," wrote Malvina Stephenson in the *Tulsa Tribune* next day. "She swung a high-heeled foot over the saddle, adjusted her long, swirling black skirt, smugly tossed her flower-decked head high and went into action.

" 'Hobby' scooted across the room with ease, bucking at regular intervals, Mabelle hanging perilously in the saddle. The crowd cheered and cheered."

After Mabelle's demonstration, others crowded around asking to ride the Oklahoma bronc. A big Irishman, Jim Maloney of the Secret Service, got first chance. Instead of gentling that horse, like Mabelle, he spurred it and let out a loud "Giddyap!"

You don't do that to any bronco first time out if you hope to come down in one piece. The man-made horse took a few fast glides, then balked, stopping dead. The muscular Maloney pitched upward and outward, landing in a thudding heap, wedged into a corner of the room, breath knocked out of him.

Those following him were more cautious. They asked

Mabelle for helpful instructions, but all were thrown except those who merely inched the critter along, sissy fashion.

The more daring were thrown. They included some of the nation's top government brass of that day, many of whom came to Mabelle after being dumped, urging, "ride him again, Mabelle, so we can see how it's done." Mabelle obliged but you don't become a bronc buster on two tries. Much of the crowd carried black and blue badges of disappointment next day, made up for by memories of a fun wild-west Oklahoma evening.

Among the bronc-busting spectators were Rose Conway, secretary to President Truman; Don Dawson, Truman's administrative assistant; Speaker Sam Rayburn; Peyton Ford, assistant to the Attorney General; and Oklahomans Harrington Wimberly, Lt. General Raymond McClain, Colonel and Mrs. Roy St. Lewis, Congressman Toby Morris, Gladys Watkins, H. W. "Coach" McNeil, Forrest McIntire, Joe Jarboe, Raymond Pope, and Mike Monroney.

Whatever it took, Mabelle came up with it. First, last and always a lady, Mabelle could nonetheless out-tough most anyone. She was also honest to the core and loyal, qualities her boss Harry Truman admired most. The two could have been brother and sister.

"He was a true friend," Mabelle said of President Truman. "He stood by his friends and those of us he appointed stood by him like the Rock of Gibraltar. He was simple, straightforward and as true to the dye as could be. And he sure loved his Bess.

"I liked that man. History will see him go down as one of the great men of this country."

Mabelle also had some insights about Bess Truman.

"Bess wasn't the shy person people thought," declared

Mabelle, "She loved Blair House better than the White House and was simply a good mother and wife who didn't care to be in the limelight but preferred being what she was, a lovely, sweet woman. She didn't let people push her any other way."

Mabelle's close friends were from all classes. What you were inside is all that mattered to her, not the glitter of fancy outer trappings. She got the topmost job of any Oklahoma woman in history because of her character.

Everyone said Harry Truman was beat in 1948. Mabelle thought so, too, I suspect. Gov. Roy Turner also figured that's how it would turn out.

A lot of skittish Democrats at the highest levels, including some of the top Democratic Roosevelts, scurried off the Truman ship they thought was sinking, seeking cheese elsewhere.

Not Mabelle Kennedy. She joined Roy Turner in a small group that paid for Truman's train and a couple national radio broadcasts that kept him in the race. Truman would otherwise have lost.

Mabelle didn't expect any cheers for this. She was just doing what came naturally. I've noticed the most honest, open people are happiest. Mabelle Kennedy was among this lucky group.

"It's a wonderful age I've been living through," said Mabelle before her death at 93. "Why, I remember riding in one of the first cars, talking on that new-fangled telephone thing. So many wonderful experiences. It's been marvelous and I've enjoyed every minute."

Nobody deserved the good times more.

19

SURE, MIKE!

God give us men!---Men who possess opinions and a will; men who have honor; men who will not lie.

Josiah Gilbert Holland

He did the unheard of, voted his conscience and expressed only honest opinions to Oklahoma voters. In spite of such poor political judgment, Mike Monroney lasted an amazing six terms in the House and three terms in the U.S. Senate.

Unwavering integrity usually bespeaks a one-termer. But Mike's warm Irish smile and personality, plus a Phi Beta Kappa brain, helped him beat the odds against intellectual honesty succeeding in politics.

Thirty years is about maximum for anyone in public office. Votes of expediency cast to placate a publisher or big campaign donor eventually catch up with you. We, the people, are slow on the uptake but finally do learn to know the fakers.

Honest votes will do you in faster than dishonest. "Political suicide" votes are usually honest and Mike Monroney cast a bunch of 'em. For 30 years he got away with putting his integrity ahead of popular opinion. He would have driven a pollster nuts.

In politics as in life, "There is a season . . . a time to be born and a time to die." They lowered the curtain on Mike in 1968.

The bottom line on Monroney: He got beat for all the right reasons. Beat himself. Did it on purpose with all those sincere votes.

I say all honor to him. He put integrity above winning an election. If you don't think that's hard, try it sometime.

Mike was that rare animal who earned the right to sleep peacefully forever with his political memories. He has no reason for tossing and turning now.

Not that he was a pious saint. Saints are dead people and Mike was very much alive to his last day in Oklahoma politics.

He was a happy, fun guy and favorite of the ladies. A lot of women voted for Mike for no better reason than his wide Irish grin and that lanky, virile body topped off by handsome head of wavy silver hair.

"Yeah, the gals liked him," admits Jay Perry, Mike's lifetime best buddy. "Sometimes I had to brush 'em away.

"There was this stacked Italian gal down around McAlester. She came up to me at a rally and started talking about Mike and how she liked his looks. I'd heard it before.

" 'Does the Senator ever fool around?' she wanted to know.

" 'Never,' I told her. 'That's my department,' " laughed Jay.

"Well," the lady responded, "if the Senator ever does decide to stray a little, will you tell him from me you know a lively Italian girl who'd really like to get right down on the precinct level with him?' "

This kind of appeal didn't hurt Mike in the voting booths of Oklahoma during his younger days. When we dummies gave women the vote, we forgot one day we'd get old and lose our charm. Which for a politician can be fatal.

From his beginning at OU as editor of the *Oklahoma Daily,* Mike was deep into politics. He started the first gridiron spoof of Oklahoma politicians back in the '30's. Put on his first show in a church in Norman while an OU student.

Later he and Dave Shackelford, a buddy of Mike's and fellow reporter on the old *Oklahoma News,* wrote Oklahoma's first official gridiron, *Desire Under the Helm,* which Ralph Sewell tells me was a takeoff on the impeachment of Gov. Henry Johnston.

Being a political writer was fun but no way to get rich. So in 1928 he joined his dad in the family business, Doc and Bill's Furniture Store. Two years later Mike's dad died and the business became Mike's to run.

No longer able to write politics, Mike started playing politics instead. Got himself elected to a lot of civic jobs. He became president of the Oklahoma City Furniture Dealers. A year later, state president of the OU Alumni Association. Next year, youngest president ever of the Oklahoma City Rotary Club. Getting acquainted.

Mike's wife, Mary Ellen, was well known in Washington's society and money crowd. Which helped nudge Mike into his first race for Congress.

Mary Ellen was a member of the prominent and wealthy Mellon family and special friend of Mrs. John G. Winant, whose husband became ambassador to Great Britain and who was, in the 30's, head of the New Deal's brand new Social Security Administration. The Winants had a kennel of fancy West Island dogs Mary Ellen liked, which later became a campaign issue when Mike was running for the Senate.

Wealthy New Dealer Winant heard Mike arguing at a cocktail party against some of his rich anti-New Deal friends. Winant liked what Mike was saying.

"Why don't you run for Congress?" he asked.

"Might just do it one of these days," Mike replied.

Which he did, sooner than expected. In 1937 Oklahoma's 5th District Congressman, R. P. Hill, died. Mike jumped into the special election race which picked a successor, along with 13 others.

Like most newcomers, Mike ran against "the politicians." Fair enough. You're not a politician until you get elected.

"We spent $279 on that race," recalls Mike's campaign manager for years, Jay Perry. "Bought some flyers to pass out at courthouse meetings. Didn't even have sound equipment then. Just word of mouth, a little radio and what we could get in the papers."

Biggest campaign cost was placards, held up before crowds at speakings, reading:

MIKE MONRONEY
Unfair To Organized Politicians

Turned out the organized politicians were unfair to Mike. He came in third behind the ultimate winner, Gomer Smith, and Homer Paul.

The next year, 1938, ol' Gomer Smith's ambition got ahead of his judgment and he ran unsuccessfully against weil-entrenched Senator Elmer Thomas.

This time Mike and Jay decided to let 'er rip with the money. They spent the grand sum of $729, edging out T-Bone McDonald in the Democratic primary and swamping Republican Harlan Deupree in the general. McDonald went on to become, along with Roy E. "Friday" Fitzgerald, Oklahoma most effective political lobbyists.

Those were simpler days. Government didn't encompass all.

It was possible for an elected official to bow only to conscience, as Monroney proved. I think it's still possible — in fact, the smart way to go — but most of today's politicians and their pollsters disagree. I remind them most candidates, rich or poor, get beat, even when all-wise pollsters and media experts are doing their thinking and spending.

Before TV took over politics, most doctors were medical practitioners, not incorporated high finance operators organizing political action committees to protect their Big Bucks stake in socialized medicine. Union priorities were higher wages and worker safety, not electing candidates favoring featherbedding. And businessmen not only talked free enterprise, they practiced it some, offering minimum agitation for special tax breaks and taxpayer subsidies.

Most candidates of that early day didn't consider holding office a lifetime job. State legislators drew $100 a month for three months every two years. A few terms of that and most happily relinquished this mainly non-paying honor.

Running for school board, city council and the legislature were things people did out of gratitude for being American. Votes bought and sold were then at least honest and open, albeit illegal, business transactions.

Your elected officials today must take money in big bunches from every special interest group under the sun if they hope to pay the campaign bills and stay in office. Most also don't hesitate to grab those juicy honorariums, up to $5,000 each, for reading dull speeches someone writes for them to various conventions for the Honorable Sons and Daughters of Free Enterprise.

If you think these donations and honorariums don't influence a Congressman or U.S. Senator, think again. This massive exchange of greenbacks between public officials and private hustlers may be a cut above bribery but the difference is razor thin.

Those from whom these blessings flow got wants that get satisfied. So don't look for any fast reduction of the federal deficit. The little guy of weak mind, strong back who works for a salary will be privileged to hold up ever more of our topheavy political house of deceit in days to come.

Mike Monroney was not in the mold of modern politicians, except for charisma, which he possessed in greater sum than today's most handsome candidates, ever on the lookout for a TV camera to smirk at.

Mike was a big worrier about money. His worry, however, was that someone might donate too much to his campaign. Ed Edmondson was like that. A little more dough and Ed might have made up the 3,835 vote difference between him and Oklahoma's Republican champ of all time, Henry Bellmon, in '74, when 778,000 votes were cast.

"In those early campaigns, Mike put a limit of $100 on what he'd accept in donations," Jay Perry told me. "Some groups he wouldn't take a dime from, like beer distributors."

Jay Perry was a smart campaign manager. In the circumstances, he wisely made a few rules of his own.

"I'd go to a guy we'd done something for and tell him, 'We need some money. Can you help us out with $2,000?' "

The fellow would agree and then Jay told him the rest.

"I'll need a list of 20 names to go with your donation," Jay explained. "Mike won't take more than $100 from one person, so tell everyone whose name you give me they donated $100 to Monroney's campaign."

Usually the system worked, Mike none the wiser. But once Jay got caught accepting billboards from a beer distributor.

"I had this beer distributor friend who liked Mike," said Jay. "Didn't want anything, just to help.

" 'Tell me how many boards Mike needs in my territory and I'll get 'em for you,' he offered. How could I turn him down?"

Jay ordered paper for those boards and a couple weeks later

they were up. Not long after, in the hot summer, Mike and Jay were driving into Lawton and spotted one of Mike's new billboards.

"The sun was setting, shining bright against that billboard," Jay recalled. "I almost dropped my teeth because the outline of a beer bottle and several letters from the word Falstaff were bleeding through the paper."

"Where'd you get that billboard?" Mike demanded to know, face getting red.

"Uh, we got boards from the auto dealers," Jay softly replied, looking straight ahead.

"You know damn well, Jay, there's no Falstaff auto dealer in Lawton," Mike shot back.

"He had me," Jay concluded, "but after the '40's, that hundred dollar limit stuff and being fussy about who we'd take billboards from didn't get the job done."

Mike Monroney went to Washington and Congress the first time with but two assistants, Vi Lesch and John Burns. These two were highly capable and did it all for Monroney. Go look at your Congressman's office today. You'll find it overflowing with aides who are mostly 365-days-a-year campaigners, paid to do whatever it takes to keep Mr. Congressman in office.

With all those campaign people, in Washington and at home, plus the solid gold franking privilege to boot, no wonder only an occasional too honest Congressman or Senator ever gets beat. More quit out of disgust with the system than lose.

I think it was good Mike lost when he did. His health was beginning to fail. It's doubtful he could have held up a full term. Defeat gave him a few years of deserved easy going.

"When I first came to the House, I blamed my inexperience for the fact it was difficult to consider legislation properly due to so many distractions," said Mike in later years. "After awhile I realized Congress was so organized and operated under such outmoded procedures we couldn't properly handle the day's needs."

Mike hit Congress running in 1939, determined to change the world, starting with Congress. Of course that Congressional world remains the same, only more so, in spite of Mike's valiant effort to streamline its snail's pace operation and self-serving actions.

Mike was able to get rid of many quill pen customs in the Congress of his day. Media people thought so highly of his efforts, in 1945 Mike was awarded the *Colliers* Congressional Award. With it went a $10,000 cash payment, which Mike promptly gave to help found the Episcopalian Casady School in north Oklahoma City.

"He is known among his colleagues as a politically courageous man, energetic and faithful to the tasks assigned him," they said of Mike at the award presentation. "He is a man who will stick his neck out whenever the occasion requires a bold stand."

Less than a year after he got this prestigious award, voters of Oklahoma's 5th district came within a hair of turning their famous son out of office for sticking his neck out, fighting the special interests.

World War II had just ended. Americans one and all were happily welcoming back from the battlefields their noble sons and daughters. Mike's election problem was caused by his bull-headed vote "against free enterprise" and for price controls.

I got out of the army after four years in 1946 and remember how it was. Those of us who went in at $21 a month and shot craps honestly came out broke, and often with a new family to support.

The big needs we had were a job, a house to live in, a new suit, white dress shirt and some kind of rattletrap car. Uncle Sam said we were entitled to $20 a week for a year, or until we landed jobs. The 52-20 Club we called it. But if you're not into begging, going to a welfare office every couple weeks to sign up for a handout is hard on your pride. Most of us went to work doing something after three or four weeks.

All that saved Mike in his '46 race against Republican Carmon Harris was a small block of votes from the few veterans who had managed to register. I guarantee we vets favored price controls, being buyers short of funds.

But some important people who got rich keeping their hands in Uncle Sam's pockets during the war were enjoying the warm rush that satisfying uncontrolled greed brings. They angrily demanded "Socialist Monroney" start waving the flag of free enterprise and opposing price controls.

Real estate people, meat packers, car dealers, clothiers and other merchants were big into under-the-table bribes if you wanted to buy their short-supply products. I favor free enterprise but oppose rape, which is what was going on.

Monroney stuck by price controls but barely escaped with his life, 47,173 votes to 43,508 for Carmon Harris. Harris was a fine man and later outstanding judge. I suspect his financial backers handed him his red hot "Dump Monroney and price controls" issue.

After that squeaker, the thought entered Monroney's mind he might be smart to lift his eggs out of the undependable Oklahoma City Chamber of Commerce's basket by running for the U. S. Senate, where he could breathe a few non-political breaths four years out of six.

Popular and rich wartime governor Bob Kerr was finishing

his term and had his eye and bankroll zeroed in on the seat held by first-termer Republican "accident," E. H. Moore. So Mike began thinking about 1950 and Senator Elmer Thomas, whom the wise pundits said was "too firmly entrenched" to lose to anyone.

Monroney decided to have a look anyway.

"He had all those young OU alumni for him so one day in '49 he came by and told me he'd like to check it out," Mike's campaign manager, Jay Perry, told me. "We got into my plane and took a 3-day tour of the state, talking to Mike's fraternity brothers who came out to the local airports to meet us."

"Who's Senator Thomas's campaign manager here?" was Mike's first question.

" 'Used to be so-and-so' was the answer we got a lot," Jay recalled, " 'but he died last year.' Or they'd say, 'He moved away;' or 'He's gettin' old and really doesn't do anything. Turns it over to others.' "

After hitting half the airports in Oklahoma with little sleep for 72 hours, Mike and Jay came back to Oklahoma City punch drunk but believing Elmer Thomas was a paper tiger. His organization was strong on paper, weak in the field.

As happened to Mike 18 years later, Senator Thomas and friends had gotten older, less hungry.

"We got back to my house and, first thing, Mike calls Mary Ellen in Washington," said Jay. "First she'd heard about it.

" 'What! Are you drunk, Mike?' was Mary Ellen's reaction. 'Let me talk to Jay.'

"So I got on and told her it was gonna be like painting a mule with a toothbrush because we didn't have a nickle for the campaign but we figured Thomas's organization was non-existent and Mike's friends could do better.

" 'Oh, my goodness,' Mary Ellen finally said; thinking, I'm sure, about the grind ahead."

Those days you campaigned on the courthouse square, at the fairgrounds and from the back of a pickup. TV was just being born in Oklahoma, so folks would still come out and crowd around for the entertainment and speaking.

WKY-TV in Oklahoma, where I worked, had been on the air only a few months. I did Oklahoma's first TV election broadcast from the *Daily Oklahoman* newsroom during that campaign. My boss, Bruce Palmer, turned the TV act over to me and Mark Weaver so he could do the more important commentary on WKY radio.

I was new in town and a little nervous doing my first ever TV election show. A little old guy kept coming up to me at every break, when I was trying to think what to say next, asking all kinds of questions. It was irritating. After the third or fourth time, I was giving this little guy hostile looks and short, quit-bothering-me answers.

Finally, at the next commercial break, I went to where Palmer was doing his radio stuff and asked, "Who the hell is this joker coming onto the set asking me dumb questions? He's driving me nuts and I'm gonna get rid of him."

"I wouldn't," Bruce cautioned. "That's E. K. Gaylord. He owns the place."

I'll say this for Gaylord. He was a hard guy to insult.

Our TV show was all ad lib, about as sophisticated as Mike Monroney's campaign. Mike and Jay had rounded up three cars, a pickup and flatbed truck to put their show on the road.

One car, with loudspeaker, went ahead blaring out music and announcing "entertainment stars" on the way and also "that great U.S. Senate candidate, Mike Monroney."

Two major appearances daily in larger towns were standards, noon and night, plus stops at all the puddle-jumper places in between. They had a lady playing an organ mounted on their flatbed truck.

Pat Brogan, a wonderful Irishman from the old country who became an Oklahoma City attorney, was a dedicated Sure, Mike! lover who became chief handyman and trouble-shooter on the campaign trail. He was in charge of solving solveable problems and burying the unsolveable. Last I saw Pat, his proudest possession was still the solid gold watch Mike presented him for his loyal efforts on the Senator's behalf.

Mike ran the identical campaign against "unbeatable" Elmer Thomas in 1950 that Henry Bellmon resurrected to blow away Mike in 1968. Both were campaigns of Seniority and Pork vs. A Fresh Start.

"If you want to continue getting benefits in dams, power and irrigation, as well as Oklahoma military and other establishments, vote for me," urged Thomas. "If you don't want these things, vote for my opponent.

"Oklahoma has gotten $1-billion in federal benefits during my years in the Senate because I have seniority as head of the Senate Agriculture Committee and chairman of the Military Affairs Subcommittee."

Monroney and voters countered with the same age-old question Bellmon and voters asked Mike 18 years later, "What have you done for us lately?"

"Under the seniority system," Mike harangued a Muskogee crowd June 1, 1950, "accident and chance have placed the nation's destiny in weak hands. Yes, seniority counts but in Senator Thomas's case, it counts Oklahoma out."

Mike declared Thomas's proposal for an $825-million

Arkansas River project would require digging 650 miles of canal, "mostly on dry land and sand bars."

"It would be easier," Mike added, appropriating a Will Rogers remark, "to pave it."

Maybe Mike's best issue was Thomas's friendship with utility companies and lack of enthusiasm for Rural Electric Cooperatives. I've been in enough Corporation Commission races to know utilities aren't worth shooting until the election's over. That's when they and their attorneys work their wiles. You can forget 'em until the election's over.

But the Duke Coopers and Czar Langstons of Oklahoma have always spilled blood on the campaign trail for REA favorites.

"You can't be an errand boy for the utilities in their fight against REC's and remain in the Senate," was a line in every Monroney speech.

Like all outsiders trying to get in, Mike demanded Thomas debate him on radio-TV.

"It has been my policy never to pay attention to what my opposition says," was Thomas's predictable answer.

Biggest thing going for Mike was popularity with the media. I was working news and special events in the Gaylord vineyard at brand new Channel 4 and WKY radio in Oklahoma City and was for former reporter Monroney, same as every newsman I knew.

Naturally, we were all impartial but Thomas kept insisting we weren't. This poor attitude hurt his campaign. He failed to realize the media, when you're scrounging for votes, is never wrong.

In desperation, Thomas prevailed upon an old fire-eater, former Congressman Gomer Smith, to go on radio to undress

Mike and the media. Ol' Gomer talked about "Monroney's millionaire wife and her society soirees."

"A soiree," Gomer stormed, "is a fancy word for cocktail party, for which the Monroneys are famous in Washington. Mike is also the darling of news columnists, big magazine publishers and parlor-pinks.

"If Monroney becomes Senator, scandalmongers of press and radio will have won an election and a Senator and Oklahoma will have lost a Senator. It seems all newspapermen look upon themselves as a special class. They think their intelligence superior to that of the ordinary man."

I have yet to meet anyone who doesn't consider his intelligence superior to the ordinary man and I guarantee there were none with such modesty among we members of the Oklahoma media. Still aren't. Of course we remained neutral and impartial, as always, but somehow all the good Monroney quotes got printed, balanced by dumb Thomas replies.

Could we help it if Thomas made a few less than brilliant comments? Which is why I always say, I'll trade you the publishers and editorial writers, plus 50,000 extra votes, if you'll give me the working media. With them I'll beat you to death every time.

Believe me, Virginia, the media writes nice Santa Claus things about those they admire.

"I kidded Mike about making 1,200 speeches in that Primary," laughed Jay. "Mike said it was one speech made 1,200 times, which is nearer the truth."

But Mike's speech was good. They sneaked up on an overconfident Thomas. He didn't know what was happening until too late. Mike led Thomas in the 1950 primary by 14,653 votes. Which meant deep trouble for Senator Thomas in the runoff.

"We woke up leading the next morning all right," Jay reminisced, "but didn't have two dimes to rub together. So we called Coach McNeil to see what he'd recommend."

H. W. McNeil had a lingo all his own and called everyone "Coach," hence his nickname. The barrel-chested and lovable McNeil, Floyd Gibson and Duke Cooper of Stillwater, head honcho of the REC's, and Fred Boston of Enid were four of Monroney's stalwarts in that campaign. Gov. Roy Turner was also for Mike and McNeil was never hesitant to use the power of the chief executive's office, where possible, in Mike's behalf.

While McNeil was figuring out how to raise money for the runoff, Jay borrowed $2,000 from Bill Atkinson to pay a few bills the first days of the runoff. By then McNeil had some things going.

There was a nameless fellow in Washington who was in charge of selling off surplus war assets.

"Coach told the guy we had a chance to elect a good Senator and got his help," Jay remembered. "Mike, of course, would have opposed taking money from people buying war assets, so we didn't tell him. It was too fine a source of funds to let Mike shut it off."

I worked with Coach McNeil in a couple campaigns and he had the sweetest campaign temperament I've seen. He croaked like a frog when talking and used Damon Runyon language but his tolerance of the cynical hustlers infesting every campaign was Christ-like.

Coach's tolerance was not matched by equal trust in his fellow man, however. First thing McNeil suggested was getting Senator Thomas shadowed. He wanted to know where the Senator was getting his money. Thomas was big dog on the Senate Agriculture Committee and reportedly played the commodities market, where he might have had inside information.

Thomas took off for New York and Wall Street right after the primary, then headed for Chicago where he spent a couple days around the commodities markets.

"Elmer just came through Chicago and he's got a bundle under his arm that doesn't look like a teakettle," is how McNeil described the Senator's travels.

Thomas got himself funded and so did Mike. But half Thomas's campaign organization went on vacation during the runoff.

"The primary election was July 4 that year," Jay recalled. "So when Thomas paid off his primary campaign people, I'll bet some didn't even vote. They loaded up Ma and the kids to take a little vacation."

Mike had the virgins and Thomas the dancehall girls. Virgins are overrated in bed but best for campaigning. Most of Mike's OU alumni friends had never been in a campaign before. They were young, energetic, clean and highly respected. They had no better sense than to work their heads off, for nothing.

So it came out Monroney, 240,432; Thomas, 213,665.

Nomination meant election for the Democratic nominee those days, except in the case of Monroney. A smart, handsome and silver-tongue redheaded preacher, Rev. Bill Alexnder, talked to the Lord one night and the Lord told him early to run for the U.S. Senate. So he said.

At the time of his conversation with what you might consider a campaign manager to outdo even Coach McNeil, Rev. Alexander was a Democrat. But some of Alexander's main backers were Republican and he changed his registration to GOP.

God may have asked him to run but I doubt if He asked Alexander to turn Republican, being an Independent Himself.

Bill Alexander was a spellbinder on the campaign trail, a charming and decent man. But he knew more about religion than politics. I remember he went over to the eastside in Oklahoma City with his Negro maid and had her testify publicly in his behalf. Not many Negroes, as blacks were then known, took pride in one of their own being elevated to the high post of maid for Rev. Alexander.

Another thing Bill didn't understand was that Baptist preachers and those of other denominations also talk to God. God rarely tells them who to vote for but most preachers I've known come away with the definite impression He doesn't want them going outside their own camp of True Believers.

If Rev. Alexander got any endorsements from preachers outside his own First Christian Church group, it was a secret.

Senator Bob Kerr wasn't crazy about Monroney beating Elmer Thomas. Bob was a practical businessman seeking pork to bring home, Mike an idealistic reformer. But in the general election Kerr took his Baptist teaching to the stump with a vengeance against Rev. Bill Alexander.

"I guess you all heard," Kerr shouted to campaign crowds, "The Lord told Bill Alexander to run when he was a Democrat. We all know the Lord doesn't make mistakes, so who you suppose it was told Bill to run as a Republican?"

Had to be the devil himself. A lot of religion talked during that campaign but not much practiced. In Little Dixie's Baptist Bible Belt, someone put out a throwaway claiming Episcopalian Mike Monroney was a roaring Roman Catholic. Episcopalians wear their collars backward, too, and are naturally suspect but not so much as a preacher of *any* denomination but

Baptist. They'd take Episcopalian Mike over the First Christian preacher any day.

If Bill Alexander hadn't been a preacher, he might have won that race because he had talent and charisma to burn, plus a lot of disenchanted Thomas Democrats. He also had well-heeled backers, Democratic and Republican, including the money crowd in Oklahoma City — C. R. Anthony, Babe Eddie, Frank Buttram and many more with proud bank balances.

Rev. Alexander also had the Republican *Tulsa Tribune* in his corner. Tribune political writer George Dixon gave wide Oklahoma distribution to a piece by a Washington society reporter that really scorched Mike, although meant to be friendly.

Evelyn Peyton Gordon was the society ace for Scripps-Howard, Monroney's old employer. She did a glowing piece about Mike and Mary Ellen which Dixon gleefully pounced on.

"Mike Monroney, the doughty Congressman from Oklahoma, has the Senate job in the bag," she started off, two months before the election.

The *Tribune* figured Oklahoma voters would be glad to know the Washington society crowd had already elected Mike.

The story went on about Mary Ellen's stylish clothes, designed to make a hit with Oklahoma farm women who still had a few depression-days feed sack dresses in their closets. The fancy writin' lady gushed about "The Monroney's pine-paneled recreation room, which stretches under the library and drawing room," a comment popular with all Oklahoma voters possessing formal home libraries and drawing rooms. Must have been 50 such, all Republicans.

For a touch of real elegance, the lady noted that Mary

Ellen's mother was a Mellon (of the multi-millionaire Mellons) and Mary Ellen had become a famous Washington breeder of snooty West Highland white terriers. Their kennels were pictured as more plush than most Oklahoma homesteads.

The Tribune saved the lady's best comment for a kicker.

"The Monroney highball and cocktail glasses," this society writer friend of Mike's said snootily, "are all marked with the heads of former champion West Highland terriers. So are their cocktail napkins and all their bar equipment."

In bone-dry Oklahoma, where voters would then consign you to hell faster for taking a drink than murder, these vital statistics about the Monroney's drinking gear were well received in two or three of our lowest-life bootlegger-owned pool halls. Elsewhere I'd say it wasn't much help to Mike's campaign.

But the *Tulsa Tribune* alone against the rest us media nonpartisans favoring Mike wasn't enough for Bill Alexander. That plus the fact he touted a different church than most Oklahomans favored, placing him on the wrong road to salvation, cut the preacher's political career short — Monroney, 345,953; Alexander, 285,224.

But in a different time and circumstance, plain Bill Alexander, without a prefix to his name, would have been one tough dude to beat.

For the next 18 years, Monroney served in the Senate and did as he pleased. He went in a liberal Democrat, came out the same. But his folks back home were growing conservative from partaking of unfamiliar prosperity.

They liked government handouts Oklahoma was getting in greater share than most. They liked the fact Oklahoma paid less federal taxes than we got back in goodies from our then powerful delegation in Congress. But they got to thinking their tax burden, even though less than a fair share, was still too much.

They also wished Mike would quit being such a do-gooder.

Mike never took a poll to find out what he believed. So he got used to back-home criticism. His style was to educate Oklahoma voters about issues on which he and they differed.

Mike and Mary Ellen were favorites of President and Bess Truman. Mike liked Truman's frankness and willingness to take a stand on tough issues. Mike himself voted what he thought best for the nation instead of concentrating on dragging everything not nailed down back to Oklahoma. Some thought this attitude selfish. So he steadily lost favor with Oklahoma's money-changers.

There was something called Model Cities, forerunner of urban renewal, providing federal money to rebuild cities. Tulsa got in early and as a result created one of the finest downtowns in America. In Oklahoma City, E. K. Gaylord decided Model Cities was at least socialistic, maybe communism. The heat he and other Big Cigars generated was so intense Senator Fred Harris, the flaming liberal of high principles, changed his firmly made up mind and voted against Model Cities after reading Gaylord's editorials.

Not Mike. He let the flames crackle around him and voted what he believed. Later, of course, when Gaylord learned what urban renewal could do to upgrade his properties, he took a liking to these beneficial federal expenditures. But he didn't forget Mike had crossed him.

In 1964 I handled the campaign against so-called right-to-work, labor's side. Our view was popular as herpes with the media and chambers of commerce. Yet Mike Monroney came out flat-footedly against right-to-work. I was there when important people were giving him hell over it. He made me proud.

Most politicians, even though we had them on record opposing right-to-work, waffled and ducked when the issue got hot. Not Mike.

"I've always been against it," Mike said. So he lost important support which he never recaptured.

Mike believed everyone deserves decent medical care. Most doctors and editorial writers were against Mike's stand for medicare. Doctors didn't yet know how rich socialized medicine was going to make them. Were Mike in the Senate now, he'd still be fighting the Docs, this time trying to cut down on their overtreating and overcharging.

Mike was on the winning side of the battle to provide medicine to all who need it but that fight earned him more new enemies who lined up with Henry Bellmon.

When Vietnam got hot, President Johnson was in deep trouble. I was in Washington then, working on LBJ's reelection campaign, and I know many Democrats running in '68 shunned the president to take up the media's chant for getting out of Vietnam, even if it required abject surrender.

Again, not Mike.

"What LBJ has done for Oklahoma far outranks whatever Henry Bellmon can do," said Mike. "I'm especially grateful to him for one of the largest military payrolls and for completion of the Arkansas River project on schedule."

Mike didn't believe Jane Fonda, Ramsey Clark and the Washington-New York TV news stars were best qualified to decide the nation's foreign policy.

"I'm ashamed of them (the media)," declared Mike. "They

can't go into Hanoi to film enemy casualties. They film only one side of the war — our side, our casualties. If we move out, no power this side of heaven can stop total takeover of Asia."

Now the takeover is well underway and another takeover just like it is looming up ahead, right off our own shores in Central America. And not many Mike Monroneys around to speak out against those in our media and government hailing Moscow-supplied Castro and other hammer and sickle fighters south of our borders as "reformers."

Shortly before his '68 race, Mike did another courageous thing, although Mike considered it only proper. He came out in favor of a sizeable surtax to help pay for the Vietnam war.

"I'm all in favor of a tax increase," Mike admitted. "I've studied it for a year. Our economy is escalating and we need the tax to avoid inflation."

To pay war costs, Mike favored luxury taxes on whiskey, wines, fur coats, movies, night clubs, cigarettes and long-distance calls.

"Solving our problems will take time, patience and determination," Mike pointed out. "We had draft card burnings and uprisings just before World War II. A few months before Pearl Harbor, extension of the draft was approved with only one vote to spare."

It has always been thus; we, the people, listening to false prophets until amost too late. Next time it may be.

Back home in Oklahoma, the toll road lobby was strong as ever when Mike hollered his last hurrah in 1968. Yet Mike didn't bend a knee to them either.

When toll roads were born in the '50's, I was in the governor's office dishing out toll-road propaganda in behalf of both the Turner and Will Rogers turnpikes.

"It's not true," I remember saying for a TV commercial we made at the Turner Turnpike gate, "that this turnpike will never be paid off, as some are suggesting. The law is ironclad; once the bonds are paid, this will be a free road forever after."

I was lying. When Raymond Gary became governor and we got some straight information about toll roads, it was obvious building toll roads is the worst possible way to furnish highways. You pay a double load in added fees and other costs, many hidden.

Toll roads are bright and shining stars for bond dealers, lawyers and consulting engineers. Consulting engineer and toll road czar Harry Baily got wealthy in a hurry building Oklahoma's turnpikes.

Monroney knew this. He also knew his opponent, Henry Bellmon, while governor, permitted the state to back down on its solemn word the Turner Turnpike would be a free road the minute its initial bonds were paid off. Which made liars out of a bunch of people besides me.

Henry once said each toll road "must stand on its own bottom." But later he got acquainted with Harry Bailey and it was arranged for the two bell cows of the toll road system — the Will Rogers and Turner Turnpikes — to be remortgaged to the tune of $188-million. The money went to build new toll roads which could no way stand on their own bottoms.

"A holdup," is the way Mike described this deal. He said it would end up costing $268-million to attain $61.9-million in new capital.

Mostly folks yawned. They're used to paying high dollar for such low value political deals.

Looking back, you tell me if Mike was much wrong on the issues. Or was it those who voted him out for taking honest stands where others ducked?

Sure, Mike!   295

By 1968 Mike was way too liberal for Oklahoma. He was also too honest for Oklahoma voters. They didn't understand the pure gold value of honesty in a politician, even when he disagrees with you.

So Mike's time had come.

They tried to modernize Mike's last campaign. Until then, his boyhood best buddy, Jay Perry, was Mike's closest campaign confidante. Jay handled the money, flew Mike around in his plane and kept Mike's schedule.

"They got a brain trust in '68," Jay complains. "Figured Mike was in trouble so they brought in outside geniuses who turned out to be useful as mares in a mule barn."

I know what Jay's talking about. In every major campaign these days, you wind up with what I call The Camel Committee. A camel, of course, is a horse created by a committee.

Trouble with The Camel Committee, those honored to serve on it feel this strong obligation to demonstrate brilliance in the fields where they are Know Nothings. They change things just enough to screw 'em up. Unless you have strong jockeys preventing The Camel Committee's nose from getting too far inside the campaign tent, you end up with everything bastardized, at double cost.

Still I don't think you can blame Mike's Camel Committee for losing to Bellmon. Give Henry Bellmon a big chunk of the credit. He's maybe the shrewdest politician who ever hit Oklahoma.

His red hot Panama Canal Treaty vote nearly set the *Daily Oklahoman* on fire. It also made Henry the darling to this day of our far-left Democrats. If Henry enters another campaign, the American Civil Liberties Union crowd will be marching shoulder to shoulder with the Eddie Gaylords of Oklahoma, singing "We Shall Overcome" in Henry's behalf.

Carter Bradley, former United Press International head in Oklahoma and later a Bob Kerr advisor, was Monroney's administrative assistant his last years in office, and during Mike's final campaign.

"Lot's of things happened to us," Carter told me. "For one, Mike's health was starting to fail. He was getting tired.

"Mike was basically religious. He didn't approve all those subsidies being handed out to business under the label, Helping Free Enterprise."

Mike's brain trust had lined up young Bill Holloway, son of the former governor, to generate Volunteers for Monroney.

"Then a federal judgeship opened and damn if Mike doesn't recommend Holloway for it," said Bradley, shaking his head. "That neutralized Holloway right quick. But getting his friend on the bench was more important to Mike than having Holloway rounding up money and votes for Mike.

"Mike always did put his beliefs and the people's welfare ahead of anything political. In the end, that's what got him."

I can't think of a better reason for getting beat.

There were tears shed by the Monroney faithful election night. Bradley, Larry Derryberry, DeVier Pearson, Mary Kay Foster, Carl Clark, David Busby, Joe Nobles, Mary Ann Harbison, Pat Brogan, Fred Boston and the rest didn't think it could happen like it did. Close maybe but not by 50,000 votes.

Jay Perry smelled it, however, and wasn't popular with The Camel Committee.

"I told my wife, Pat, 'I'm not going down there tonight and watch Mike get beat,' " Jay told me. "I knew from being with Mike, listening to the polite applause at business club meetings and the like, we were in bad trouble, especially in Oklahoma City and Tulsa."

Then Jay changed the subject, told me a story about Mike always forgetting people's names. Didn't spend the time he should stroking egoes.

I knew about Mike's poor memory for names. For years Wayne Mackey played Monroney in the Oklahoma City gridiron and most of that time Mike couldn't remember Mackey's name. This cut down on Wayne's sense of importance playing the important U.S. Senator role.

"He was like that with everyone," Jay laughed. "Handling Mike in a crowd was like leading a cow out of a herd. On his own, he'd finish working the crowd, then head back in again to say goodbye a second and third time."

Jay's job was that of lookout.

"I'd spot someone I knew Mike would want to talk to, tell Mike his name and any pertinent facts I thought he ought to know," Jay explained. "This one guy out in western Oklahoma had just lost his brother, so I whispered that to Mike.

" 'Well, hello,' says Mike solicitously, putting an arm around his shoulder. 'So sorry to hear about your brother. It's a darn shame."

A week later they meet the same guy at a district Monroney rally.

"Mike spots him first," Jay shook his head in the telling, "and rushes over to give him the glad hand and a big hello. First thing Mike asks the guy, 'How's your brother?'

"Clouds start forming on the fellow's face and his eyes get narrow. 'My brother's still dead, Mike,' he spits out, then walks away fast, mad as hell.

"It was his worst campaign fault but I never knew a man in or out of politics more conscientious, more devoted to his job. Never gave you watermelon conversation. Never told you he'd do something if he didn't think he could. Never."

Bellmon labeled Mike "Alibi Mike" and "wild-eyed spender."

"Henry's administration as governor looked good," Jay admitted. "He cut the ribbons and took credit for federal projects, then blamed Mike for the spending."

Mary Kay Foster, who now works for Gov. Nigh, has been around the horn in Oklahoma politics. Mary Kay is typical of Mike's longtime employees—capable, kind and helpful to one and all. She worked for Mike several years and for the Oklahoma Democratic Party before becoming Nigh's main gal for keeping his organization updated between elections.

"I didn't believe it, that they'd vote Senator Monroney out," said Mary Kay, eyes clouding over, recalling the 1968 election night. "He was just good. So sincere, maybe the best who ever served. I was always proud working for the Senator."

"I don't think any political turn of events will diminish the reputation, honesty and goodness of our senior United States Senator," Bill Kerr, State Democratic Chairman, told Mike's friends on the final sad election night.

"If you cry, I'll cry, so don't," said Alice, Mike's granddaughter, to a friend that same night.

A lot of people were holding wet handkerchiefs when Mike finally walked in, with his usual big grin.

"I hope because we ran into a downdraft, some turbulence and landed a little short of the runway you won't give up on Oklahoma politics," Mike told his friends. "I've had 30 marvelous years, for which I thank you. Now I've been relieved, I'm going to take off my shoes and see a little of the country."

Mike had a few good years after that. He came back to

Oklahoma City the last time February 14, 1980, two days after he died.

"I want to take him home," said Mary Ellen at the end.

As Mary Ellen stood waving goodbye, trying to smile through tears, a small yellow plane took off into a brisk wind over the FAA Center in Oklahoma City. Paul Odom was at the controls and Mike's best buddy, Jay Perry, sat beside him.

Within seconds a flapdown door on the plane's fuselage opened and Jay held up a brown leather box containing his best friend's ashes. He watched as Mike's ashes were sucked up and out to mingle with air and earth above and around the national aeronautical center which Mike, "Mr. Aviation," had brought to Oklahoma.

They said nice things about Mike that day.

"He was the same in Oklahoma and at home as in the halls of Congress," stated son, John Michael. "His innate gentleness and warmth of character were apparent above all. He had faith in the Democratic system and faith in his code of ethics, which he never broke."

"He was a self-confident man of principle who wouldn't bend his principles to reach goals," put in DeVier Pierson. "He was without ego in a calling where men with ego are not an endangered species."

I see Mike now, tall and slender with blue eyes twinkling, crinkled at the corners from much smiling.

"I'm not liberal and I'm not conservative," I remember Mike saying once. "The liberals won't have me, nor the conservatives. I've always just followed my nose."

Which is a pretty good road map if you want to get somewhere.

Sure, Mike!

20

GOOD GUY, GOOD GOVERNOR

When a man assumes a public trust, he should consider himself as public property.

Thomas Jefferson

That nice kid from McAlester who cut the widest swath ever in Oklahoma politics knew when he was delivering groceries to Carl Albert's back door that one day he would reach for the brass ring — governor of Oklahoma.

He wasn't sure he could grab it but was gonna try. Nobody worked harder to get there than George Nigh. Nobody had a better helper than Donna. They're a team nobody could beat.

At this writing in 1983 I hear it said, "George won't quit now. It's too deep in his blood. He'll run against Don Nickles or something, you watch."

He'll fool me if he does. I've known George since he was the youngest to hit the Oklahoma legislature in 1951, the year I became Gov. Johnston Murray's press secretary.

I've been with George in his every statewide race except one and never heard him express ambition for any office but governor. He's one of God's rare creatures who fulfilled his highest ambition, twice.

So I figure he'll quit ahead and happy. He has laurels enough to rest on.

You never really know another person deep down. I guess Paul Carris knows George Nigh better than anyone, being the same best buddy today he was when they were kids together.

"Paul Carris was literally my best friend from birth," George now says. "We lived a block and a half from each other and did everything together. His mother was my mother's nurse when my older brother was born. Our parents ran around together. We were in the same grade, enlisted in the navy together, best man at each other's wedding. To this day we're still that close."

If anyone knows George it's Carris, now George's eyes and ears on the Oklahoma Racing Commission. I can tell you Paul Carris was never surprised by any of his best friend's accomplishments. Neither am I. There's more behind Gov. Nigh's pleasant countenance than Eddie Gaylord suspects.

If George and Eddie Gaylord started even in any contest under the sun, I guarantee George would win. You suppose that's why Eddie can't stand him?

I was with George in Hollywood long ago when he was Oklahoma's official representative at the movie premier of *Oklahoma!* I remember my wife, Helen, telling him to go rent a tuxedo. He was a State Representative but looked more like the college cheerleader he had been only a couple years before.

The master of ceremonies got mixed up and billed him as "Senator George Nigh of Oklahoma." Those movie people were amazed Oklahomans would elect "such a young U. S. Senator." Of course George was years short of being able to even qualify for the job.

During a radio network broadcast, George interrupted his interviewer to explain he wasn't really a U. S. Senator, only State Representative. But I kinda think he liked the title and I know that trip, his peek at the tinsel and shine of Hollywood's land of make-believe, didn't lessen his political ambition.

Hollywood stars and important politicians aren't that far apart. Both get catered to and imposed upon a lot. They also thrive on center stage.

George carried off the *Oklahoma!* premier in fine shape, for himself and Oklahoma. I think he came home with confidence his dream of someday becoming governor could come true. He had the basic ingredients — parents who taught him right from wrong, training in Little Dixie's school of higher education politics, firm determination and perfect political temperament.

There were several key turning points in George's outstanding career. More than once he was ready to throw in the towel on his dream. Had Gov. David Boren run for reelection instead of the U. S. Senate, I'm convinced Nigh's political career would have ended right there. He wasn't ready to remain a life-long Lt. Governor. He could do far better on the knife and fork circuit as a speaker-entertainer, leaving the aggravations of politics behind.

I think they breed politicians in southeast Oklahoma like race horses in Kentucky. George Nigh is such a born politician. He knows anything can happen in a horse or political race. He knows you must be the right horse or person in the right place at the right time to win. That's what makes it exciting.

"As long as I've ever thought about what I wanted to be, it's always been governor," says George. "When I was in Junior High, before TV, my folks wouldn't let me stay up late to hear the Republican and Democratic conventions on radio. Those days they sometimes went on all night, without recess.

"So I'd arrange to stay with my grandmother, who'd let me do anything. I'd listen to the convention proceedings far into the night. Fun to me."

Nigh's first campaign was as Youth for Tom Haile leader in a Pittsburg County judge race. George organized a bicycle parade for Haile.

"I was 13 or 14," George remembers, "and we decorated our

bikes with crepe paper and cardboard held onto the spokes by clothespins. About 40 of us kids, me chairman. The crepe paper was pretty and the cardboard clickety-clicked as we rode our bikes around. My candidate won!" George laughed happily.

His heroes were politicians and some movie stars, especially Oklahoman Will Rogers who, with his common man humor, represented we, the people, well against the over-privileged. George listened to Franklin Roosevelt's fireside chats and counted him his hero then, but passing time has elevated Harry Truman to that spot.

"Roosevelt was a great motivator, could move people through his speeches," said George. "Back then, coming out of the depression, I thought Roosevelt was everyone's hero.

"But when Truman became president, I became a strong admirer because of his courage in making decisions. I think history will record Roosevelt an outstanding president, Truman a great president. Truman's my hero now."

Will Rogers is George's all-time Oklahoma hero. He can recite every detail of what happened on a street in Colorado Springs in 1935, the day word came Will Rogers had gone down with Wiley Post off Point Barrow, Alaska.

I remember exactly where I was, who with and what I was doing when I heard Kennedy was shot, when VJ Day came and when the anti-Vietnam kooks tried to take over my office at the wild Democratic Convention of '68 in Chicago. George has the same graphic recall about when he learned of Will Rogers' death.

"I remember it for two reasons," George says. "One, it was the first time dad ever went with us on vacation. We didn't have much money and dad worked hard, so when we took a

Good Guy, Good Governor

trip dad could never go. This time he did.

"That day was the first time I saw a traffic jam. We went to buy donuts and traffic completely stopped. People were getting out of their cars, standing there crying. Newsboys were hollering, 'Extra, extra, read all about it. Will Rogers killed.'

"I've never forgotten that day nor what Will Rogers meant to Oklahoma and the world. As an eight year old boy it never crossed my mind that many years later, as Lt. Governor, I'd be national co-chairman along with movie actor Joel McCray, of the celebration honoring the 100th anniversary of Will Rogers' birth.

"A lot of water went under the bridge for this little boy, believe me, between 1935 and the occasion of Will Rogers' 100th anniversary celebration."

George Nigh always has heroes. He's seen most of what's to see but he's not cynical like most people in politics and the media. He's upbeat, positive, striving to make things better. Sometimes he succeeds.

That's because he never lost sight of his star. His nickname was "Senator" in high school. The fake Gypsy seer with bandana and upside-down goldfish bowl before her, giving the class prophecy, announced dramatically, "I see George Nigh has just been elected President of the United States (pause) Street Cleaners Association."

When he came back from the navy and folks asked what he would do next, "Go to college and run for office," was George's reply. He started with pre-law, "because I thought you had to be a lawyer to succeed in politics." He found out there were already too many political lawyers, so changed his mind and, when a senior at East Central University, Ada, filed for the House of Representative in McAlester.

He ran his campaign by commuting to rallies on week-ends until graduation in June, 1950. The first primary that year was July 4 and George got to celebrate his first election victory.

George and his campaign crew were all in their early 20's during this campaign, doing their darndest to look like 30. His crew chief was Paul Carris. Others included Joe Gravitt, Quentin Mantooth and Howard McGee. All were still in school or just graduating.

"Dad was an old farm boy who had a neighborhood grocery store," George related. "He convinced me no one trusted anyone who didn't wear a hat. It was 1950 and men wore hats. So we all went out and bought cheap straw dress hats, short-sleeve shirts and ties. Went to all the rallies with these dumb looking hats on. It was terrible!"

What I think came through to Pittsburg County voters was, here are some trustworthy young guys of serious mien wanting one of their own to pick up the torch of conformity and carry on the best traditions of what, up to then, at least, was the world's greatest democracy. It wasn't until after George went to the legislature the next January that he found out his dad was registered Republican.

"I didn't know what my parents were," George explained. "Didn't know I was supposed to be either a Democrat or Republican. I just chose to be a Democrat."

Which of course was the only sensible choice in Pittsburg County. George also got his dad switched.

George's mother and dad were "salt of the earth" people. They worked hard, prayed hard and demanded integrity of their kids. I asked George what traits he got from his folks.

"Fairness. My folks were fair," George said first. "Dad worked hard as any man I've known. I work hard.

"From my mother, sense of humor. Dad couldn't tell or catch onto a joke. Mother had a joke for every occasion, jovial. Neither was interested in politics. Our only family politician was a Republican uncle."

George favors his mother. His timing with a joke is that of a master comedian. He can ad lib one-liners faster and better than some big time comics. If you don't think he inherited his dad's capacity for work, try following him a couple days.

George cleared his first hurdle to the governor's chair when he decided to leave the House after eight years. Like most things in life, the decision was forced on him. He was trapped as a teacher in one school, no option to move anywhere else without giving up his House seat.

In those more sensible days, before we, the people, lost our minds and changed it, the legislature met only three months every two years. So George could teach one full school year and half another before taking leave of absence to be a legislator.

George didn't aspire to House leadership. He was shooting for bigger things. His most memorable act as a legislator was getting Rodgers and Hammerstein to permit use of the theme song from *Oklahoma!* as Oklahoma's state song.

After eight years, George had to either spit or get off the spot. He had chances to become a principal or superintendent but not in his home district. So at 30 he decided to let Oklahoma voters make up his mind what to do next. He filed for Lt. Governor and everybody said he didn't have a prayer.

"I decided it was time to either be in politics or education, not both," George explained.

In this campaign he faced a tougher task than picking out a hat. 77 counties is a lot of territory to cover without a horse and no money for a train ticket, which was George's situation.

Every Nigh campaign is based on friendship. There were no paid workers in George's 1958 Lt. Governor race against the famous Cowboy Pink Williams. Those straw hat boys of his House race got into the saddle again and his family played a big role. So did some Jaycees, his students and the Young Democrats George had served as president.

Bob Bartheld, now a dentist, and a lot of folks in Pittsburg County, led by Bill Edwards, can also take bows for this Nigh miracle. The same with Bob Scarbrough, Jim Hazenbeck and Ted Bonham. I also recall Raymond Gary his last days as governor telling the State Democratic Party to give George a little money when he got past the primary.

We spent it for TV spots David Hudson, Larry Frazier and I put together with rubber bands one crazy midnight in Larry's recording studio.

Nigh couldn't get publicity in the primary. He wasn't news because everyone knew Cowboy Pink had it sacked up. So George decided to hold a Nigh campout on the capitol grounds.

"I was an unknown school teacher without a chance but I had a brother, Wib, bus agent in McAlester, who owned a bus himself," said George. "Brother Sam managed our one-person office in McAlester and brother Bill, who worked for the Katy Railroad in Texas, came home week-ends to campaign with my folks and sister, Mary.

"After school Friday we'd load Wib's bus and go to some new part of the state—family, students and McAlester towns-people—to campaign. But we got no statewide publicity. I decided the only way to break into the big media was round up a busload of kids with pup tents, sleeping bags or whatever and to camp out on the capitol grounds.

"It worked. TV and newspapers came out and took pictures

of us pitching tents, building fires, having fun. I got noticed for the first time. People started telling me they'd vote for a teacher who could get his students working like that."

At the heart of this first Lt. Governor campaign was just one guy really believing George might win, George himself. Polls were predicting Cowboy Pink in a runaway.

Pink Williams got famous and defeated Jim Berry, who served 20 years as Lt. Governor, by sending out a postcard poking fun at Republican Secretary of Agriculture Ezra Taft Benson, royally disliked in rural Oklahoma. Cowboy Pink's postcard featured a donkey, or ass, with a caption urging voters to kick their own asses for voting Republican.

Not everyone considered it funny. They thought Pink a character, which he was, but a shrewd and plenty smart money-making businessman.

Republicans who hated him elected Pink by needling the postal department into bringing vague charges against him for circulating what they claimed was "an indecently captioned picture on a postal card." This silly complaint succeeded only in getting Williams tons of publicity, causing Oklahoma voters to go laughingly to the polls and electing Pink, the ass-kicker, by more than 100,000 votes over Stillwater banker Jim Berry, who everyone figured would die in office.

The ass-kicking joke got worn a little thin after four years and George thought he could win if he got in a runoff. He figured it right.

He sneaked into the runoff with 80,000 votes to 176,000 for Williams. Everyone was congratulating George for making the runoff, while consoling him for his certain upcoming defeat. No one believed he could overcome Cowboy Pink's massive lead.

"There were 11 in that primary and George Norvell of Tulsa and Neville Kerr of Muskogee got more votes combined than I did," George explained. "Almost all votes not for Cowboy Pink were against him.

"That three weeks of the runoff we really put together an organization. Joe Johnson, former state president of the Jaycees, had advised me against running, saying I didn't have a ghost of a chance. He was in Texas, refused to come home to help.

"At 3:00 in the morning the day after the first primary, there was a knock on my door at the Biltmore Hotel. It was Joe Johnson.

" 'I've come to give you three weeks of my life,' " said Joe. "Joe was a mainstay in putting together my runoff campaign. I at last became an item the press would cover and we took the momentum. In three weeks I went from 100,000 votes behind to 111,000 votes ahead."

I've been in enough campaigns with George Nigh to get well acquainted with the Good Fairy watching over him. His Good Fairy was waving her wand wildly in both the runoff and general elections of 1958.

It was Howard Edmondson against Bill Atkinson in the Democratic runoff for governor and George vs. Cowboy Pink. Edmondson's people didn't want elderly, Old Guard Pink Williams on the ticket. They were saying, "Vote for two fine young men."

Atkinson's people tried to offset this appeal by saying, "Mature and experienced Atkinson and young Nigh will be a balanced team." George got the best of both worlds, each camp in the governor's race favoring him.

In the general election, George's Good Fairy performed a

true miracle. Even his Republican opponent, George B. Sherritt, wound up voting for Nigh.

"I went to a rally on Tishomingo's Main Street and my opponent, who was mayor, introduced me," George recalls. "I didn't know he was the Republican Lt. Governor candidate until Senator Joe Bailey Cobb told me. I couldn't believe the guy running against me would introduce me at a Democratic rally. As I was leaving he wished me luck. Not only that, he contributed to my campaign!

"Election day there was a letter in my mail from Mr. Sherritt. He said he wanted to be first to congratulate me and assure me I had his vote. Only reason he got in the race, he said, was to make sure Cowboy Pink got an opponent."

How's that for political planning and high strategy?

Before Nigh took over as Lt. Governor it was an office of small prestige and no duties. It was rare to find the office open. A typed card pasted on the door told the phone number of the man just a heartbeat away from becoming the state's chief executive, in case you wanted to get 'hold of him, which nobody did.

George thought he got elected to a job. When he learned he didn't, he went out and made one for himself. He took over the state's tourism promotion for one thing, making it into one of Oklahoma's biggest industries. Before he quit as Number 2, he brought the national Lt. Governors' Conference to the state, as he did the National Governors' Association after becoming governor.

He also made a few thousand speeches at high school graduations and to every civic, women's, men's and professional club you can find in Oklahoma. His easy manner and humorous master of ceremonies talents made him popular with

Lt. Governors, which now has made him big in the National Governors' Association, largely run by former Lt. Governors.

As Number 2, George had time to meet every Oklahoma newspaper publisher and radio-TV station manager. He made friends of most, got his picture in the paper a lot and these media friends came in handy when he tried jumping his bggest hurdle of all.

After Senator Bob Kerr died and Howard Edmondson resigned as governor so Lt. Governor Nigh could appoint him to the vacancy, George demonstrated his strong desire to become governor on his own. He was governor only nine days but made good use of his time. Since he was single then, George rattled around in that big mansion like one pea pod in a huge iron pot.

"So I invited my staff in for a couple nights," said George. "I think there were seven, plus my family, including nieces and nephews, for a slumber party. After the slumber party, we held open house. I'll never forget it!

"That one Sunday I was governor we scheduled the open house from 1:00 to 5:00," George chuckled. "It was one of the coldest days of the year, way below freezing. The crowd was forming at 9:00 and by 11:00 I said, 'Open the gate, it's too cold to stand out there.' We were scheduled to close at 5:00 but didn't until 11:00.

"They estimated 10,000 people went through before we closed up. I shook hands with every single one. It was fun!"

The play of a man who might be thinking of running for governor himself.

But after 16 years as Lt. Governor and one try for the governor's chair in 1962 which failed, it began to look as 1978 approached that George Nigh's boyhood dream would die with him. I told you George's parents preached fairness. George had a rule: "I'll never run against an incumbent governor, regardless of party affiliation."

Dewey Bartlett ran for reelection so George bowed out. The same with David Hall. Both got beat but George still wouldn't change his tune.

"I wanted to be governor but was resigned to never getting there," says George. "Donna and I were even talking about things we might do instead. I wasn't going to undercut a governor I served as Lt. Governor."

Why not U. S. Senator?

"All my interest is Oklahoma," Nigh confesses. "I have great love for this state. It's my center, eye of my storm. Always has been. I'm not interested in national politics."

So George's Good Fairy whispered in David Boren's ear, "Why not leave that mean ol' legislature behind? Become a big statesman on the national scene." Boren smiled and replied, "Hey, good idea!" Next day George and Donna were on a dead run for the job offering free house rent.

Before going into the Nigh Good Guy campaign of '78, I must tell you about the 1953 Oklahoma legislative session, of which George was a part and helped make famous. Made up of ambitious World War II veterans, the '53 legislature provided more important political leaders for Oklahoma than any other session.

It produced two governors, Raymond Gary and George Nigh; a Lt. Governor, Nigh; State Treasurer, Bill Burkhart; State Auditor, Joe Bailey Cobb; Congressman, John N. "Happy" Camp; Leo Winters, House and Senate employee, became Chairman of State Election Board, State Treasurer and Lt. Governor; two highway commissioners, K. D. Bailey and Tom

Kight, Jr.; OU Board of Regents, K. D. Bailey; Tax Commissioner, Bob Wadley; Commissioner of Charities and Corrections, Jim Cook; Democratic National Committeeman, Jim Arrington; State Supreme Court, Pat Irwin; Court of Criminal Appeals, Kirksey Nix; State Court of Appeals, Charles Wilson; Wildlife Commissioner, Roy Boecher; Clerk of Western U. S. District Court and Director, State Selective Service Board, Herbert Hope; and Chairman, State Election Board, Basil Wilson.

Two members of that session set the record for legislative service of 30 years—Bill Bradley and Wiley Sparkman. Five members of the '53 House served as Speaker a total of nine terms and nine members of the '53 Senate served as President Pro Tempore. This session also produced nine district judges, three district attorneys, two industrial court judges, three mayors, a postmaster and a sheriff.

Mentor for many in this talented group was then House Speaker Jim Nance, the wise old pro. Nance always put his eggs in the governor's basket and profited thereby. It was he and Bill Doenges during Johnston Murray's administration who blunted J. D. McCarty's constant efforts to incite mutiny and take over the House himself.

About the only members of the '53 session who quit politics were those carried out feet first. One-third of them died within 10 years, telling you something about the double curse of ambition and politics.

Just before George Nigh got ready to run for governor, he was almost blown out of the water. His luck deserted him March 1, 1978, when Gov. Boren went to Washington the day several Langston University students staged a sit-in at the state capitol. They demanded more money for their "mistreated" university.

In my view, the all-time champion state institution for over-funding is Langston. Its only excuse for being, in a state loaded with colleges, is the fact it has clout with the federal Department of Education and Oklahoma's regents are afraid of being called racists if they get rid of the state's last all-black college. If all-white colleges are racist, I'd like to know something: Why aren't all-black ones racist?

A group of 25 Langston students, some real huskies, overcame House security and took control inside a corridor leading to the Speaker's office. Secretaries and girl pages were quickly shunted to the House lounge for protection while they and House members were being held hostage.

House members were incensed by this arrogance, especially Speaker Bill Willis. He demanded immediate action from the man on the hot seat, Lt. Gov. George Nigh. Members of the House, although helpless themselves, were irate because Lt. Gov. Nigh couldn't ready his Good Fairy to free them instantly.

They became angrier by the minute while Nigh was contacting Gov. Boren in Washington, and law enforcement people. They wanted action, preferably revengeful action, wanted it immediately. George is not a guy you stampede. He took all precautions to avoid bloodshed while a few legislators tried their own negotiating.

Senator Gene Stipe emerged, moving freely through the intruders. "See, I told you he could walk on water," said one captive House member.

Some demonstrators were spoiling for a fight. They wanted to be forcibly arrested and removed, become martyrs to "racism." Heightening danger was a former black civil rights leader appealing via radio for more blacks in the area to join student protestors. The capitol is very near Oklahoma City's black ghetto, holding 50,000 potential reinforcements for the student militants.

His political future hanging in the balance, Nigh nonetheless remained calmer than his House critics. He got all his ducks in a row before taking action, making sure all exits and entrances were covered by troopers or other police. Once that was accomplished, his orders were, move fast and firmly but without undue force.

First Nigh asked demonstrators to clear the aisle, allow access to the House. Nobody budged. Nigh told them, "You are forcing me to have you removed or arrested." Then he got his troops together and moved them in.

Demonstrators were isolated on each floor and forcibly removed from the third floor exit, letting House members leave. Trying to take earlier action with only a few outmanned capitol police would have been suicidal.

Yet next day some insulted House members, egos at half mast and resenting their forced captivity, were faulting Nigh for not saving them quicker. The media began speculating Nigh might be dead in the water for his governor's race. Some questioned whether he was "strong enough" for the job.

"Should I have called in storm troopers, cracked a few heads and caused a race riot for national television?" asked the frustrated Lt. Governor.

The California student president of Langston, Bill Strother, was big man during Nigh's time of strife. He said if Langston got the state's highest per-student funding, "that would put us close to $3-million, which is a good start.

"I think the next thing is to go back to Langston, rest, evaluate our progress and develop some system of direct cor-

316   *Good Guy, Good Governor*

respondence with the House, Senate and governor's office," he added. "We've made our move. It's their time to prove, back up what they talk. I think," he concluded, "the students should be commended for their behavior."

Not many agreed. Police, in more danger than House members, were happy about Nigh's deliberate actions. Oklahoma City police chief Tom Heggy said he knew of only one arrest, another California student demonstrator who slugged a highway patrolman.

Gov. Boren came to Nigh's defense, saying the only suggestion he made during the demonstration was be sure enough law officers were present to handle any problem before removing demonstrators. He said Nigh talked to him several times, outlining steps he planned to take, "and in each case I concurred. I'd say, overall, results of Nigh's handling were very good."

Some of us in Nigh's campaign worried over fallout from this near riot. Looking back, I'm convinced it helped George. He lost a few hotheads but more than made up for it in gains among the sensible, influential 30 per cent of voters in the moderate middle who always come down on the side of reason. They are George's home base.

Attorney General Larry Derryberry, $500,000 in hand, was the favorite as Oklahoma's '78 governor's race started. Nigh had less than half this sum but his worries weren't about money. He knew it would come if his campaign took off. If it didn't take off, Fort Knox wouldn't help.

The other important contender was former State Senator Bob Funston, Tulsa, an attractive candidate but poor and unknown by most voters.

Nigh demonstrated political savvy when the '78 election was over by appointing both Funston and Derryberry's top aide, Odie Nance, to important state posts, a move that didn't hurt when '82 rolled around. Nothing makes a friend of a political enemy faster than providing him love and bread on the table after he's been rejected by voters.

Larry Derryberry had the bankers and a bunch of fellow lawyers to go with his sturdy campaign fund. George had something more important — 213 out of the state's 245 newspapers endorsing him. His payoff for never failing to salve every publisher's ego by seeking out his opinion on the issue of the day whenever George came to town. George came often for good causes affecting the community, which publishers remember.

Having 213 impartial newspapers on his side, believe me, assured George at least a fair shake in the press of Oklahoma, Eddie Gaylord and the *Daily Oklahoman* to the contrary notwithstanding.

Considerable credit for this public relations miracle goes to Ben Langdon, former publisher, who bird-dogged his colleagues for Nigh endorsements. George was also blessed with the best ever campaign treasurers in his two governor races — J. D. Helms and Bob Parks. You need people with smarts like them handling your money. And George's longtime executive secretary, Margaret Hall, is the coolest, most efficient person around, juggling 20 things at once with one hand.

Among other key headquarters people in the '78 race were Ted Coombes, Larry Wood, Robert White, Jeannette Edmondson, Georgia Boulton, Larry Brawner, Bob and Genny Carter, Shirley Cassil, Carl Clark, Jack and Berma Craig, Bill Crain, Del Cravens, Donna Sentell, Jim Echols, Bob Hodder, Mary K. Foster, Delmas and Carol Ford, Bert Galloway, Dean Gandy, Ellen Garrett, Tom Kielhorn, Terry Linhart,

Mike Mashburn, Jay Mitchell, Crystal Mounts, Calvin and Mary Newsom, Jim and Madalynne Norick, Steve Olim, Herb Pate, Sue Peck, Dan Rambo, Pete Reed, John Reid, Harold Rogers, Doug Sanderson, Bill and Marcia Shockey, Bob Wadley, Cindy Davis, Cindy Worley, Billie Worwag, Wayne Chandler, Bill Morgan, John Orr, Henry Roberts, Brad and Betty Ward, Pat Perry, Gary Jones, Norris and Betty Price, Sam Nigh, David Hudson, John and Shirlene Glenn and Roger Sweeney.

A Nigh word-of-mouth secret weapon was the fact his two main opponents, Derryberry and Funston, were lawyers. Many voters sorta feel lawyers already have their fair share of political offices. They own the courts and control the legislature so, like my AAA friend Bruce Palmer says, "Maybe we could struggle along without the entire government in the hands of these complicators."

The sorely missed *Oklahoma Journal* asked, "Do you want a lawyer as governor? Half the Oklahoma Senate is now lawyers. Elect another in this race and lawyers would dominate the legislative, judicial and executive branches. What then happens to the cherished divisions of power in state government? We think it would be too much lawyer control."

Larry Derryberry is an excellent lawyer and more than able debater. He understands the technique of asking your opponent in a debate five questions, each requiring a fat book for proper answer.

Yet George didn't get hurt debating Derryberry. He kept his cool and his own counsel and schedule, in spite of a Derryberry effort to get him involved in constant debating. George came through as what he is — Good Guy, Good Governor — the slogan used for his campaign four years later.

"Good guys can't cope with the problems of crime," shouted Derryberry. "Good guys can't deal with Judge Bohanon and good guys can't handle the question of pardons and paroles.

"While George has been out cutting ribbons, we've been in court fighting the state's legal battles. He's known as a good guy. One thing that hasn't been said of me is that I'm a nice guy. I've been known as controversial and a battler."

I think Derryberry forgot George had been in office 20 years with no hint of scandal. He took the nothing job of Lt. Governor and made it into a plus for Oklahoma industrial development and tourism. To this day George has no stronger interest than industrial development, where he has appointed top people, including Jay Casey as director, Oklahoma Department of Economic Development.

"It's awkward going around yourself saying you're a nice guy," George laughed in talking about the '78 campaign, "but when the nice guy idea evolved, my opponents reinforced it by *attacking* me because I was a good guy. We sat around wondering how being a good guy was hurting our campaign, until finally we said, 'What's *wrong* with being a good guy?' We decided if they were ridiculing being a good guy, we'd take the opposite view and build on it."

That's where the white hats came from, the caravans, jeans, sweatshirts, boots and all the rest of the Good Guy stuff, handed us by the opposition.

"I spent four months in nothing but jeans and a white hat," George remembers. "It became our symbol and was fun. When we went to a rally and looked out over the crowd, my white hat support was visible. Made us look like winners."

Campaigns where opposing hates are the issue and the meanest slasher wins used to be the rule in Oklahoma. Not

Good Guy, Good Governor

anymore and definitely not running against George Nigh. He's smart enough to never hate back publicly. The biblical admonition to turn the other cheek works for him, and will for anyone practiced in biting his own tongue when the inevitable insults come.

Before the filing period, Nigh came up with a great idea that helped him catch up to Derryberry fast. He prevailed upon Jeannette Edmondson to head a petition drive for signatures from voters urging him to run. The law provides you may omit the filing fee if you obtain enough signatures from qualified voters.

To avoid lawsuits from his lawyer opponents, George both filed his petitions and paid the fee. He said his goal was 50,000 signatures. At filing time he was able to present petitions carrying 72,000 names!

Anytime you start a campaign with 72,000 publicly promised votes in the box before filing, you're in the race. Those petition signers became George's hard-core organization.

A voter who comes out publicly has his reputation on the line with yours. He's going to persuade others his judgment is sound. If he gives money, he's doubly locked in. He'll gather greenbacks from others to protect his investment.

George got 72,000 walking, talking Good Guys in his pocket before filing. "Just a gimmick," sneered his opponents, wishing to hell it was their gimmick.

But before the general election ended, our Nigh campaign was fading. Had it not been for these petitions and the caravans, which locked in solid support that never left, we could have had a sad ending.

George and Donna criss-crossed all Oklahoma. Their trucks and vans went to every village and crossroads store.

They seemed everywhere because George's workers were everywhere. George or Donna's picture appeared in all papers, proof they had been to *your* town seeking *your* vote. We, the people, like that.

Donna often got more notice than George. George has been some places so often, he's old hat. Not Donna. She has a lively personality and can and will speak on the issues. She was also blessed with the livest-wire sidekick around, Shirley Cassil, best dancer in the Nigh campaign and a personality kid from way back. Like Donna, you can see in her face what she thinks. I promise you this pair made votes wherever they went.

George and Donna might see only a dozen people in some town. Yet everyone knew they were there because volunteers saw to it every car and business got a Nigh brochure.

George has words of praise for his good luck charmer, Donna.

"Donna's an issue person more than a tea-sipper," explains George. "We had people on the caravans would rather go with Donna. We had press asking to go with her. She's strong, knowledgeable, discussing issues from my vantage point but not afraid to come right out with how she feels. She brought people in who wanted to help Donna."

George had something else going that didn't show. For 16 years as Lt. Governor, he had *time* for people. When a visitor showed up, George might spend a half hour, maybe drink coffee. He had spoken to more high school graduates than McGuffey's Reader, all voters in '78.

As a result he had strong support in every little town. This broad voter support makes the difference election day. Every tiny puddle-jumper burg and crossroads store in Oklahoma had somebody preaching Nigh.

Derryberry barely squeaked into the runoff, which made it bad for both him and Nigh. Since what he was doing up to then didn't work, Derryberry began taking bad advice and came out slugging. Had there been no runoff, I'm convinced Nigh would have breezed through the general election.

As it was, George got cut up in the runoff, although not enough to help Derryberry. It aided only Republican Ron Shotts.

Two things in particular killed Derryberry—his effort to make George look soft on crime because he did his duty and signed some paroles, and a series of phony "debates" Derryberry's people set up.

While Lt. Governor, Nigh signed about 2,000 paroles recommended by the Parole Board and the governor's staff. Derryberry implied something wrong in this action. Intelligent voters knew it was no issue, lining up with Nigh.

A worse mistake was Derryberry's people buying time on rural Oklahoma TV stations, then advertising to the public a Derryberry-Nigh "debate." Ads urging voters to tune in were circulated. George didn't even know about the "debates," although I'm sure Derryberry's people sent him a notice. George and Donna were out campaigning, not waiting around for letters from Derryberry.

George is too smart to walk into the trap of a "debate" loaded in his opponent's favor. It wouldn't even be a real debate. Derryberry's people arranged for two strong newspaper supporters of Larry's to ask the two candidates questions.

At "debate" time, Derryberry's paid spokesman comes on TV, sorrowfully announcing that fraidy-cat Nigh didn't show up. They would go ahead anyway, he said, an empty chair representing Nigh.

Every question Derryberry got was right over the plate and he hit 'em out of the park. The Attorney General proved he was unafraid of embracing mom, apple pie and the flag.

The sad thing about this elaborate "debate" was everyone watching knew it was fake. The show was embarrassing to watch. Next day they were joking about this "debate" in the capitol press room.

"It may be the first debate between a candidate and empty chair when the empty chair won," chuckled the *Tulsa Tribune's* Richard Tapscott.

Why do "media experts" talk candidates into such things when the campaign gets wobbly? Because it hurts bad to lose and there's no money for second place.

One "break" Derryberry got was getting endorsed by the Oklahoma Education Association. Some of our people worried about it. Not me. In politics as in life, nothing is what it seems to be.

I'd have worried had George been the teachers' pet and gotten their endorsement. Not everyone loved our educators' constant clamor for more pay, while student test scores were heading south.

George got his share of teachers, having been one himself, while escaping antagonism from voters who know they learned more in the one-room little red schoolhouse than most kids absorb today inside elaborate brick and mortar from teachers frustrated by bureaucracy and no discipline.

In spite of the "debates" where Nigh didn't show and Larry's endorsement by the OEA early in the campaign, it turned out to be Nigh time. I remember after a real debate between Nigh and Derryberry on channel 2 in Tulsa, Larry's inner circle came away smiling, thinking they'd won something.

If they did, it didn't show up in the voting machines. Nigh beat Derryberry in Tulsa 29,556 to 11,918, won in Oklahoma County 43,919 to 29,820. Larry was no doubt surprised but took his loss manfully and followed time-honored tradition by actively helping George, his longtime seatmate at OU football games, when Nigh came up against the handsome football star, Ron Shotts.

"I'm disappointed but not destroyed," said Larry election night. "I can't quarrel with the people; I love the system."

Facing Republican Shotts was a different ballgame. He had things going for him you couldn't counteract. He was young, handsome, OU football star, a fresh face and another lawyer for George to duel.

Issues were even thinner against Shotts than during the Democratic primaries. Polls, wrong again, showed Nigh running away with it. They failed to discern George had been campaigning a long time. Voters knew his story too well, while Shotts' tale was just unfolding.

Shotts also had Eddie Gaylord and the *Daily Oklahoman* on his side, spewing out cur-nasty editorials daily. Cold winds were blowing hard against George. Thank God Shotts followed the harsh Gaylord line. Had he come with a positive program of his own, an upset might have been possible.

Instead, Shotts' strategists decided votes could be mined out of a mini-vacation Nigh took in California after the runoff. Rick Shelby, now in the Reagan ranks in Washington, came to bat for Shotts.

"I find it absolutely incredible," declared Shelby, in fake shock, "that George Nigh would urge all Oklahoma Democrats to work to make sure he gets elected, while he heads for a vacation in sunny California. He's vacationing in California with a movie star while, as usual, he leaves the work and tough decisions to someone else."

George let that one slide. But when they picked on his girl, Donna, he came with strong words of rebuttal.

Before George knew he would run for governor, Donna opened a small gift shop where she sold moderately priced items, mostly made in Oklahoma. She opened the shop when they were thinking of leaving politics. In two years, I doubt if they made $5,000 profit.

Shotts trumpeted to the press that Donna Nigh was selling Christmas gifts to lobbyists, whose arms, he claimed, were being twisted by George. He also complained about "a meeting of lobbyists to solicit $200,000 in campaign funds" for Nigh's race.

Leo Cravens of the Oklahoma Home Builders Association called a meeting of members of the Oklahoma Society of Association Executives, a group George belonged to for years. Most of its members were happily helping Nigh in the campaign. Both Cravens and Ed Kelsey, president of the group, denied Shotts' claim members were being pressured to buy tickets, "up to $5,000 worth," for the Nigh campaign.

Tickets were available at the meeting but no pressure was applied. Most members were in the $100 contributor range, a far cry from $5,000. In the end it was determined some lobbyists gave to Nigh, others to Shotts, a goodly number to both.

So what else is new? Lobbyists of one kind or another—people with wants—supply most money for campaigns. George gets more pure friendship money than any candidate I've known.

"Issues" in this '78 campaign were nothing to write a book about. But constant criticism of George in the primaries, and now the general election, was taking its toll. I hate to admit it but those front page *Daily Oklahoman* diatribes day after endless day also started hurting.

A poll published October 21, two weeks before the election, showed Nigh the choice of 67.01 per cent of voters, Shotts getting only 30.19 per cent. Feeding in the undecided, George's vote would have been at least 70 per cent had this poll been correct. Those in our camp who believed the poll's optimistic forecast stuck thumbs in their lapels, grinned proudly and saw no reason to shake the bushes election day.

So the vote comes in only 52.27 per cent for George, 47.30 for Shotts. I keep telling you about polls. Don't trust 'em. George had absorbed too many low blows. He won because he has staying power and most voters knew in their hearts George Nigh wasn't guilty of anything shady.

Thinking back, I recall a few things that turned out funny.

George's press secretary, John Reid, has a sly sense of humor. He and George were campaigning at a nursing home where one sprightly little lady in her 80's kept cackling about how much she loved George.

"The way that lady carried on, I was wondering in there," needled Reid when they got outside, "did you speak to her graduating class, too, George?"

When Donna's caravan was in western Oklahoma one day, Don Price of Midwest City was driving the van when it exploded and caught fire. So did Don.

"That's when you know who your friends are," said Donna later. "We almost knocked each other down getting out of there."

Don's clothes were aflame so they rolled him around in the stubble of a field beside the road and damned if the field didn't catch fire. Donna flagged down a passing motorist and they took Don to the hospital. Other Nigh workers stayed behind, trying to put out the fire.

Next week the local paper carried a letter to the editor.

"I wasn't sure who I'd vote for," a lady wrote, "until the other day I passed a van parked beside the road with big George Nigh signs. All Nigh's workers were out in a field trying to beat out the flames with campaign signs. A candidate whose people are that concerned about others gets my vote."

We didn't ever tell 'em who *set* the fire.

George had enthusiastic workers willing to go the extra mile. I recall one shapely gal early in the campaign who came squealing up to George exclaiming, "Oh, George, I can hardly wait to go banging door to door for you."

I believe George thanked her, while cautioning the lady against extending herself too much.

When it was all over election night and bone weary George and Donna finally got home, Donna kicked off her shoes, prepared a small medication and leaned back smiling. They were elected! Years of strife and turmoil rewarded at last. She was savoring the moment, dreaming of the happy times ahead.

As they made ready for bed, George reminded Donna they must be up early next day because "I've got a million things to do before the legislative session." The remark brought Donna down to the real world fast.

"George," she said quietly, tapping him on the shoulder and turning him around, "tell me, when does all the fun start?"

The fun starts, if it ever does, when you're no longer in office or trying to get in. George and Donna Nigh have had few calm, non-turbulent days since election night, 1978. Nor will they until George leaves office.

People ask me, "What kind of governor is George?" Thus

far evidence shows he's deliberate, thorough, considerate, master at balancing House and Senate and smarter, tougher and more conservative than critics realized.

I have half a book left over. If God is kind, I'll do another. Part will be Nigh's happy 1982 campaign, plus a definitive study of George's struggles and triumphs as chief executive.

Many moons will pass before anyone nears his political records. Youngest person elected to the House and as Lt. Governor. First Lt. Governor elected governor. First governor to succeed himself, first elected twice. Served as governor four times.

Only governor carrying all 77 counties. In 50 counties he carried every precinct! Got more votes than any other governor.

"History will record how you perform," George says of these records. "But it makes you proud to know every skeleton you've had in your closet has been out there for 28 years in public office, yet you get the largest vote and carry every county."

I hear it said George's first four years were easy because the tax money poured in. That has changed, yet indications are Nigh can handle bad times, too. He held out against the tax increase legislative leaders wanted in '83 and adopted policies which reduced the state payroll, first time in 30 years, by at least 2,000.

Bryce Baggett gets credit for being Oklahoma's expert on legislation. He wasn't a big Nigh supporter, yet Nigh sought him out and prevailed upon Bryce to run the Employment Security Commission six months. Bryce got to know the real George Nigh.

"While in this job," Baggett stated, "I've been impressed with the governor's perception and skill dealing with the legislature. On at least two occasions, when I decided a certain strategy was appropriate and recommended it, he overruled me and planned things I didn't think could work. He did it so adroitly, the difficult problems were handled without disruption and no hurt feelings. I shook my head in amazement at the skills George Nigh showed. He is one whale of a governor."

Listen to what George Nigh says a governor should be.

"Patient, a workaholic and, somewhere in there, have some kind of ideal to go by," is his short answer.

"Then desire to serve. I worry," he adds, "about a candidate whose goal is just to win the election.

"It helps to have experience with public service. People who want to run the government like a business don't understand government is a business you can't run like a business. In private business, if I have a friend I want to trade with, I do. In government, I'd be accused of kickbacks or wasting tax money.

"It's important a governor try to get along with the legislature. I make recommendations but if the legislature doesn't like 'em, they don't pass 'em. I work on what I think is best long as there's a chance to pass it but I don't get mad everytime somebody disagrees with me.

"I want my relationship with legislators to be a partnership. Only way to be a partner is be friendly with the House and Senate. Where the public's concerned, you might be politically better off being at odds with the legislature. I try not to be.

"There are different styles of governors. Raymond Gary and David Hall achieved their programs because they got along with the legislature. Howard Edmondson and David Boren could achieve with the public but had a difficult time getting things passed by the legislature.

"I think you need kind of a middle ground. Be friendly and get along but be apart enough to make sure you keep your independence. Too many things in life are extreme. I like the middle ground."

George has a special saying I think tells you what his insides are all about: "America has always been run by people who stay until the end of the meeting."

Whether as governor or helping a friend in trouble who could never help him back, you'll always find George present at the start and finish.

Good guy, good governor.

"Nigh for Oklahoma" says it all about George and Donna. Their life and dreams begin and end right here at home. They've given a lot to Oklahoma and gotten a lot back, for which they and we, the people, can be grateful.

21

LAUGHTER AND TEARS

When you pay people to be poor, you're going to have a lot of poor people.

Thompson, Iowa *Courier*

Heading into the west, I catch myself looking back to where I left the happiest fun times. I hear the joking and laughter better now than when I was helping create the din. I've wiped away the tears.

It's a bit murky up ahead, clouds graying, dimming the sun. I think I see a rainbow peeking through, though it's hard to tell looking into a setting sun behind a cloud. Sailors say that means rain tomorrow.

Tomorrow never comes, I believe. I'm moving toward the sunset maybe a bit more reluctantly than some other roads I've traveled, yet with light heart and happy for any chance to travel more.

Tomorrow never comes but is always our greatest hope. Today is never perfect but better than we maybe deserve. Politics is like that, never perfect but better than we think. About as good and bad as you and I.

I'm with Huck Finn who said, "I never seen anybody but lied one time or another." Huck wasn't high on Aunt Polly's sainted old maid sister, Miss Watson, who never missed church and always behaved "so as to go to the good place." Huck could see no fun going where she was going.

He'd rather go to hell with his friends. I'm kinda like that. I'd hate to spend eternity looking down on the fallen, resenting the fun they had. I believe whatever brought me here will take me out OK.

Wherever I end up, I don't expect to see those I've known who plan on playing lead trumpet in the heavenly orchestra. I won't miss 'em. There is little joy in those never tempted nor understanding in those never shedding tears of transgression. I think kindness the greatest word in the dictionary, righteous the most overrated.

Apologies now to those I've interviewed who must wait until my next book for their wisdom to be properly showcased because I flat ran out of space in this opus.

There's Granville Scanland, former Oklahoma County District Attorney, who told me, among other things, how Oklahoma City got the Cowboy Hall of Fame. Final choice was between Oklahoma City, Dodge City and Colorado Springs.

A governor of one state whose vote was crucial had a close friend whose son was in the penitentiary. The governor wanted him paroled but feared he'd be picked up on a "hold" from Oklahoma, where he was wanted for escape after conviction of armed robbery. County Attorney Scanland turned down several requests to release his hold on the young man.

One day Scanland got a call from Gov. Gary's secretary, asking him to come meet with the governor.

"This governor wrote Gary complaining about 'that hard-nose county attorney' who wouldn't release the hold on his friend's son," laughed Scanland. "He offered to produce his state's crucial vote for Oklahoma City as the Cowboy Hall of Fame site if Gary would get me to release my hold on the boy.

"So I told Gary, 'I'll go along if it'll bring the Cowboy Hall of Fame to Oklahoma City.' "

Such nose-picking reasons are common in gaining approval for some of our great civic projects.

There have been no better qualified Corporation Commissioners than Jan Cartwright and Bill Dawson. Both left the commission because one vote equals zero when there are two votes against you.

As Attorney General, Cartwright got bad-rapped by the business community for giving an honest opinion, when asked, about industrial trusts. His opinion was upheld by the state supreme court. True, it gave Oklahoma a black eye with some out-of-state industrialists but blame that on those who set up illegal trusts without court approval, considering themselves above the law. Nor was their cause helped by rinky-dink tax exemptions they granted their buddies in retail businesses not deserving them.

Cartwright and Dawson were thoroughly honest, fearless and conservative public officials. Cartwright's enemies try to brand him a flaming liberal. Not at all. He voted straight conservative as a legislator and figured he should also try saving people's money as corporation commissioner.

"I'm not anti-business," says Cartwright, "I'm anti-monkey-business. Utility lobbyists thought I was a wonderful fellow when I was voting to keep taxes down.

"But when it comes to their own business, utilities don't want to realize they're a monopoly and supposed to be regulated. They act insulted when you question their practices.

"They have *everything* in the fuel adjustment clause. I'm still looking for the kitchen sink."

Bill Dawson is now in the State Senate. He pointed out to me when leaving the Corporation Commission that the commission's chief hearing officer for several years was recruited from the biggest lobbyist before the commission. When this hearing officer quit the commission he went back to work with the lobbyist, after handling some of the largest cases involving companies the lobbyist represented. It is common for commission employees looked upon with favor by companies seeking favorable rulings to be offered, and accept, fine jobs from these companies.

That's why I've been buying utilities stock. I'd do a book about the Corporation Commission except it would be so dull from explaining involved details nobody would read it. Those being regulated too often hide behind mountains of red tape they purposely weave into the commission's operation.

Bill Reynolds has a bunch of great Bob Kerr stories. He was an important member of maybe the best U. S. Senate staff ever and loved Bob Kerr like a father. Reynolds also worked for Roy Turner when he ran for governor. He's the one responsible for bringing Kerr and Turner together again after their bitter 1954 battle for Kerr's Senate seat.

"There was bad animosity between Turner and Kerr after that race," said Bill. "They didn't speak for years."

By 1962 Kerr's power was so great he could beckon President Kennedy to southeast Oklahoma to dedicate a lonesome road in the Kiamichis, not far from Kerr's ranch. Kerr planned a bull show for the president and the secret service gave permission to invite a select group, which didn't include one of Oklahoma's top cattlemen, Roy Turner.

"I decided their feud had gone on long enough and told Kerr's ranch manager Turner should be invited," said Reynolds. "He agreed but assured me he wasn't going to be the one mentioning it to Kerr.

"That night I picked Kerr up at the Ft. Smith airport and on the way to his hotel gingerly suggested maybe Roy Turner should be asked to meet President Kennedy. Kerr's silence could be louder than most people's shouting. For 20 minutes he didn't say a word, then finally asked, 'Why?'

"I told him he had won, could afford to be magnanimous, that Kennedy knew Turner and would expect to meet him when he came to Oklahoma."

More silence but when they reached the hotel Kerr turned and said, "OK, you call him."

By then Bill had his courage up a little and told Kerr he was properly the one to make the call.

"I put the call in for him and told Mrs. Turner Senator Kerr wanted to talk to Roy but he wasn't home," Reynolds related. "When he called back next day I told Roy the Senator wanted him to be part of welcoming the president. I could tell he was pleased.

"At the ranch Kerr was introducing Turner to Kennedy and the president broke in, 'Why, I know Roy Turner. He headed the Truman-Barkley Club, did more to elect Harry Truman than anyone.'

"Roy lit up like a Christmas tree. That night some of us got a little tight, including Roy, and he was so joyful he bawled. Said it was just as well he got beat, that he couldn't have done for Oklahoma what Kerr did."

Kerr died not long after but before he did Turner and he became good friends, visiting together at each other's ranches, even doing some business together.

"I was always glad I had a hand in bringing them together," concluded Reynolds. "Two of Oklahoma's greatest Democrats needed to bury the hatchet. It thrilled both of them when they finally did."

For some reason I usually ended up opposite Kerr in Democratic Party politics, which means I wasn't always on the winning side. Kerr cultivated a following of potent people who went to bat for him and you better be ready to duck when they came out shooting. Kerr was the mastermind but preferred it not be known he was messing in party doings, a practices that can make political enemies.

I remember one bloody, whiskey-soaked night in 1960 when Smith Hester, Dean Hart, Dean Rinehart and I outfoxed the original foxes of Oklahoma politics — Senator Kerr, J. D. McCarty, George Miskovsky and the old man of the mountain, Ray Fine. They were a rugged crew in those darkest hours after midnight before convening of the State Democratic Convention.

Senator Kerr was trying to upset our plans to elect Mary Catherine Mason Democratic National Committeewoman. She had supported Roy Turner against him and Kerr always tried to stay at least even. In this case, he was pretending to support a woman from southwest Oklahoma but his real choice was a lady from Oklahoma City they planned to present as a last-minute "compromise choice for the sake of party harmony."

The old political trick of getting two people fighting, then a third steps in and runs off with the prize. Kerr was master of this strategy and it helped him to take party control away from more than one governor.

About 2:00 a.m. we got word J. D. McCarty, Fine and Miskovsky were roaming the halls and visiting all lighted rooms, lobbying delegates against our candidate. They carefully avoided us.

Meantime, the Oklahoma County lady Kerr really wanted for the post paid me a visit, pleading that I had every right and should support her for committeewoman since we were both from Oklahoma County and Mrs. Mason was from western Oklahoma.

"Not after I've given my word," I told her, "and especially not since you Kerr people already beat her once before."

McCarty and Miskovsky were pretty clever on their own. Two weeks earlier they talked us into naming them delegates to the Democratic National Convention from the 5th district. So now they felt free to oppose Mrs. Mason without fear of retaliation, except it didn't work out that way.

We were pondering what to do in the wee hours when Dean Hart suddenly slapped his knee and yelled, "I've got it! What the 5th district has given, the 5th district can take away.

"J. D. and Miskovsky just *think* they're delegates. No law says we can't rescind that action and pick us some new ones."

Dean Rinehart was dispatched to roust out members of the 5th district executive committee for a new vote. I went to work drawing up a resolution rescinding appointment of McCarty and Miskovsky as delegates. As the early morning sun raised its head, Smith Hester and Hart trotted off happily to give J. D. the bad news.

There was cursing, gnashing of teeth and threats but Hester and Hart don't scare easily. We knew Kerr wanted J. D. and Miskovsky as delegates to support his best buddy Lyndon Johnson against Kennedy in Los Angeles. We figured if Kerr couldn't pull off his "compromise," he might just put his arms around J. D. and Miskovsky and tell them not to risk losing out as delegates.

We let Kerr know we knew who was behind the deal and that hatreds could develop to hurt him in Oklahoma later, as well as losing support for LBJ.

A couple hours before the convention was to start, I was

sawing wood in my room, trying to get some red out of my eyes, when there was a loud rap on the door. When I sleepily opened it, Rex Hawks walked in. Rex was Kerr's eyes and ears whenever a political snooker game was going on.

"The Senator wants to know, are you guys still gonna try forcing through Mason as National Committeewoman?" he asked.

"Tell the Senator," I boasted, "that he beat Mary Catherine once but this time she's going to be elected or there'll be blood all over the convention floor."

Rex scowled but went his way and Mrs. Mason was quietly elected a few hours later, after which J. D. and Miskovsky were finally approved as delegates to the national convention.

Sometimes when you believe the other guy's bluffing, a bluff of your own works pretty well.

In 1960 Kerr took control of the Oklahoma delegation away from J. Howard Edmondson and voted them for LBJ. I was one of the delegates whose vote Kerr cast. In 1952, when Kerr himself ran for president, he took the Oklahoma delegation away from Gov. Johnston Murray. He never could have done it, I'm convinced, had not then "assistant governor" Bill Doenges been in his corner.

Kerr controlled the Democratic Party operations under most governors but not when Raymond Gary was chief executive. Gary knew how to handle power, too, and the party was his baby because he knew how to turn its money faucet off and on.

Murray was plenty hacked about Kerr taking over the '52 delegation but put on a front of friendship. Gov. Roy Turner and his close friend, "Coach" McNeil, were also at the '52 convention in Chicago. They were against Kerr, too, although putting up a show of support for Oklahoma's favorite son.

The thing about governors when Kerr was in the Senate, he always figured them as possible opponents when their terms were up. So he didn't want them holding strings on the Democratic Party machine. His fears were well-founded, as Turner's later race against him proved.

With not votes to broker, Gov. Murray was a lonely figure at that '52 convention. Nobody paid him any mind. When Kerr was nominated and the noisy, colorful demonstration for him began, an angry Murray strode from the convention hall and got in line for a hot dog. Ahead of him were Otis Sullivant of the *Daily Oklahoman* and Mike Monroney aide Jay Perry.

"Better get back in there, governor," chided Sullivant, "can't you see the Kerr demonstration just started? You'll miss it."

"Gov. Turner just went in," added Perry, feeding more fuel on Murray's fire, "and oh, my God, there goes Coach McNeil."

"Where's your Kerr banner?" Sullivant kept the razz going. "Young lady," he told the hot dog stand attendant, "give the governor here my hot dog. He's in a hurry to get back to the big Bob Kerr demonstration."

Murray gave Otis a look that would slice your throat.

"You *are* going in for the demonstration, aren't you?" Perry needled again.

"I'd rather flunk my Wasserman," Murray spit at them, stalking away.

The world's greatest political speech ever, bar none, was delivered by Sam Rayburn at a Democratic dinner in Oklahoma City honoring Speaker Carl Albert. Rayburn had retired and Speaker Albert, his successor, was being honored because the Democratic Party needed money. Rayburn was featured speaker.

Such affairs are always a bore but this one was the worst ever. Two-thirds of the audience was introduced. Everyone from House members on up were invited to "say a few words." Rayburn, resembling an angry Buddah, sat through it all stoicly.

9:00 p.m. turned into 10:00, 10:00 to 11:00, then 11:30. Rayburn's tight face got redder and redder. A few minutes before midnight they finally got around to introducing the featured speaker.

Rayburn rose stiffly and headed to the podium. He'd been sitting so long he had a hard time tracking. At the rostrum, he stood a full minute glaring balefully at the crowd, eyes blinking, eyebrows twitching madly. Then he turned slowly, bestowing an especially hateful look at self-important party officials who had spent more than three hours introducing their friends.

"It says here," Rayburn finally began, holding the dinner program out for all to see and reading from it, "Address: Sam Rayburn. Well, my address is Bonham, Texas. You can write me there if you like."

Then he sat down. Not another word did he utter.

A few embarrassed titters, a sprinkling of applause and then, when everyone realized this was his whole speech, the crowd stood as one, laughing uproariously and stomping their feet, giving Sam Rayburn the greatest ovation I've seen.

You remember funny things like that and I could go on but am running out of paper with still a few personal prejudices to get off my chest. Everything's not funny anymore in the good ol' U. S. A. or Oklahoma politics as we get ready to enter a new century.

The clash of cymbals and beating drums are getting louder.

Everyone's shouting, nobody listening. We need to circulate a petition bringing back kindness, consideration of others and honest opinions honestly expressed.

One of these days we will, I hope, squash this quota thing, the idea all people and all things must be made equal by government decree. Believe me, if we ever do get to where everyone is equal, you ain't gonna like equal.

Who wants a doctor sent to medical school on a quota, ahead of better qualified students? Not anyone with common sense. Neither should government or private contracts be awarded on the basis of quotas for this group or that, rather than low bid and ability to perform.

One man's pleasure is still another's pain. This won't change but when something brings pain all around, it ought to be routed out. Congress is producing too many things like our binding cheese support program costing $2-billion a year. Nobody's deeper into buying political advantage than Senator Proxmire's Golden Fleece Award Wisconsin dairymen. They've fixed it so only people on welfare who get it free can afford cheese.

We're tired of schools where everyone passes and discipline is not part of the curriculum. Our colleges have become universities by legislative decree but some of our best football player graduates have trouble reading the sports page.

I see a new leadership about to rise among blacks, more intellectually honest and less noisy than the present crop of self-appointed breast beaters. Black racism isn't any nicer than white racism and there's a lot of it around today.

I'm fed up with professional blacks leading their people still deeper into the wilderness of ever more welfare handouts, their battle cry, 'Gimme or I'll burn the place down!' The truth is blacks willing to give it the old try are doing just fine, thank you.

We'll be electing more women to office down the road and I think most will be the mama type believing in family first, concerned about better education and a healthy environment. I'll be voting for 'em. They're our best antidote to today's main political crop of aggressive male lawyers who are writing all our laws and the loopholes to go with them.

Let us, however, pray we don't start replacing male lawyers in office with even more aggressive female lawyers. They could destroy the Phase II charge for the Equal Rights Amendment.

Marriage will never replace shacking up but I sense revulsion setting in against the more radical permissiveness tainting our society. Girls made of sugar and spice remain more popular than those flavored lemon or vinegar. And when you speak of equality, don't forget no mere male can ever be equal to a demure lass bringing forth that greatest of all miracles, a child.

Our society has always put this squalling brat first. Don't bet on it ever changing.

Worst disease in government today is staff infection. You catch it inside the government and it spreads fast.

For years our courts have been legislating and now ambitious staffers working for congress and state legislatures are the true wielders of power. Those of greatest influence are combination press agent-investigator. They ride to power on the desire of elected officials for certain reelection above all and forever.

In Washington, one of every three people is a congressional committee staffer. The other two are members of the media they leak to.

You don't amount to much on a committee unless you control some alter ego staff making you famous for doing things you weren't elected to do. The media loves these excessive staffs providing them endless reams of "news" copy.

When your Oklahoma Congressman or Senator comes home with a couple colleagues to "investigate" why they're picking on our oil industry, that's a staff infection operation. They hold hearings, attended mainly by the media, and their "findings"are that your local Congressman or Senator is daily fighting fearsome dragons blowing poisonous fire on our poor oil people. Works the same with military installations, farmers or whatever. Such "hearings" play well on the 6:00 o'clock news and in the next election.

A month later your Congressman or Senator is apt to turn up in Detroit, where he'll be part of a congressional team "investigating" why the Japanese have been making better cars than ours. Their "finding" will be that the Detroit Congressman is courageously slaying Japanese car manufacturers in Washington fast as he can.

One hand washes the other, all in behalf of keeping these people in office, their inflated investigative staffs occupied and the media supplied with "news."

Congressmen and Senators who do a good job on these local scams next take week-end jaunts to places like Central America where, after 48 hours "investigatng," they return with the wisdom necessary to solve all this hemisphere's problems in 20 seconds on the next newscast.

Do we need all these congressional and state legislative "investigators?" Of course not. Their only purpose is to come out of every "investigation" with what they went in for. They know who hires 'em, who pays 'em and who can fire 'em. They discover what they're paid to discover, even when it ain't so.

I wish the media would get up clear-headed some morning and look itself in the eye. A few hundred Washington columnists, each scrambling for three "exclusive" sensations a week, have hyped the news so much we can't tell fact from fiction. Where they leave off, TV extends the hype even more. Any little ol' lie passed around two days among the Washington media becomes a sort of sad truth in the public mind.

The media, pollsters and Political Action Committee lobbyists have taken over most elected officials, and with them our government. Diogenes can blow out his lantern. That honest man he's looking for is out taking a poll, leaking a government secret, or explaining why some loophole favoring a major campaign contributor is going to create more joy than anything since the pill.

So we've got a few little problems. Can we solve them? Certainly, without much trouble.

I remember when J. Howard Edmondson was elected governor of Oklahoma. An evangelical fervor gripped Oklahoma. Tiny kids and little old ladies were proudly singing Howard's campaign song. Thousands never before in politics got in up to their elbows. They had fun and put the Oklahoma train on a different track briefly.

Jay Casey is a happy, handsome fellow, now director of the Oklahoma Department of Economic Development. He was a young crewcut out beating the bushes for Howard in that '58 campaign. One of his greatest creations was the "Truth Tree," a huge cedar Casey and others cut down on Peaceable Mountain outside McAlester. They went to work with spray paint and made that tree into the conscience of Oklahoma and theme for Edmondson's campaign.

"It had one old rotten limb we designated OLD GUARD,"

Casey laughed. "Then our Ora J. Fox limb had a live fox in a box tied to it. Folks really laughed at that."

Ora Fox was a promoter of that time who lived off donations from pensioners listening to his weekly radio broadcast, wherein he endlessly promised to "protect your pension from the politicians." Fox always had a special candidate in each governor and U. S. Senate race, the one who came up with the high dollar. Since Howard Edmondson didn't have any campaign money until he got in the runoff, Fox was against him.

"I'll never forget when I claimed Howard's mother was on the pension rolls," Casey told me. "It was at Hartshorne, where they had plenty pensioners. Ora Fox was haranguing the crowd, claiming Howard would cut off their pensions.

" 'It's a lie,' I shouted, really steamed up. 'Why, Howard Edmondson's own dear mother is an old-age pensioner.' "

After the meeting the local editor, who was for Howard, came over to Casey.

"What you just said will make a helluva headline if true," said the editor. "Is Howard's mother really on the pension rolls?"

"Oh, my God, no!" replied Casey. "Did I say that? I meant to say she's old enough to be."

"That's what I thought," said the editor, grinning, "so that's what I'll put in my story."

In that campaign, Casey and friends painted the front of an old Studebaker to look like a skull and crossbones, with a huge sign reading TRUTH SQUAD

"For the life of me," Casey laughed, "I can't remember why we thought a skull and crossbones had something to do with truth but our Studebaker did attract attention. With it and a loudspeaker, we drew crowds."

Those young Oklahomans 25 years ago were idealistic, eager to make things better in their government. Once their crusade got underway, other Oklahomans joined them. It would be the same again, in Oklahoma and throughout the nation. All it takes is doing what we must do in a democracy if we want to keep it, pay attention to what's going on.

We're starting to do that again. For the long haul, I'm convinced we have what it takes.

Cowardly politicians with no true beliefs cluttering the landscape are getting replaced. The public relations games they play no longer fool us.

Main thing wrong today, as I see it, is that we're all choosing up sides to fight each other. Everyone pursuing his own special interest, with politicians struggling to keep 51 per cent of these special interests on their warm side for the next election.

We need a change of attitude, supporting our government instead of always milking it for something. Replace "What's in it for me?" with "What can I do to help?"

There's no doomsday approaching. Everything will be just fine when you and I quit bellyaching and start pulling on our own oar to make things better. Quit blaming everyone except ourselves when things go wrong.

America is home of the common man, a great little guy when he gets going. The common man is still king when he wants to be and uses his common sense. So quit looking over your shoulder to see who's screwing up. Go look in the mirror.

There's nothing wrong here you and I can't fix. It's strictly up to us. That's right, you and me. If we don't fix it, who will?